THE MASKS OF
JONATHAN SWIFT

By

WILLIAM BRAGG EWALD, Jr.

O Thou! whatever title please thine ear,
Dean, Drapier, Bickerstaff, or Gulliver!
The Dunciad, I, 19–20.

BASIL BLACKWELL . OXFORD
1954

PRINTED IN GREAT BRITAIN
BY A. T. BROOME AND SON,
ST. CLEMENTS, OXFORD.

To
Professor George Sherburn

PREFACE

I owe sincere thanks to a number of people for generous assistance. The research was supported in part by grants from the American Philosophical Society and from the Harvard Foundation for Advanced Study and Research. It is a real privilege to be able to thank two highly distinguished Swift scholars—Dr. Herbert Davis of Oxford University and Professor Ricardo Quintana of the University of Wisconsin—for having read the manuscript; their suggestions have been extremely valuable. Dr. R. J. Hayes, Director of the National Library in Dublin, and Mr. Desmond J. Clarke, Librarian of the Royal Dublin Society, greatly facilitated my investigations in Ireland. Through many revisions Mrs. Kathleen M. Hall has been an excellent typist. But my largest debt is to Professor George Sherburn. For his wisdom and kindness I can express my gratitude only inadequately, in the dedication.

WILLIAM BRAGG EWALD, JR.

Harvard University
April 15, 1953.

CONTENTS

SWIFT AND THE MASKS OF OTHER WRITERS

'In writing,' Jonathan Swift told the Duchess of Queensberry in a letter dated August 12, 1732, 'you are too lazy to give yourself the trouble of acting a part.'[1] He was remarking on the naturalness and sincerity of her letters (though not of her conversation!). But as he wrote these words he may well have recalled his own habits over the past three decades of his busy career, may well have reflected on his own love of impersonation, his seemingly inexhaustible capacity for 'acting a part.' It was significant that his friend Pope had addressed him with four well-known titles : Dean, Drapier, Bickerstaff, and Gulliver. The last three had been among his most famous rôles. But there had been many others.[2]

Because of the great interest in *personae* and the faculty of impersonation (as well as in the larger problem of point of view) during the past century and a half, one is invited to wonder how much Swift, in this respect, resembles more recent writers. Can study of these authors, about whom so much more can be learned, throw light on Swift as a creator of masks? Yeats, for example, played the rôles of 'Michael Robartes', 'Owen Aherne', and many others. And, as Professor Ellmann shows, Yeats was only one of a number of *fin-de-siècle* literary men—including Wilde, Pater, Lionel Johnson, Aubrey Beardsley, William Sharp, Valéry and Mallarmé—who tended to create personalities different from their real ones in their writings and even in their lives.[3]

Writers frequently, of course, use *personae* for primarily artistic reasons. Browning speaks as a Bishop, Fra Lippo Lippi, Caliban, and Andrea del Sarto. A. E. Housman, the apparently austere Latinist, uses again and again the voice of a 'Shropshire Lad'. Ezra Pound writes lyrics in the disguise of various *Personae*, and T. S. Eliot conceives Prufrock, Gerontion, the Hollow Men, and Teiresias.

Did Swift, like these men, use masks for mainly literary reasons? Or were there more specific psychological causes? Is he similar to Robert Schumann, who signed his musical criticism in the *Allgemeine Musikalische Zeitung* with the names 'Florestan', 'Eusebius', and 'Raro', each apparently standing for a particular side of his nature?[4] Does he resemble Henri Beyle ('Stendhal'), whom Professor Levin has called 'a single elusive personality masking under many disguises', and who consciously played many rôles, using one hundred and seventy-one different pseudonyms and leaving thirty-two wills?[5]

An answer to these questions depends upon what we know of Swift's psychology. This has always been an irresistible field for speculation, though it has continued to be something of a mystery. Did he distrust facing the world as himself, as a single integrated personality? At once proud and sensitive, did he desire mastery over large political and religious issues while fearing to enter controversies as Jonathan Swift? What exactly lies behind his curious statement in *The History of the Four Last Years of the Queen* that any man of learning would oppose a law requiring an author to sign his name to his printed works, since ' all Persons of true Genius or Knowledge have an invincible Modesty and Suspiciousness of themselves upon their first sending their thoughts into the World ' ?

Unfortunately our biographical information is inadequate to provide a final answer. We do know that Swift seems to enjoy assuming poses in everyday life. He likes pretending. Early in his career (1703) he writes to Stella's suitor, Tisdall, urging him (perhaps ironically) to fool her with a ' bite '—the ' witty ' trick, popular at court, of telling a complete lie in a perfectly serious manner. Swift's friends frequently reported (primarily in his later years) his habit of assuming various unusual attitudes. One remembers the dinner parties described (the historicity is questionable) by Mrs. Laetitia Pilkington : the Dean ordered the cook to make the overdone meat less done, demanded that Mrs. Pilkington tell him all her faults, and accused her of stealing a bottle-screw of his because it was she who was the least wealthy of the company. He had a cabinet, he told her, which contained all the money he had gained from the Ministry ; when opened, the cabinet was found to be empty. When once Mrs. Pilkington touched his hand with her glove, he acted like a prudish lady. The Dean's playful farewell to another group of guests is also familiar : ' Good night, God bless you, and I hope I never see you again ! ' There are many other stories.

We also know that Swift's early life had certain unhappy aspects, which might possibly have made him insecure. His father died before Jonathan Swift was born. The son and his mother were rather poor relations of an uncle, Godwin Swift, who gave the boy (by one account) ' the education of a dog ' and sent him to Trinity College, Dublin, instead of to England, as he wished, for higher education.[6] In 1689, he began his first residence with Sir William Temple, by whom he was treated as an inferior. Following this residence Swift probably stayed in Ireland with his uncle William, without being able to find a suitable occupation.[7] When Swift left Temple in anger after a second residence, in 1694, it was no doubt humiliating for the young man to have to request his former employer to write a letter of recommendation to the Archbishop of Dublin because Temple was the only person who could have done so. And what effect the 'first' love letter to Varina and her hesitating to marry him might have had on him, one can only guess. One usually thinks of the years 1691–93 as those in which Swift was producing Cowleyan pindarics, poems in a style with more abandon than that of his later verse and prose. Could the decade of the 1690's (from Swift's twenty-third to thirty-third year) have seen a relatively secure young man turn into another sort, who never liked to admit that he was Jonathan Swift? One cannot be absolutely certain. The information, particularly about Swift's childhood, is too scanty. Furthermore, we are glad to know, during the 1690's he had things to be proud of : King William taught him how to cut asparagus in the Dutch way, and Oxford gave him an M.A. Most important, there is no clear-cut connection between ' sufferings,' ' insecurities ', and his created characters.

Much more illuminating than these biographical details is the fact that, unlike those writers for whom the device is an indispensable instrument for self-expression and who tend to identify themselves with their masks, Swift seems to have been able to use it or not as the occasion demanded. Of the works in the Temple Scott edition, only about one-third (by rough estimate) are written from behind a full *persona*. Though the percentage of these tends to be higher in Swift's early career, the device turns up constantly throughout the course of his production. The remaining two-thirds, of course, are for the most part anonymous ; they may also contain irony based upon affectation. But though Swift may have found it nearly always wise to conceal his identity, he does not seem in any period to have been self-compelled to create *personae*. His mask and non-mask works generally appear together throughout his life. And, significantly, he never used any mask a second time, after it had done the work for which he created it.

In these respects Swift resembles less the nineteenth and twentieth century writers using masks than he does some of the writers of his own time. The use of impersonation for satiric and literary purposes becomes very popular in the later years of the seventeenth century and continues into the eighteenth. A striking number of Swift's immediate predecessors and contemporaries—for the most part tough-minded journalists—were likewise writing under pseudonyms. Both Professor Sherburn[8] and Professor Sutherland[9] have called attention to this fact, though both have observed that the *personae* of these various writers

are for the most part not clearly and consistently conceived. It is
unlikely that inner psychology is necessary to explain the practices of
all of these men.

Roger L'Estrange, for example, the Tory ' Observator ', (he was
imprisoned at the Glorious Revolution), stoutly defended the Anglican
Church and attacked the Whigs. From April to July of 1681 his
paper consists of a series of quick questions and answers. Then he
writes dialogues between a Tory (the Observator) and a Whig, the
latter of whom frankly admits that his religion is opportunistic (July
2, 1681), that he does not tell the real reasons for his beliefs (July 6,
1681), and that his conscience changes with necessity (July 9, 1681).
There are other dialogues between the Observator and a Trimmer
and between the Whig and a Courantier.

The ' Observator ' of John Tutchin, in the first decade of the
eighteenth century, is a Whig. Beginning with straightforward essays
(April 1, 1702—June 24, 1702), the paper later shifts to dialogues
between the ' Observator ' and a ' countryman ' named Roger. The
latter asks simple questions about the ' Laudian papists ' who are
perpetrators of the Sacramental Test Act, and the ' Observator ' gives
plain answers to them. Roger can if necessary drop his naïveté, in
order to make an informative attack on such a danger as the Irish
papists (May 18, 1709).

These journalistic *personae* receive practically no characterization.[10]
They exist mainly to enable the author to make his political position
convincing through a semi-dramatic medium, and to present his
arguments freshly, as though they came from several speakers instead
of one. In another more literary tradition it was important to have the
' authors ' portrayed with some degree of distinctness. G. P. Marana's
Letters of a Turkish Spy, for instance, are supposedly written by Mamut,
an Arabian who lives forty-five years unobserved in Paris, sending
dispatches home to the Divan at Constantinople on the intrigues in
European society between 1637 and 1682. Ostensibly his ' manuscript '
has been ' discovered ' in a Paris lodging-house by an Italian man of
letters who learns Arabic in order to translate it. From Italian the
work goes into French and finally English. To the ' translator ' the
Parisian landlord describes the strange Oriental who mysteriously
disappeared, leaving his writings behind. A studious Moldavian,
short of stature and coarse of face, he dresses like an ecclesiastic,
possesses among few other things the works of Augustine and Tacitus,
and the *Alcoran*, and exhibits an irreproachable goodness in his way of
life. He is a contemplative Oriental in the midst of strange western

ways. His naive descriptions become quiet satire. It seems to him that the French and Spanish sing the *Te Deum* to give thanks for the evil they have done. His description of the Prince of Orange's great victory at Breda is tempered by his belief that the Mohammedans, who don't honor war, are superior to the Christians. He reports objectively on the curious behaviour of popes and kings. (This type of writing occurs later in Goldsmith's *Letters from a Citizen of the World*.)

Ned Ward used a similar technique in *The London Spy* (1700). The 'author' spends seven years in the country, reading and reflecting. Then he decides to quit his books, go to London, and expose in a journal the vices and follies of the city. He gives the reader an *ingénu's* impressions of card-sharps, taverns, coffee-houses, the Royal Society, and Bartholomew Fair. In both Marana and Ward the emphasis is still primarily on what the 'spy' (a rather uncomplicated character) sees, rather than upon the 'spy' himself.

Far more significant instances of the *persona* device in the eighteenth century are the *Tatler* and the *Spectator*, the 'authors' of the periodical essays of Addison and Steele. The *Tatler* is Isaac Bickerstaff, a sixty-four year old astrologer,[11] who retains some of the amusing pomposity Swift had given him in the Bickerstaff papers. A relation of the Wagstaffs and Falstaffs, he says his club considers him 'their oracle', a man of great learning, and small knowledge of the world. Although Bickerstaff constantly refers to himself as an old man, his personal characteristics seem in a number of the essays to be more or less neglected : the writing appears to be as appropriate to Steele as to his mask. Some of the essays, of course, are based on reports of various assistants who go regularly to Will's, White's, the Grecian, and St. James's. But even after excluding these essays, the reader does not receive a particularly convincing picture of Bickerstaff. For example, the Tatler's essay on the death of his father (one of Steele's best) does not well fit the character of the humorous Isaac, as it is presented elsewhere ; nor does the eulogistic article on the death of Betterton. One of Steele's main interests in Bickerstaff may have been merely the widespread popularity which Swift had given to the name.[12] Another is explained in the last issue of the periodical (No. 271, January 2, 1710–11), where Steele writes that he chose 'to talk in a mask' of an 'old man, philosopher, humorist, astrologer, and censor', because 'severity of manners' is necessary to anyone who would censure the faults of others. Bickerstaff could chastise vice, but Steele could not because, he says, his own life 'is at best but pardonable'. This statement does suggest that, for Steele's moral purposes, it was not essential

that the Tatler be clearly individualized. It was only important that
he be distinguished in some way from Steele himself.

The Spectator has also a moral aim in writing, ' to enliven morality
with wit, and to temper wit with morality.'[13] And his attributes are
hardly more consistently maintained than the Tatler's. But certain
details of his character, in various essays, are striking. The Spectator's
most unique quality is supposedly his taciturn objectivity ; he is a mere
observer of life. At the age of two he threw away his rattle. Nothing
unusual happened in his infancy, he says. In eight years at the university he read much but spoke scarcely a hundred words. He quietly
travelled to Egypt to measure to his own satisfaction the height of a
pyramid. He refuses to tell his name, his age, or his address. Needless
to say, he is a neutral between the Whigs and Tories.[14]

Although the ostensibly quiet author frequently impresses us as a
gossip like the Tatler (he exercises with dumb-bells[15]), the character
established in the first essay does effectively reappear. The Spectator
indulges in melancholy reflections on the graves in Westminster
Abbey (No. 26). He repeats he is only an observer of life (No. 49).
As he walks among the ruins of an old abbey, he admits he believes in
ghosts (No. 110). When he is in the country visiting Sir Roger de
Coverley, the country people are suspicious of his taciturnity and love
of solitude. They conjecture that he is a ' White Witch ', a Jesuit, a
discarded Whig, or a murderer. And so he returns to London in order
to be alone (No. 131). These details of personality are memorable,
and they constitute an important device in the Spectator papers.

Daniel Defoe is a more versatile and habitual creator of characters
than any of these writers. In his novels *Moll Flanders*, *Colonel Jacque*,
and *Robinson Crusoe*, written with the leading character as narrator, the
point of view of the speaker is maintained in the narrative, and even
moralistic comments on the story can be introduced without one's
feeling strongly that they are inappropriate to the speaker. For
example, Moll's advice to women—' She is always married too soon
who gets a bad husband, and she is never married too late who gets
a good one '—seems, except for the phrasing perhaps, to come as
naturally from her as from Defoe.

One of the excellences of Defoe's *True Relation of the Apparition of
Mrs. Veal* (1706) is the convincingly gossipy tone of the woman who
tells how her neighbour, Mrs. Bargrave, was visited by an old friend,
Mrs. Veal, after the latter's death. The narrator, who has heard the
whole story directly from Mrs. Bargrave, breathlessly passes it on to
her audience, even getting ahead of her narrative and having to retrace

her steps : 'I should have told you before that . . .' Similarly, the *Journal of the Plague Year* owes much to the point of view and reflections of its ' author ', a prosperous, pious saddler who remained in London during the great plague of 1665 because he felt that the divine justice could not be escaped. The details of the plague, which alone would have made an interesting story, become much more absorbing as we see the saddler's personal reaction to the terrible events he reports. When a comet flames in the sky, he records, there is a general feeling, which he shares, that doom is impending ; but, he adds, he is less superstitious than some of the women, who also heard voices. A man sees a ghost ; others believe him, but not the saddler, who did not see for himself. He can be shocked, however, when he sees a watchman climb a ladder to enter a house which a family has abandoned, leaving a dead woman behind, or when he secretly steals into the Aldgate churchyard at night to see the dead thrown into a great pit. Throughout his horrible experiences he remains pious, praying for those who blaspheme God.

These *personae*, like the others already mentioned, enable the author to present philosophic questions, ideas, or a series of events from a fresh point of view. They help him to make the details of a narrative credible : we are more likely to take the word of an eye-witness than of an historian. And, through the ' author's ' reaction to them, events take on a new life. These advantages of the mask are present even when the ' author ' writes in a style more expertly literary than one might expect of him. Swift knew well all these potentialities in the mask. But there is a crucial difference between Swift and these other writers : for him the mask became primarily a tool of irony. In brilliantly making this combination, Swift stands alone in English literature.

One can detect Swift's methods—more than in any of the previous writers—in several of the prose works of Alexander Pope. One is reminded of the Bickerstaff papers by Pope's *The Narrative of Dr. Robert Norris* (July, 1713).[16] This ' Doctor ' describes the ravings of Pope's enemy John Dennis on his deathbed, as witnessed by the Doctor, an old woman, and Lintot, the publisher.[17] Satire appears through the factual ' report ', as in Swift's account of Partridge's ' death '. Other recurrent devices of Swift's, used as early as *A Tale of a Tub* (1704), appear in Pope's essay on pastoral in No. 40 of *The Guardian* (April 27, 1713). The anonymous author ' praises ' Ambrose Philips for his rustic language and for his skill in having lilies, roses, and daffodils all grow at the same time. Conversely, he attacks Virgil for his inappropriate courtly style and Pope for his deviations into poetry. In No. 78 of *The Guardian* Pope recommends writing an epic by mechanical means : arts and sciences, after all, can be learned from indexes and dictionaries, Greek from translations. A less noted work, perhaps by Pope,[18] the *Sermon Preached to a Congregation of Glass Bottles* (1715), is presented as by the ' author of *A Tale of a Tub* '. Some of the latter's qualities appear in the extensive exhibitionistic quotations from the *Bible*, Latin and Greek writers, and the church fathers, as well as in his far-fetched metaphysical comparisons, such as that between men and bottles. Esdras Barnivelt, ' author ' of Pope's *Key to the Lock* (1715), is a pedant who explains all the dangerous meanings hidden in *The Rape of the Lock* : the author is a Papist, Belinda is Great Britain or Queen Anne, the lock is the Barrier Treaty, the Baron is Oxford, Shock is Sacheverell, Belinda's toilet is the celebration of the Mass.

The most important of these works of Pope (one which illuminates a number of his critical ideas) is the *Peri Bathous*, ' written ' by Martinus Scriblerus. Scriblerus scorns the rules of the ancients and praises the bathos of true modern poetry. Common sense is to him a destroyer of wit. In poetry discordant things should be mixed. The design of a poem should be a labyrinth from which only the author should escape. Scriblerus is like several of Swift's *personae* : his sense of values is inverted so that he praises what is bad and condemns what is good.

Henry Fielding, incidentally, later used some of these same methods. The preface and notes to his *Tom Thumb* (purportedly a recently dis-covered Elizabethan play) are supposedly by H. Scriblerus Secundus, who admires bombast as the proper language for joy and doggerel as proper for grief. The notes are mock-serious exaggerations of the methods of Bentley and other textual critics, who had suffered in *A Tale of a Tub*. In *Jonathan Wild*, again as in the *Tale*, the ' author ' can think of constancy as a ' low vice ' not characteristic of the ' great ' Wild ; Heartfree, not ' great ', is merely an ethically good man, whose ideas—as the ' author ' sees them—are inferior and base.

A list of later impersonators—including such non-Swiftian writers as Chatterton, Goldsmith and Blake—could be extended at great length. Impersonation, of course, is by no means new with the Augus-tan Age. As far back as Theocritus and Virgil, fictitious shepherds could be the spokesmen in pastorals. Ovid wrote, in his *Heroides*, imaginary letters of famous dead heroes and heroines. Even in satirical (or partially satirical) works, men long before Swift created characters or used pseudonyms : one remembers not only the occasional participants in dialogues of Horace, Juvenal, and Persius, but more specifically Skelton's Colin Clout, the shepherds in Spenser's *Shepheardes Calender*, Martin Marprelate, and the mourner for Lycidas.

In singling out all these creators of masks, one should not imply that the *persona* is an isolated literary technique. By an explicit definition it is a clear fictitious character who is represented as the supposed author of a work (or the spokesman in a monologue). It is related to other devices. On the one hand, it has an affinity with any other form of created character, particularly dramatic characters, who can be revealed only through their own speeches ; in this respect Hamlet, Pamela, and Gulliver, for example, all have something in common, and Swift has something in common with Shakespeare and Richardson. A *persona*, like any character, can be vivid or colourless. And an author may identify himself wholly or partially with any character, whether or not it is technically a *persona* : Ivan Karamazov and Alyosha may represent opposing sides of Dostoyevsky, Samson may speak for Milton, Shelley may be the real singer of the ' Indian Serenade ', Johnson may express himself through various characters in *Rasselas*. This broad problem of identification can occur with any work of fiction and with any created character, regardless of how clearly or indistinctly drawn it is.

On the other hand, in being the supposed author, the *persona* has a relation to the various attitudes and poses adopted by real authors. Any author, or any person, one must assume, has a ' true ' or ' genuine ' nature. But this is not always perfectly clear. Most people adapt their speech to an audience : the schoolboy uses different words on the athletic field, in church, or in a thank-you letter after his birthday ; a public official speaks one way in a campaign address, another way to private friends, a third way to his family, and even a fourth way in his diary. Similarly a writer frequently adopts a serious or playful attitude or tone—such as nobility, levity, solemnity, objectivity—in response to the prospective demands of his audience and the situation he is writing in. One can certainly not call these various and multiple poses masks. Yet if a pose is definite enough and extended enough, it has certain similarities to a created character. Fielding, as narrator in his novels, adopts poses which certainly do not reveal all of his ' true ' character. It is not all of the ' real ' Thackeray who fastidiously gathers up the puppet show at the end of *Vanity Fair*. The Alexander Pope of the *Epistle to Dr. Arbuthnot* is still Alexander Pope,[19] using various rhetorical attitudes (similar to those of Horace)[20] by which he presents himself as mild, noble, or contemptuous : ' I wished the man a dinner and sat still ' The Jonathan Swift of the sermons is still Jonathan

Swift when he writes indecent verses, even though his attitude is so different that he seems to be almost another person. To begin to understand the ' whole man ', one must recognize all his poses.

Moreover, the *persona* has a relation to the specific pose which occurs in irony. Most irony, it can be said, involves a surface statement which at the same time contains a clue to a real meaning underneath. In making the surface statement the writer must (however briefly) adopt a pose which—superficially, at least—differs from his ' true ' nature. Gibbon, for example, pretends strict fairness to the early Christians. Wilde and Shaw habitually say things they don't really mean. But irony, to deserve its name, must indicate its true meaning ; otherwise—as when Wilde says in the *Intentions* that he doesn't agree with all his own statements, without specifying which ones he rejects—we have posing or impersonation which is usually insincere or at least deceptive. This is the problem in Defoe's *The Shortest Way with Dissenters*, in which—behind the undeveloped disguise of an Anglican extremist—he urges that all dissenters be eliminated. The tract is ironical only if one feels that the extremity of the proposal is enough to make the Anglican argument ridiculous, and thus show the real meaning.[21] Unfortunately many of his contemporaries took Defoe seriously.

The figures Swift creates are at times quite close to mere poses, rhetorical or ironic. But at his best he conceives lifelike characters who are distinct from himself, who tell his tales, and who exist to express the surface meanings of his irony. This irony has been a source of difficulty largely because to understand Swift's ideas, it is essential for the reader to distinguish Swift's own attitudes from those of his *personae*. If one wishes to get to the substance of a work by Swift, one must hear the voice through the mask.

The *persona* device has, to be sure, attracted writers who desired to play the rôles of other people not only in their writings but also in their lives.[22] Swift, however, must be considered not only among Yeats, Wilde, and other *fin-de-siècle* writers, but rather among the much larger number of impersonators and creators of characters who were not trying to fuse their own identity with that of their *personae*. Swift must be seen among other ironists. The regularity with which he reveals his true meaning, unlike a *poseur*, reminds one that for the most part he wrote in response to immediate, practical situations. At various times he had to defend religion and learning against their modern enemies, fight the repeal of the Sacramental Test Act, ridicule astrologers, defend the Tory ministry of Harley and St. John against the Whigs, protest against English injustices in Ireland, as well as deplore man's abuses of reason. In all these efforts it was through irony and created character that he chiefly appealed to his audiences, and with astonishing success.

FOOTNOTES TO CHAPTER I

[1] *The Correspondence of Jonathan Swift,* ed. F. Elrington Ball (1910–4), IV, 337.

[2] There has been a tendency recently to distinguish Swift from his *personae.* See particularly : Ricardo Quintana, ' Swift as a Situational Satirist ', *University of Toronto Quarterly,* XVII (1947–48), 130–6 ; John F. Ross, ' The Final Comedy of Lemuel Gulliver ', in *Studies in the Comic* (University of California Publications in English, vol. VIII, no. 2, 1941), 175–96 ; Robert C. Elliott, ' Swift's *Tale of a Tub* : an Essay in Problems of Structure,' *PMLA,* LXVI (June, 1951), 441–55. Professor Quintana calls Swift's method as a whole ' situational satire '. The ' situation ' results from the setting up of an ' imaginative point of view, making possible and controlling a kind of translation into terms familiar to a certain angle of perception '. Within the framework of the ' situation ', the drama resulting from created characters is only one of several possible devices. Others are parody, allegory, myth, and ' discoveries, projects, and Machines '.

Professor Quintana argues for the ' imaginative point of view ' as a basic unity for these varied devices. It seems very necessary, however, to recognize exactly how the *persona* technique is related to each of them. The character Swift pretends to be can affect all these devices, though some far more than others. The drama contained in the activities of an ' author ' (such as Gulliver) ; an author's style (which frequently amounts to parody) ; his enthusiasm for ' discoveries, projects, and machines'—whether they are his own, as in *A Modest Proposal,* or those of other people, as in Book III of *Gulliver*—all these devices (and others) are inextricable from the nature of the mask.

On the other hand, allegory (as found in the narrative of *A Tale of a Tub* and in the spider and the bee passage of the *Battle of the Books*) and myth (as in the ' animal myth ' in the fourth voyage of *Gulliver*), these devices—in themselves— are relatively independent of an author's personality. Yet even they owe much to the fact that they involve a report, though fairly objective, by an ' author ' who clearly is not Swift.

[3] *Yeats, the Man and the Masks* (1948), pp. 70–3.

[4] *Gesammelte Schriften über Musik und Musiker* (Leipzig, 1854).

[5] Harry Levin, *Toward Stendhal* (Murray, Utah, 1945), pp. 14–15.

[6] See Arthur E. Case, ' Swift's Supposed Ingratitude toward his Uncle Godwin ', in *Pope and his Contemporaries : Essays Presented to George Sherburn* (ed. James L. Clifford and Louis A. Landa, Oxford, 1949), pp. 129–34.

[7] Émile Pons, *Swift : Les Années de Jeunesse et le Conte de Tonneau* (Strasbourg, 1925), p. 158.

[8] 'Addison, Steele, and the Periodical Essay ', in *A Literary History of England,* ed. Albert C. Baugh (1948), p. 871.

[9] ' Some Aspects of Eighteenth-Century Prose ', in *Essays on the Eighteenth Century Presented to David Nichol Smith* (Oxford, 1945), pp. 98–9.

[10] See also, for undeveloped ' authors ', the *Miscellaneous Letters and Essays* (1694), which contains pieces signed by Charles Gildon.

[11] No. 59, August 25, 1709.

[12] ' The Dedication : to Mr. Maynwaring.'

[13] No. 10, March 12, 1711.

[14] No. 1, March 1, 1711.

[15] No. 115, July 12, 1711.

[16] George Sherburn, *The Early Career of Alexander Pope* (Oxford, 1934), pp. 106-7.

[17] Norman Ault, ed. *The Prose Works of Alexander Pope* (Oxford, 1936), I, 153 ff.

[18] *Ibid.*, pp. lxxv-xcii, 203 ff.

[19] For a broader use of the term ' mask ', see : Austin Warren, ' The Mask of Pope ', *Sewanee Review*, LIV (1946), 19-33.

[20] Cf. Book I, Satires IV and VI.

[21] See : John F. Ross, *Swift and Defoe : a Study in Relationship* (Berkeley and Los Angeles, 1941), pp. 81-4.

[22] Ellmann, *op. cit.*, pp. 70-3. Cf. Yeats' statement that every passionate man is ' linked with another age, historical or imaginary, where alone he finds images that rouse his energy.' Napoleon, he says, modelled himself on a Roman emperor, or a *condottiere* (*Autobiography* (1938), p. 133). One should not conclude, however, that imitation is the property of only a few eccentrics and writers. The broader questions of the function of imitation, identification, and impersonation in the education and development of the individual, and of their function in enabling an adult to deal with the present by identifying himself with a past model—these questions have been discussed by Sigmund Freud (' The Anatomy of the Mental Personality ', *New Introductory Lectures on Psycho-Analysis* [1933]) as well as by Thomas Mann (' Freud and the Future ', *Essays of Three Decades* [1947]). Professor Werner Jaeger points out the importance of examples and ' pattern-lives ' drawn from myth in the education of Homeric and later noblemen : Telemachus, for example, models himself after Orestes (*Paideia : the Ideals of Greek Culture* (1945), I, 32-4, 40-1). And Mr. Arnold Toynbee says that the only way the ' creative minority ' can carry the ' uncreative rank and file ' along with them is ' by enlisting the primitive and universal faculty of mimesis '. (*A Study of History*, abridgement by D. C. Somervell [1947], p. 276).

Clearly, the problem of imitation is not confined merely to literary men, hypocrites, or paranoiacs ! Its importance in the psychology of normal people—children and adults—would appear to be enormous. It would account for a child's desire to imitate (seriously) Buffalo Bill, for a business man's or a scholar's desire to imitate (even to the mannerisms) a successful salesman or professor (and thus result in certain ' professional characteristics '), for a sincere Christian's desire to imitate Christ. It would perhaps account (all this is mere hypothesis) for the interest people have in writing, acting, and seeing plays, and—ultimately—for some of the emotional power of an impersonator like Swift.

II

THE AUTHOR OF *A TALE OF A TUB*: PARODY

A Tale of a Tub, the *Battle of the Books*, and *A Discourse Concerning the Mechanical Operation of the Spirit* were published together in 1704, anonymously. The real author, though no one knew it, was of course Swift, a thirty-six year old clergyman in the Church of Ireland. Most definitely in the digressions of the *Tale*, however, a supposed author appears : a fictitious person whom Swift detested, a ' modern ' Grub Street literary hack.[1] In his misuse of learning, his unwavering devotion to all things contemporary, and his pride, the 'author' is an object of ridicule. With this character, Swift at once establishes himself, early in his career, as a superb creator of masks. The intellectual brilliance and energy of the ironical satire, which give the *Tale* a place among Swift's major works, result in large part from his *persona*.

This particular ' author ', however, does not figure equally clearly in the rest of the composite book. Even in the narrative sections of the *Tale*, he is of lesser importance. Furthermore, it is a real question whether Swift intended the mask of the *Mechanical Operation* to be identical with that of the *Tale* ; and the method of the *Battle of the Books*, like that of the narrative sections of *A Tale of a Tub*, differs noticeably from that of the digressions.

The main function of the ' author ' of the *Battle* is to add an air of great significance to the trivial ancient-modern controversy. When his forewarning is neglected—to mix in the library the champions of the ancients with those of the moderns—the ' terrible fight ' breaks out. ' I, being possessed of all qualifications requisite in an historian ', he writes, ' and retained by neither party, have resolved to comply with the urgent importunity of my friends, by writing down a full impartial account thereof.' This clearly is not Swift speaking.[2] Through the author's serious-minded description, as well as his use of epic devices, the battle takes on an inflated significance. The point of view is certainly important. But little emphasis is on his own character. The reader's attention (the spider and the bee passage is a good example) is instead directed to the concrete details of the story and to the allegory.

One comes to the same conclusion about the narrative sections of the *Tale*. The author's inverted sense of values enables him to describe certain of the ludicrous activities of Peter, Martin, and Jack (Catholicism, Lutheranism, and Calvinism) as though they were of great importance. His handling of the superficially mysterious allegory (which conceals the inconclusive story of the three brothers) as well as his frequent comments on his own technique may remind one of the qualities of the modern writers whom the ' author ' represents. Still, the allegorical symbols themselves and the details of events are the primary objects of our interest. Of course, in these sections the characteristics of the author do not contradict those presented in the digressions. The narrative contains evidence about him. But it is in the digressions that the *persona* is of really central significance to the satire.

Even in these digressions, however, three sections are not written by the supposed ' author ' of the book. Swift himself writes (anonymously, of course) the 'Apology', which first appeared in the fifth edition of 1710. Although this section adds to the already humorously long list of introductory units, it is for the most part a sincere explanation of certain aspects of the *Tale*. Swift says he satirizes only the abuses of religion and learning, that his work contains nothing against religion, that it contains parodies and irony.[3]   One may with less certainty accept Swift's remark that he had never seen the second set of explanatory notes[4] and that there were fewer *lacunae* in the original manuscript than in the printed book.[5] Some of the remarks in the 'Apology' partially fit the *persona*, though they apply primarily to Swift himself : the statement, for example, that in 1696 the young author's invention was at its height and his reading fresh in his head, and that the method of the *Tale*—alternating narrative and digression— is altogether new.[6] More in the character of the *persona* is the compliment to Wotton for having elucidated certain difficult passages in the text.[7]

The bookseller, ' author ' of ' The Bookseller to the Reader ' and the ' Dedication ' to Lord Somers, is even more clearly distinguished from the author of the *Tale*. The bookseller is not a learned man. He cannot translate *Detur Dignissimo*, and to him ' Socrates, Aristides, Epaminondas, Cato, Tully, Atticus ' are merely ' hard names '. He shows a mercenary interest in the dedication to Somers, since he is sure that having Somers' name in the front of the book will help sell it, whether it is good or not. He is disappointed to find he must praise Somers for the wit, eloquence, and learning, which everyone knows he has, rather than for the more dramatic virtues, common in dedications, such as military skill or profound knowledge of metaphysics and ' the Oriental tongues '.[8] Thus, while the ' Dedication ' is an adroit compliment to Somers,[9] it is also a criticism of Grub Street, in showing the empty flatteries that usually constitute a dedication ; the mercenary attitude behind the compliments ;[10] the life of the wits, whom the author visits—to find out the meaning of the Latin phrase —by climbing dark winding stairs ; and, most important, the pride of the poets and wits, each of whom thought *Detur Dignissimo* meant the dedication should be made to him.[11]

But it is the ' author ' of the *Tale* who is Swift's first major mask character. With this creation, Swift at once establishes his claim to a corrosive intellectuality. The *persona* resembles more the wits whom the bookseller visits than the bookseller himself. The author is of the Grub Street Brotherhood, and he has a partisan resentment against the arrogant success (but not the modern ideas) of the Royal Society at Gresham College and the group of poets who meet at Will's Coffee-House.[12] The ' shrewdest pieces ' of the *Tale*, he says, were conceived when he was in his bed in a garret, after he had sharpened his invention with hunger ; he worked under the influence of a long course of physic, and a great want of money.[13] From this garret he can hear the loud whispers of the modernists that Wotton's brains are shaken.[14] A ' most devoted servant of all modern forms,'[15] the author can list to his credit such works (not yet published) as *A Character of the Present Set of Wits in this Island, A Dissertation Upon the Principal Pro-ductions of Grub Street, Lectures Upon a Dissection of Human Nature*, and *A Critical Essay Upon the Art of Canting*.[16] As a political hack he has written ninety-one pamphlets in three reigns for thirty-six factions.[17] When the ' grandees of Church and State ' became worried about the attacks the ' terrible wits ' of the age were making on religion and government, they decided to build an academy to hold all nine thousand seven hundred and forty-three of them in the kingdom.[18] But until that time, the grandees selected the author to divert the wits, as seamen do a whale, by *A Tale of a Tub*. Thus the author can say with perfect frankness that the *Tale*, from his point of view, contains no satire.[19] In fact, he has ' neither a talent nor an inclination for satire ', being more interested in writing a panegyric on the (modern) world.[20]

In keeping with this characterization, the author composes in the manner of a number of his brother moderns as well as in the manner of several ancients whom the moderns particularly admired. This fact accounts for much of the style of the digressions.[21] As a parody of the formlessness of modern writing (Dryden is a chief offender), the *Tale* contains six prefatory sections—'Apology ', ' Dedication ', ' The Bookseller to the Reader ', ' Epistle to Prince Posterity ', ' Preface ', and ' Introduction '—in addition to the ten alternating sections of narrative and digression, and a ' Conclusion '.[22] Swift himself points out in the 'Apology' as well as in a footnote (supposedly written by an ' editor ') that both Dryden and L'Estrange are parodied when the author (who, like them, has been a partisan writer) speaks of his plan to finish his great and noble work and thus employ well ' the poor remains of an unfortunate life ' ; his conscience, like theirs, is ' void of offense '.[23]

More extensively the author writes in the manner of Richard Bentley. The author cites the words of a writer whose works have long been completely lost, just as Bentley refers to a statement in Aristotle's lost treatise on the Sicilian government.[24] Like Bentley, the author can find things in an ancient text that are not really there. He is sure, for example, that ancient writers mention true critics (textual critics like Bentley and Wotton), though these references are hidden under an allegory. Thus when Pausanias mentions asses that pruned the vines of the Nauplians, when Herodotus speaks of asses with horns in western Libya, when Ctesias mentions the bitter taste of the flesh of the horned asses in India, and when Herodotus speaks of how an army of Scythians was routed by the braying of an ass, they are referring to the critics of their day.[25] Using the ancients for his own purposes, the author disregards the facts that Pausanias considers the detail about the Nauplian asses a trifle[26] and that Herodotus mentions asses in passing, in a list of ten other wonderful animals, including dog-headed men.[27]

The reason the ancients could not refer openly to the critics, the author thinks, was that the writers feared the critics' power. So even the symbol of the ass, being too close to the original, was discarded for others ' more cautious and mystical '. Both Diodorus and Lucretius refer to a weed in the mountains of Helicon that has a poisonous scent, and Ctesias, angry with the critics, more boldly mentions a toothless serpent of India which kills by its vomit and a poisonous juice. These, the author says, are undoubtedly hidden allusions to ancient critics.[28]

This passage in the ' Digression Concerning Critics ' proving the antiquity of ' true ' critics, as Dr. Starkman points out, parodies the method of Bentley through its collation of abstruse sources, its digressive interpolations, its display of assurance, and its erudition, which is carried down to the most absurd details. Swift's satiric achievement here results from the fact that he can ridicule Bentley's manner, prove Bentley is an ass through his matter, and compete with Bentley in Bentley's own specialty, classical criticism.[29]

Elsewhere the author writes specifically in the style of recent mystics, cabalists, alchemists, and Rosicrucians. Thomas Vaughan, author of the *Anthroposophia Theomagica*,[30] was typical of these 'dark authors'. Like them, the author of the *Tale* refers to the mystical significance of the numbers seven, nine,[31] and three.[32] In section X, which contains the most extended parody, the author refers to himself as a 'mysterious' writer the deciphering of whose *Tale* will require 'seven ample commentaries' by seven deepest scholars in every kingdom in Christendom, who have been shut up for seven years in seven chambers. But he leaves a number of innuendoes to aid future commentators. First, he has 'couched a very profound mystery in the number of O's multiplied by Seven and divided by Nine'. Second, he advises a devout Rosicrucian to 'pray fervently for sixty-three mornings, . . . and then transpose certain letters and syllables according to prescription, in the second and fifth section'; this will reveal a recipe for the *Opus Magnum* (the great work of alchemy). Finally, if someone will 'calculate the whole number of each letter in this treatise, and sum up the difference exactly between the several numbers, assigning the true natural cause for every such difference', his labours will be plentifully rewarded. But, the author warns,

> he must beware of *Bythus* and *Sigè*, and be sure not to forget the qualities of *Acamoth*; *a cujus lacrymis humecta prodit Substantia, a risu lucida, a tristitia solida, and a timore mobilis*, wherein *Eugenius Philalethes* hath committed an unpardonable mistake.[33]

The cryptic references to the magic numbers—seven, nine, and their multiple, sixty-three; to alchemy; to the mysterious words and the Latin phrase from Irenaeus's *Contra Haereses*; and to the error of Philalethes (a pseudonym of Thomas Vaughan) mark this passage as a humorous imitation of the occultists. As the accompanying 'editorial' notes (written by Swift) indicate, Irenaeus (his account of the doctrines of Valentinus the Gnostic, according to Guthkelch and Nichol Smith)[34] is really the source for *Bythus*, *Sigè*, and *Acamoth* as well as for the description of the tears, from which comes the moist substance of rare attributes. The note goes on to point out that the quotation from Irenaeus on the title-page of the *Tale*, ' *Basima eacabasa eanaa irraurista, diarba da caeotaba fobor camelanthi* ', is an example of the 'cant or jargon of certain heretics '.[35] Probably the phrases from Irenaeus in Section X are also examples of similarly undecipherable jargon. One suspects Swift has played a trick on the reader who expects to make sense out of these phrases. This conclusion is reinforced by the 'editor's'

C

saying (the note appeared first in 1710, after learned readers had had
six years to puzzle over meanings) that though Vaughan quotes the
Latin description of the tears, he makes no mention of Acamoth, ' so
that this is nothing but amusement, and a ridicule of dark, unintelligible
writers '. Swift would doubtless have considered his parody a success
if he had accomplished his design (which the ' editor ' suspects) ' to
set curious men a hunting through indexes, and enquiring for books
out of the common road,'[36] and then had been able (in the note of
1710) to laugh at their useless efforts.

This parody on the ' dark authors ' stays as close to an original as
possible ; it achieves its effect through the absurdity of exaggeration.
One can say the same thing about the parody on Dryden and L'Estrange,
once one recognizes the contrast between the record of the author's
past life and his present claim to peace of soul. The parody on Bentley,
however, is of the sort in which the author utters Swift's ideas, but in
a manner like Bentley's.

These are all three parodies of specific literary texts. Elsewhere
the author adopts mannerisms typical of whole groups of modern
writers. For example, the author, though he elsewhere mentions his
working hard and writing in a garret, can say that the *Tale* is the result
of ' a very few leisure hours, stolen from . . . an employment quite
alien from such amusements as this '.[37] Later in the book the author
says that such a display of amateurism is common among modern
writers.[38] The author of the *Mechanical Operation of the Spirit*, too,
urges his friend ' T.H. ' to tell others how hastily and carelessly the
discourse was written.[39]

The author of the *Tale* can also repeat certain trite expressions of
the moderns. The main reason for the poor reception of current Grub
Street writings, he says in the ' Introduction ', is ' the transitory state
of all sublunary things '. The second reason is the fact that present
superficial readers refuse to go beneath the surface of a work. For, he
says, Wisdom is a fox, who must be hunted and dug out. It is a cheese,
the richer having the coarser coat. It is a sack-posset, which becomes
sweeter the deeper one drinks. It is a hen, ' whose cackling we must
value and consider, because it is attended with an egg.' Lastly, it is a
nut, but to be chosen with judgment.[40]

Though Swift probably agreed with this commonplace, it is also
likely that the author, proud of ' these momentous truths ', is humorously belabouring the obvious. The ideas that only mutability is
constant[41] and that truth is hard to find because she lives at the bottom
of a well occur also in the *Tritical Essay Upon the Faculties of the Mind*

(1707–8), an essay which is almost entirely a composite of pseudo-philosophical commonplaces. The author of the *Tritical Essay*, in this same vein, reminds the reader that man is a microcosm, that nature does nothing in vain, that death ends all, and that ' all rivers go to the sea, but none return from it '.

Another similarity between the author of the *Tale* and the author of the *Tritical Essay* is that both tend to rely more on extravagant analogies than on careful logic. In the *Tritical Essay* (which incidentally never mentions the ' faculties of the mind ') the author feels that facile references to the classics are enough to support any argument. To prove that the world cannot be a fortuitous concourse of atoms he says that Alexander wept because he had no more worlds to conquer, ' which he need not have done if the fortuitous concourse of atoms could create one '. After thus refuting Epicurus he immediately says, in an incoherent transition, that ' the first step to the cure is to know the disease '; this statement prefaces an explanation of how an unlearned man may sometimes contribute to a learned argument; and he follows his explanation by irrelevant allusions to Aristotle and Socrates. The author returns from ' this digression ' to continue his main argument—that nature does nothing in vain, but that ' the various opinions of philosophers have scattered through the world as many plagues of the mind, as Pandora's box did those of the body ', except that the philosophers have not left hope at the bottom. And so, ' if Truth be not fled with Astrea, she is certainly as hidden as the source of Nile, and can be found only in Utopia.' [42]

This parody is effective because of its patent exaggeration. Though in the *Tale* Swift often conceals a second meaning in the words of the author (as in the parody on Bentley previously discussed), sometimes the author of the *Tale*, like the author of the *Tritical Essay*, proudly displays mere illogical comparisons. It is curious, for example, that in the ' Introduction ' to the *Tale*, Wisdom should be compared to a cheese, ' whereof to a judicious palate the maggots are the best '. And it is strange that the author should illustrate the fact that Wisdom is found beneath the surfaces of things by saying that Wisdom is a nut, ' which unless you choose with judgment, may cost you a tooth, and pay you with nothing but a worm '. But it is the use of such jocose figurative language by the *persona* that establishes a bridge between the created character and Swift, the master of these ceremonies.

Elsewhere in the *Tale* the author backs up his *ex cathedra* pronouncements by metaphors alone. In the first maxim at the end of the ' Digres-

sion Concerning Critics ', he says that criticism is truest and best
when it is the very first result of the critic's mind : As fowlers
reckon the first aim for the surest, and seldom fail of missing the
mark if they stay not for a second.

In the second maxim, true critics are to be known by ' their talent of
swarming about the noblest writers ', just as a king on horseback is
sure to be the dirtiest person of the company.[43] To show that the best
way to know books is, of course, through the index, the author gives
three analogies : that ' the arts are in a flying march ' and are best
attacked from the rear ; that physicians discover the state of the body
by examining excrement ; and that to catch sparrows, boys throw salt
on their tails.[44] (The author, in a similarly inconclusive manner, cites
the fact that the moderns are running out of material for deducing
' similitudes, allusions, and applications . . . from the *pudenda* of either
sex,' as an ' uncontestable argument that our Modern wits are not to
reckon upon the infinity of matter for a constant supply.')[45]

The author's fondness for daring metaphysical comparisons is
evident in his description of worldly Fame. It is a fruit grafted on the
body, which cannot grow and ripen ' till the stock is in the earth ' ; it is
a bird of prey lured ' to pursue after the scent of a carcass ' ; perhaps
it is on a tomb that her trumpet sounds best, ' by the advantage of a
rising ground, and the echo of a hollow vault'.[46] Even more strikingly,
the author describes the state of the human mind. Man's liberated
imagination leads him to depths as well as heights, for

> not well perceiving how near the frontiers of height and depth
> border upon each other; with the same course and wing, he falls
> down plum into the lowest bottom of things.

And he proceeds in a characteristically involved sentence to
analyse the causes of this phenomenon :

> Whether a tincture of malice in our natures makes us fond of
> furnishing every bright idea with its reverse ; or whether reason
> reflecting upon the sum of things, can, like the sun, serve only to
> enlighten one half of the globe, leaving the other half, by necessity
> under shade and darkness ; or, whether Fancy, flying up to the
> imagination of what is highest and best, becomes over-short, and
> spent, and weary, and suddenly falls like a dead bird of paradise,
> to the ground.

Swift could possibly agree with the basic idea in this passage : man
cannot rise to the thought of God without descending to the thought of

the Devil. And one may see a nearly poetical excellence in its language and imagery. But it is reasonably clear that Swift is imitating a modern style of argument, because the author, having speculated on 'the frontiers of height and depth ', comes back to plain modern prose. He doubts, ' whether after all these metaphysical conjectures, I have not entirely missed the true reason.' [47]

The author goes far beyond these passages in his disregard for logic when he attacks Homer and other ancients. Taking the argument that the moderns, being able to profit from all progress since antiquity, are really more mature than the ancients, the author carries it to an absurd conclusion. The ancients, he says, conscious of their imperfections, tried to divert the censorious reader ' by satire or panegyric upon the true critics, in imitation of their masters, the moderns '. He can agree with Wotton that the finest inventions of the ancients have been long since thought of by transcendent modern geniuses,[48] and, in the manner of Wotton and other moderns, he can note Homer's limited knowledge of science and experimental philosophy.[49] This description of Homer's scientific, not literary, limitations amounts to an attack : Homer has read none of the works of recent alchemists and cabalists, he makes no mention of the useful save-all, he knows nothing of English law, or of the doctrine and discipline of the Church of England. Although Homer is admittedly the inventor of the compass, gunpowder, and the circulation of the blood, he gives no account of the spleen.[50] The effectiveness of this passage depends upon the author's illogical and literal acceptance of the claim that the moderns are the true ancients.

Finally, the author shows a lack of clear logical reasoning, in a way which is an exaggeration of the manner of certain moderns, by his belief in mechanical systems. Since he wrote the best parts of the *Tale* in bed in a garret, the reader will, he says, understand the *Tale* better if he assumes the same position as the writer.[51] The author is sure there is not enough matter left in nature to make up a volume on any one subject, because ' a very skillful computer ' has demonstrated this fact by the rules of arithmetic.[52] In a glance at John Dunton, who said extracts of books were better than the originals, and at Dunton's *Athenian Gazette*, which supplied short cuts to learning,[53] the author says he regrets that no modern has ' attempted an universal system in a small portable volume, of all things that are to be known, or believed, or imagined, or practiced in life '. Then, in a reference to the occultists, he describes such a system, projected by ' a great philosopher of O. Brazile '. Books are to be dissolved in *balneo mariae* with Quintessence of Poppy and three pints of Lethe. The resulting elixir,

snuffed up the nose, will produce ' an infinite number of abstracts,
summaries, compendiums, extracts,' all well ordered in the head and
' reducible upon paper '.[54]

Alluding to modern materialism, in the ' Introduction ' the author
analyzes how a speaker must stand above his audience so that his
words, which have weight, will fall into their open mouths.[55] Madness,
in his diagnosis, has mechanical causes. As vapours rise from the earth
and make clouds and rain, so human vapours ascend from the body to
the brain and make invention flourish.[56] This is what ' the Moderns
mean by madness '. The important thing is not the origin of the vapour,
but at what angles it strikes the understanding and what kind of mind
it hits ; thus it is merely a numerical difference which produces the
distinction between Alexander the Great, Jack of Leyden, and Descartes. The author claims that by his system the two main types of
madness ' are mystically displayed ' as results of but a single cause : the
vapours either carry away a piece of the mind or ' stay at home and
fling it all out of the windows '. He looks down upon other less
careful philosophers, who said the two types are due to two causes,
deficiency and redundance.

The author believes the manner of proselytizing to be similarly
mechanical :

> there is a peculiar string in the harmony of human understanding,
> which in several individuals is exactly of the same tuning. This,
> if you can dexterously screw up to its right key, and then strike
> gently upon it ; whenever you have the good fortune to light
> among those of the same pitch, they will by a secret necessary
> sympathy, strike exactly at the same time.

' In this one circumstance,' he says assuredly, ' lies all the skill or luck
of the matter.' For if a person jars his string out of tune with others,
he will be called mad. Therefore a person should adapt his talents to
his environment, for it is ' a fatal miscarriage . . . to pass for a fool in
one company, when, in another, you might be treated as a
philosopher '.[57] Swift agrees with his ' author ' on the fact of madness
and on the similarity between madmen and successful proselytizers.
But the mechanical explanation of the nature of madness is fitting only
to the *persona*, who is a true modern accepting fully such a materialistic
philosophy as that of Hobbes.[58]

These are some of the primary examples of parody in the *Tale*.
The author may write specifically in the manner of Dryden, Bentley, or
Vaughan, or he may imitate certain characteristics of a group of writers.
Swift's satiric message may come through the author's exaggeration, or

it may be part of the author's own message. But the analytical nature of this discussion should not make one forget that all these types of parody fuse in such a way that the reader is hardly conscious of passing from one to another. Much of the brilliance of the *Tale* is due to the way in which the author shifts quickly from resembling one writer to resembling another, or in which he resembles several at once. It may well have been this quality which led Johnson, in his *Life of Swift*, to praise in the *Tale* 'vehemence and rapidity of mind'. Certainly this process strengthens our conception of the author—as a modern who is capable of exhibiting any of the varied faults peculiar to the large and heterogeneous group he symbolically represents. Swift reminds the reader forcefully of certain clear convictions : that religion demands reason, emotional control, and order, that learning requires humility and intelligence. The amazing fact is that he can do these things by pretending to be a Grub Street hack who admires faulty logic, mechanical systems, and dark unintelligible mystery.

FOOTNOTES TO CHAPTER II

[1] Professor Robert C. Elliott (*op. cit.*) has pointed out the significance of the author's point of view in the *Tale*. But in describing the writer merely as an *ingénu* (the author of *A Modest Proposal* is also one) capable of 'idiocies', he does not fully explain the exact character of the *persona*.

[2] Moreover, the well-known 'Preface of the Author', frequently quoted as a statement of Swift's, is not exactly appropriate to the character of the supposed author. Like the author of the *Tale*, he remarks favourably on ineffectual modern satire :

Satire is a sort of glass, wherein beholders do generally discover everybody's face but their own ; which is the chief reason for that kind reception it meets in the world.

Unlike the author of the *Tale*, he seems here to be admittedly a satirist :

. . . I have learned from long experience, never to apprehend mischief from those understandings, I have been able to provoke ; For, anger and fury, though they add strength to the sinews of the body, yet are found to relax those of the mind, and to render all its efforts feeble and impotent.

There is a brain that will endure but one scumming ; let the owner gather it with discretion, and manage his little stock with husbandry ; but of all things, let him beware of bringing it under the lash of his betters . . .

This satiric spirit does not properly belong to the 'impartial historian' of the great battle. But does it with complete sincerity belong to Swift, who could hardly speak of his 'long experience', at least in literary controversy; who in the *Tale* ridicules the modern satirists who lash the world ; and who seems throughout the *Battle* to be laughing more or less at both sides of the overblown controversy ? If the 'Preface' is a warning to Wotton and Bentley, it is still amusingly ironical.

[3] *A Tale of a Tub, The Battle of the Books, and the Mechanical Operation of the Spirit* (ed. A. C. Guthkelch and D. Nichol Smith, Oxford, 1920), pp. 4–8. Referred to hereinafter as Guthkelch-Nichol Smith.

[4] Guthkelch-Nichol Smith, p. 20. See the 'Introduction' of Guthkelch-Nichol Smith, pp. xx–xxi.

[5] *Ibid.*, p. 17.

[6] *Ibid.*, p. 4. Swift could be called young ; in 1696 he was twenty-nine. But the author is supposedly a veteran of factional quarrels in three reigns. (*Ibid.*, p. 70).

[7] *Ibid.*, p. 15.

[8] *Ibid.*, pp. 23–6.

[9] As Émile Pons points out (*op. cit.*, p. 287).

[10] See Miriam K. Starkman, *Swift's Satire on Learning in A Tale of a Tub* (Princeton, 1950), pp. 112–13.

[11] Guthkelch-Nichol Smith, pp. 23–4.

[12] *Ibid.*, p. 64.

[13] *Ibid.*, p. 44.

[14] *Ibid.*, p. 169.

[15] *Ibid.*, p. 45.

[16] *Ibid.*, p. 2.

[17] *Ibid.*, p. 70.

[18] *Ibid.*, pp. 39–42. This academy, suggestive of the Academy of Lagado, in certain aspects resembles the French Academy of Cardinal Richelieu (*ibid.*, p. 39, note), the Academy of Leibnitz (Starkman, *op. cit.*, pp. 77–8), and Rabelais's Academy of La Reine Quinte (Huntington Brown, *Rabelais in English Literature* [Cambridge, Mass., 1933], pp. 155–6). Without inconsistency, the 'author' of the *Tale* admires the modern wits and yet gladly arranges to serve the 'grandees' by writing the *Tale* in order to divert the wits (he does not attack them) from their formidable attacks on church and state. Characteristically he does not consider a 'tale of a tub' (see Guthkelch-Nichol Smith, pp. xxvi–viii, note) an unworthy literary form.

[19] Guthkelch-Nichol Smith, p. 48.

[20] *Ibid.*, pp. 53–4.

[21] For a detailed discussion of Swift's views on language, see : Harold D. Kelling, *The Appeal to Reason : a Study of Jonathan Swift's Critical Theory and its Relation to his Writings* (unpublished doctoral dissertation, Yale University, 1948), chapter 2. Swift, who evidently had clearly defined ideas on how words should be used, faced a technical problem when he wrote in the person of someone he disliked, someone who might be expected to misuse language. Although—as in the *Tale* and *Gulliver's Travels*—Swift can obviously ridicule certain abuses of language, he must often of necessity grant the supposed author an ability to use words effectively, though not (on the whole) to understand the significance of these words.

[22] See Herbert Davis, *The Satire of Jonathan Swift* (1947), pp. 28–9 ; and Starkman, *op. cit.*, pp. 106–7.

[23] Guthkelch-Nichol Smith, pp. 69–71.

[24] *Ibid.*, p. 102, and note.

[25] *Ibid.*, pp. 98–9.

[26] *Description of Greece* (tr. W. H. S. Jones, 1918), II, xxxviii, 1.

[27] *Herodotus* (tr. A. D. Godley, Cambridge, Mass., and London, 1938), book IV, section 191.

[28] Guthkelch-Nichol Smith, pp. 99–100. The reference in Diodorus has not been found (*ibid.*, note). Lucretius is misquoted : '*Floris odore hominem taetro consueta necare*' (*De Rerum Natura* [tr. W. H. D. Rouse, 1931], bk. VI, ll. 786–7) becomes '*Floris odore hominem retro consueta necare*'. The author is probably being ridiculed here for his mistaken substitution of *retro*, which contains a scatological suggestion.

[29] Starkman, *op. cit.*, pp. 101–3.

[30] The principal sources of Swift's parodies on these writers have been well summarized in Guthkelch-Nichol Smith, 'Appendix F'. See also Starkman, *op. cit.*, pp. 51–4.

[31] Guthkelch-Nichol Smith, pp. 58, 187.

32 Guthkelch-Nichol Smith, p. 57.

33 *Ibid.*, pp. 185-7. Note also the author's use of such dark polysyllabic words as 'exantlation' and 'reincrudation' (*ibid.*, pp. 67-8).

34 *Ibid.*, p. 352, note.

35 *Ibid.*, p. 187, note. The quotation on the title page is from Irenaeus's description of the mysterious practices of the Heretic Marcus. (See Nichols's note, *ibid.*, p. 347).

36 Guthkelch-Nichol Smith, p. 187, note.

37 *Ibid.*, p. 30.

38 *Ibid.*, p. 182. The editors cite an example of such affectation in Blackmore's *Prince Arthur* (*ibid.*, note).

39 *Ibid.*, p. 265. There are many close similarities between the author of the *Tale* and the author of the *Mechanical Operation*, a number of which will be pointed out. It is difficult to say whether Swift intended both works to be seen as the product of a single author. In the prefatory list of other treatises by the author of the *Tale* and in the *Tale* itself, the *Mechanical Operation* is not mentioned. The title *An Analytical Discourse Upon Zeal, Histori-theo-physiologically Considered* suggests some of the contents of the *Mechanical Operation*, but it is unlikely the two works are the same, because the non-existent *Analytical Discourse* is later said to be three large folio volumes long (*ibid.*, p. 137). Furthermore, the author of the *Tale* dislikes the attacks which those of Gresham College have made against his fellow Grubeans (*ibid.*, p. 64), while the author of the *Mechanical Operation* says he will send an account of certain phenomena to the Iroquois *virtuosi*, 'as soon as we can determine them at Gresham' (*ibid.*, p. 265). On the other hand, Edmund Curll, in his *Complete Key to the Tale of a Tub*, says that the *Mechanical Operation* was intended to come 'in about the middle of the *Tale*, as a preliminary to Jack's character' (*ibid.*, p. 328). Curll's conjecture is of far less significance than the fact that the author of the *Mechanical Operation*, like the author of the *Tale*, promises the world a *Critical Essay Upon the Art of Canting, Philosophically, Physically, and Musically Considered* (*ibid.*, p. 282). The important thing is that both authors exhibit certain modern faults. See, however, an article of Professor James Clifford in which he insists upon the unity of the *Tale*, the *Battle*, and the *Mechanical Operation*, basing part of his conclusions on the observation that the imaginary titles hold the three works together. ('Swift's *Mechanical Operation of the Spirit*', in *Pope and his Contemporaries*: *Essays Presented to George Sherburn*, pp. 135-46). The 'same author' mentioned by the Bookseller at the beginning of *Battle* is probably Swift, as in the 'Apology'.

40 Guthkelch-Nichol Smith, p. 66.

41 *The Prose Works of Jonathan Swift, D.D.*, ed. Temple Scott (1897-1908), I, 295. Referred to hereinafter as *Works*.

42 *Ibid.*, 291-5.

43 Guthkelch-Nichol Smith, p. 103.

44 *Ibid.*, p. 145.

45 *Ibid.*, p. 147. The author of the *Mechanical Operation* proves that the English are the posterity of the Scythians by the analogy between the Scythian Long-heads and the English Round-heads (*ibid.*, pp. 270-1).

46 *Ibid.*, pp. 185-6.

47 *Ibid.*, pp. 157-8.

48 *Ibid.*, pp. 96-7.

49 See Pons., *op. cit.*, p. 289; and Starkman, *op. cit.*, p. 91.

50 Guthkelch-Nichol Smith, pp. 127-9.

51 *Ibid.*, p. 44.

52 *Ibid.*, p. 146.

53 Starkman, *op. cit.*, p. 84.

54 Guthkelch-Nichol Smith, pp. 125-7.

55 *Ibid.*, pp. 60-1.

56 *Ibid.*, p. 163.

[57] Guthkelch-Nichol Smith, pp. 167–74.

[58] For the background of the theory of vapours and of sympathetic vibrations, see Starkman, *op. cit.*, pp. 24–32. In using them, Swift seems above all to be showing his dislike of mechanical systems. This is even more evident in the *Mechanical Operation of the Spirit*. The author praises the ' famous art ' of mechanical operations (Guthkelch-Nichol Smith, p. 271). He shows how modern 'spirit' proceeds completely from within, so that modern enthusiasts cover their heads to prevent perspiration, a great ' spender of mechanic light ' (*ibid.*, pp. 272–3). He argues that ' the seed or principle ' which has given men visions of invisible things ' is of a corporeal nature ' (*ibid.*, p. 289), and that *virtuosi* say that ' the brain is only a crowd of little animals ' (*ibid.*, p. 279).

III

THE AUTHOR OF *A TALE OF A TUB* : PANEGYRIC

The fact that the author of the *Tale* writes in the fashion of a group of people whom Swift disliked does not mean that the author is a complete fool. His parade of erudition is vast but corrupted. One sign of his learning is his ability to use conspicuously a wide range of classical quotations in his discourse. Though the footnotes occasionally give such modern translations as Dryden's Virgil[1] or Creech's Lucretius,[2] the text usually gives the original, with the exact source frequently indicated in a marginal note. Some of the author's (or Swift's) mistakes have been mentioned—the misquotation of Lucretius and mistaken reference to Diodorus.[3] The author also cites Plutarch as the source for a story which the *Lives* does not contain.[4]

Perhaps more significant is the changing of Lucretius's ' *Musaeo contingens cuncta lepore* '[5] to ' *Melloeo contingens cuncta lepore* ' ;[6] there may be a reflection on the author in his promising that his description of the Aeolists will have a honey-like charm rather than the grace of the Muses. A humorous error that clearly belongs to the author rather than to Swift is the reference to Socrates's being suspended in a basket to aid contemplation ; here the author accepts Aristophanes's satirical account in the *Clouds* as fact.[7]

But the author is not a person to make this sort of error often. Most of his references are minute and accurate ; one is impressed by his erudition. He cites a pamphlet falsely attributed to Xenophon to show that the Athenians were allowed to criticize any prominent person.[8] His discussion of the frustrated love of Henri IV of France contains relevant quotations from Lucretius's discussion of the physiology of sex ;[9] and it is not extravagant for the author to compare the writers' faults collected by the true critics to Cacus in his den, Hydra's heads, and Augeas's dung.[10] More frequently the author's allusions are novel and unusual. The reader is surprised to find a minute passage from Pausanias about the inhabitants of Megalopolis—' of all the gods they honour the North Wind the most '—in a discussion of the Aeolists ;[11] to find Horace's description of a monster with the tail of a fish and the wings of a bird referred to in a description of Peter's Bulls ;[12] and to hear Horace's description of the reason men work—' *senes ut in otia tuta recedant* '—applied to old judges on the bench.[13]

Frequently, however, the author's allusions are obviously far-fetched. He goes out of his way to quote Virgil's

> . . . *Evadere ad auras*
> *Hoc opus, hic labor est*

in order to show a parallel between getting out of Hell and rising above the heads of a crowd in order to address them.[14] With equal inappropriateness, arguing that it is difficult for proselytizers to hold men fast by their ears, he cites Horace: '*Effugiet tamen haec sceleratus vincula Proteus.*'[15]

Other passages illustrate even more clearly the author's habit of bringing the words of great ancients to bear on his own trivial arguments. Cicero, he concludes, knew the necessity of adapting vibrations to persons and times, for Cicero wrote to a friend in England, '*Est quod gaudeas te in ista loca venisse, ubi aliquid sapere viderere*'. Actually Cicero is saying that Trebatius has had the good fortune in Gaul to be recognized as a lawyer by Caesar; Cicero adds that even if Trebatius should go to Britain, he would still be regarded as a foremost legal expert.[16]

Similarly, in Ctesias's description of the *pudenda* of Indian pygmies the author finds a prophetical foreshadowing of the modern genius of English writers. But he makes the most trivial applications of quotations from Herodotus. Solon advises Croesus to 'regard the end' of life; the author uses the phrase to strengthen his argument for indexes. The Scythians stimulated their mares with bone pipes to produce more milk; the author applies the description to the modern effort to find new ways of 'deducing similitudes' from the sexual organs. In the north, Herodotus says, one cannot travel because the air is filled with showers of feathers; the author of the *Tale* concludes that the region must have contained a multitude of authors, and he looks for a similar success of writers in England.[17] This extravagance reminds one of the parody on Bentley.

The author of the *Tale*, in his misapplication of wide learning as well as in his resemblance to many modern writers, is markedly different from Swift himself. How, then, does Swift speak to the reader? Or, more exactly, how does Swift express or imply his satiric message? For this is frequently, throughout his work, not a strictly literal truth but rather, for rhetorical purposes (invective is an example), an extreme statement or an exaggeration. One obvious way of communicating is through an 'editorial' note—equivocal in tone—like the one which says that the heretical jargon on the title-page is a proper prefix to such a work as the *Tale*.[18] The reader gets the point also as the author mentions the first two types of critics (not, to him, ' true ' critics) : those who distinguish excellence from false imitation, and those who keep ancient learning from being forgotten. Still another method is through having the *persona* quote someone he disagrees with. He mentions the ' morose, detracting, ill-bred people ' who dislike digressions, which jumble together fifty things introduced to please ' a depraved and debauched appetite ' as well as a ' crazy con-stitution '.[19] He cites the suggestion of some people, that every true critic should commit suicide after finishing his work.[20] This is not, of course, Swift's whole view : it is an exaggeration intended for ridicule.

But these are minor instances. The author speaks for Swift primarily by praising things that Swift would blame, by false panegyric. For instance, the author answers the detractors of true criticism, who say a critic is like a tailor, by saying that it requires more to become a true critic than to become anything else ; for just as to become a true beggar costs a man all his money, so to become a true critic costs a man all the good qualities of his mind.[21] Similarly, the author answers those who object to digressions by saying that the number of writers would be greatly reduced if they couldn't write beyond what is to the purpose.[22] Such ' defences ' as these do not indicate that Swift has abandoned his *persona*. The author is defending his modern brotherhood in the manner appropriate to him. Thus he can lament the ravages Time has made among never-dying Modern works ;[23] show the antiquity of criticism by noting that a critic, like a whore or an alderman, never changes his title or his nature;[24] say that true critics are so possessed with the defects of other pens that the quintessence of what is bad distils into their own ;[25] and conclude (illogically) that the true critic is essential to the commonwealth of learning—for he has never been penalized (as he deserves) for being unable to fiddle or build a city.[26] In the ' Preface ' he can remark on the world's failure to reform in response to modern satire, as he praises modern satirists.

These passages indicate the nature of the author. His sense of values is inverted : he does not accept the common judgment of what is good and bad. Therefore, as he says, the *Tale* is not a satire. It is rather a panegyric by one who is completely happy with ' the whole present procedure of human things '.[27] The tensions generated between this view and Swift's make for ironical satire of the first order.

The author's inverted sense of values enables him in Section VIII to give a sympathetic and mildly panegyrical exposition of the Aeolists[28] —the religious sectarians, pretenders to enthusiastic inspiration. An outsider to this group, he has made a study of their doctrines as they appear in old records.[29] He discusses admiringly the spirit, breath, or wind of the world, which such occultists as Thomas Vaughan call the *anima mundi*; for in the Old Testament life itself is called ' the breath of our nostrils '. He records the belief that, as Aquinas said, man is endowed ' with three distinct *anima's* '; the ' sage Aeolists ', noting the correspondence between man and the world, call these souls ' winds ' and to them have added a fourth; they also believe in a *quintessence*, ' extracted from the other four '. Because they believe that this *quintessence* must not be hoarded, these ' wise Aeolists ' say that belching is the ' noblest act of a rational creature '. The author accepts the Aeolists' two ' proofs ' that all learning comes from the principle of wind. The first ' proof ' is the commonly accepted opinion that ' learning puffeth men up '. The second is a syllogism : ' words are but wind; and learning is nothing but words; *ergo*, learning is nothing but wind '.

The author thus admires various parts of the doctrines of Vaughan (' *anima mundi* ') and Paracelsus (who placed ' the body of man in due position to the four cardinal points ').[30] The Delphic oracle is shown to be associated with the Aeolists. But the author is unsure whether their system is a copy of that of the oracle (with modern emendations) or whether it was completely invented by Jack, who in the allegory of the *Tale* stands for the dissenters. The Scottish sectarians, the author finds, are darkly alluded to in the classics. For Pausanias mentioned that the people of Megalopolis worshipped the north wind. Diodorus supposedly called the habitation of this god *Scotia*, ' or the land of darkness '; it is certain that from a similar region ' the most refined Aeolists ' take their origin.[31] (Actually Diodorus is referring not to a land but to ' the " shades " which is a temple of Hecate ').[32]

Whether or not the author speaks for Swift in stating the ' altogether true ' proposition—that uncivilized people arrive at some conception of a deity and then create a devil who is antipathetic to him—the author does use this proposition to show that the Aeolists, when their sect began, succeeded in creating deities—the four winds— as well as two devils—the Camelion and Moulinavent. This sect is thus associated with ' the most uncivilized parts of mankind ' in creating their gods and devils out of their own minds. And now, the author says, this sect makes an illustrious figure in the world.[33]. He is thankful to have had this opportunity to do justice to the Aeolists, whose ideas have been misrepresented by their enemies. For he holds this sect in ' peculiar honour '.[34]

He has even more admiration for modern books and writers. He praises the modern book, which is without grammar; which never has to be chained in a library, for no one wants to read it; and which finally goes through the trial of purgatory in order to ascend the sky.[35] Modern satire, which is general and hurts no one, he prefers (by implication) to the Attic satire of personal abuse.[36] Dryden, Tate, D'Urfey Rymer, Dennis, Bentley, and Wotton,[37] to name only a few, he admires. Conversely he dislikes those who malign Blackmore and L'Estrange. Characteristically he can praise at once modern critics and occultists; commentators on Rosicrucian writings, he says approvingly, bring out many new meanings which the author never intended.[38]

This adulation of modern writers assumes mock-heroic proportions in the famous passage describing the true critic and tracing his genealogy:

> Every true critic is a hero born, descending in a direct line from a celestial stem, by Momus and Hybris, who begat Zoilus, who begat Tigellius, who begat Etcaetera the Elder, who begat Bentley, and Rymer, and Wotton, and Perrault, and Dennis, who begat Etcaetera the Younger.[39]

The author confesses he would never have suspected the connection between the moderns and those obscure ancients who criticized the great writers of antiquity, had he not been enlightened by the ' noble moderns; whose most edifying volumes I turn indefatigably over night and day, for the improvement of my mind, and the good of my country.'[40] The satire in this praise of modern critics is the result of the author's subtle exaggeration. For his exposition of true criticism has no weakness of logic in its organization. He establishes his definition of true critics, proceeds to show their antiquity, and concludes with three maxims on how they can be recognized. The exaggeration is not violent, as in his praise of Wotton's ' sublime discoveries ' on the subject of flies and spittle.[41]

The author's most important object of panegyric, however, is himself. This is Swift's method of attacking one of the moderns' worst faults, their self-sufficient pride.[42] The author wants to hear Fame praising him before he dies.[43] Meanwhile, he has no hesitation about praising himself, because all moderns do so.[44]. Therefore he points out the beauties of his own writing; if other moderns (particularly Dryden) had failed to do this, no one would ever have noticed the sublime or admirable qualities in their works.[45] Foolishly displaying his modern self-sufficiency, he reports that after carefully dissecting human nature he has made a wonderful new discovery : ' that the public good of mankind is performed by two ways, instruction and diversion ' ; and so the *Tale* contains alternating layers of *utile* and *dulce*.[46]

There is an echo of the Pharisee's ' I thank thee that I am not as other men are ' in the author's saying that he does not, like other men, envy a talent (satirical ability) which he cannot reach.[47] But the major source of the author's proud statements is Lucretius, an ancient whom the moderns admired,[48] and whose work Swift (mimicking Anthony Collins) elsewhere calls ' a complete system of atheism '.[49] On the title page of the *Tale* is a quotation from Book IV of *De Rerum Natura*, lines three to five :

> . . . *Juvatque novos decerpere flores,*
> *Insignemque meo capiti petere inde coronam*
> *Unde prius nulli velarint tempora Musae.*

In this passage Lucretius speaks of how he seeks garlands from the Muses which they have given to none before him. In the following lines (six to nine) Lucretius speaks of the lofty content of his teachings, of how he desires to free the mind from superstition, of the darkness of his subject and the clarity of his verses, touched with the Muses' grace. Similarly, the author of the *Tale* can praise not only his own manner but also his matter : ' where I am not understood . . . something very useful and profound is couched underneath.'[50]

The author says that he writes to give matter for a lifetime of speculation to ' the reader truly learned, chiefly for whose benefit I wake when others sleep, and sleep when others wake.'[51] This is an amusing echo of two lines from Lucretius, which are quoted as the author discusses the universal value of modern writing :

> . . . *quemvis perferre laborem*
> *Suadet, et inducit noctes vigilare serenas.*[52]

The sentence in the *Tale* which precedes this quotation—' This, O Universe, is the adventurous attempt of me thy secretary '—contains an attitude remotely similar to that of Lucretius, who asks that a keen and attentive intelligence be applied to what he says, for he plans to reveal the nature of heaven and the gods as well as to disclose the original and end of all things.[53]

But an even closer parallel to this last quotation from the *Tale* is found in the work of such a Rosicrucian as John Heydon, who called himself a ' secretary of nature '.[54] There is likewise a glance at the

Rosicrucians[55] and the new scientists[56] as well as at Lucretius in the author's frequent iteration that he writes for the universal benefit of mankind.[57] This desire to free his work from the bounds of a particular time and place is shared by the author of the *Mechanical Operation of the Spirit*.[58]

The satirical implication is that a person who has such an infatuation for modern writers, himself included, must be a person whose rationality is not normal. Such a man is well qualified to write on madness and proselytizing. Although the author seems at times to speak for Swift in his discussion of these subjects, one should remember that these discussions are merely another form of panegyric, in which everything the author says perfectly fits his character as a person whose sense of values is radically different from Swift's.

Swift's sincere opinion about proselytizing is perfectly clear. In his sermon *On the Martyrdom of Charles I* he urges toleration for those whose religion is unorthodox. But he feels that anyone with 'new visions of his own' ought to 'possess them in silence, without disturbing the community by a furious zeal for making proselytes.'[59] The author of the *Tale*, in contrast, begins the 'Introduction' with an attitude which shows he is not only tolerant of proselytizers but actually seeks to become one himself:

> Whoever hath an ambition to be heard in a crowd, must press, and squeeze, and thrust, and climb with indefatigable pains, till he has exalted himself to a certain degree of altitude above them.[60]

Professor Sherburn has pointed out that Swift thus speaks contemptuously of the deluding power of perverted reason,[61] and Dr. Davis has added that there is an irony, at Swift's expense, in the fact that he, too, desires to be heard.[62] But Swift's contempt is skilfully incorporated in what the author intends to be an admirably careful set of instructions on how to become a successful proselytizer. After thoughtfully eliminating certain unsatisfactory 'edifices in the air' for attaining this end, he decides that there remain only three methods 'toward the just performance of this great work'—the pulpit, the ladder, and the stage-itinerant.[63]

Each edifice stands for a particular set of proselytizers. 'By the pulpit are adumbrated the writings of our modern saints in Great Britain, as they have spiritualized and refined them from the dross and grossness of sense and human reason'. The ladder is a symbol of

D

faction and of poetry. The stage-itinerant stands for the productions of Grub Street :

> It is under this classis, I have presumed to list my present treatise, being just come from having the honour conferred upon me, to be adopted a member of that illustrious fraternity.[64]

Thus at the beginning of the *Tale* the author is shown to be completely in favour of an idea which Swift despised. The contrast between enthusiasm and ' sense and human reason ' is merely suggested here. It is in the ' Digression on Madness ' that the author's admiration for proselytizing, and Swift's satire on it, come to a climax. Here the author praises the great actions possible to a man whose intelligence is overturned and whose brain is ' shaken out of its natural position '. Jack, the dissenter, is the first of these. But the list includes great princes who sought military glory—Henri IV of France, an ' ancient ' king who much resembles Louis XIV,[65] and Alexander the Great ;[66] and those who introduced ' new schemes in philosophy '—Epicurus, Diogenes, Apollonius, Lucretius, Paracelsus, Descartes, and others.[67] The brain of such a critic as Wotton has been similarly shaken, but unfortunately he has not gained a following by applying his talents to ' dreams and visions ', and so the ungrateful world merely calls him mad.[68]

In the opinion of the author with his inverted evaluation of things, to call a person mad and a proselytizer is to bestow upon him heroic praise. He scorns those who, ' in this our undistinguishing age ', would certainly consign the great innovators of philosophical systems to ' whips, chains, and dark chambers '. He has only contempt for the ' vulgar dictates of unrefined reason '. Without madness, the world would not only lack ' those two great blessings, conquests and systems, but even all mankind would unhappily be reduced to the same belief in things invisible.'[69] It is the author's opinion which is summed up in the famous passage on how, when the brain is in its natural state, a person is content ' to pass his life in the common forms '[70] without any desire to make converts.

> But when a man's fancy gets astride on his reason, when imagination is at cuffs with the senses, and common understanding, as well as common sense, is kicked out of doors ; the first proselyte he makes, is himself, and when that is once compassed, the difficulty is not so great in bringing over others.[71]

Proselytes are easily made, the author says, because delusion is better than reason. He believes everyone would agree on the definition that happiness ' is a perpetual possession of being well deceived '. He argues in favour of the definition by contrasting the pleasant appearances of things with the reality underneath :

> How fading and insipid do all objects accost us that are not conveyed in the vehicle of delusion ? How shrunk is everything as it appears in the glass of nature ? So, that if it were not for the assistance of artificial mediums, false lights, refracted angles, varnish, and tinsel ; there would be a mighty level in the felicity and enjoyments of mortal men.[72]

This contrast appears most strikingly in the picture of the woman— ' last week I saw a woman flayed, and you will hardly believe, how much it altered her person for the worse '. But it is also in that of the beau whose faults increase as first his clothes are stripped off and then his brain, heart, and spleen are exposed. The author seriously reports that these experiments prove conclusively that ' the outside ' is ' infinitely preferable to the in '.

Swift might agree that specious appearances are often more pleasant than reality. But he would not follow the author in his conclusion that credulity is preferable to ' that pretended philosophy which enters into the depth of things '. To Swift, delusion and proselytizing go together, as do reason and respect for ' the common forms '. And though the facts beneath the surface may be sobering, Swift would not conclude about all things, ' that in the inside they are good for nothing '. Curiosity and reason, piercing beneath surfaces, are to the author a perversion of nature. Instead, he admires a ' philosopher or projector ' who can delude the senses. Fully consistently with his character, he praises the person who ' can with Epicurus content his ideas with the films and images that fly off upon his senses from the superficies of things '. For such a ' truly wise ' person leaves the worst part of nature, ' the sower and the dregs ', to ' philosophy and reason '. He has arrived at

> the sublime and refined point of felicity, called the possession of being well deceived, the serene peaceful state of being a fool among knaves.[73]

Every step of his argument is coherent. It would be valid if one could agree with the assumption that happiness consists in some sort of sensory enjoyment. But Swift does not agree ; or, if he does, he does not believe that ' happiness ' should be the goal of a wise man's life. The words ' deceived ', ' fool ', and ' knaves ' make his position clear.

For they have a value for him diametrically opposite from that for the ' author '.[74] No passage in Swift is better than this in illustrating the brilliance of his irony. He gives the reader the absurd opinion of a modern proselytizer; he gives his own just reasoning by contrast; and he makes every man recall the shock of at some time thinking himself a fool among knaves. In the tension among all three meanings lies Swift's power.

This skilful parallelism, between what the author says and what Swift means, continues as the author proposes a scheme to utilize the vast genius in Bedlam. The madmen confined there would make admirable public officials—in civil and military offices.[75] The author describes the insane behaviour of a number of the inmates, and laments that they are not free to exercise their talents in the army, at Westminster Hall, in the City, in the medical Society of Warwick-Lane, and in many smaller occupations.[76] To him, the inmates of Bedlam are so excellent that they could well take over prominent offices in the state. To Swift, there is a great resemblance between the madmen in Bedlam and the officials who live outside.[77]

Swift brings his attack on the author and the moderns he represents to a climax in this ' Digression '. The author commences his panegyric on Bedlam by saying he was once a member of that ' honourable society '.[78] Furthermore—as a conclusive proof that the inmates of Bedlam can excel in the offices of the world !—he says that he, like them, is a person whose imagination is apt to usurp the place of his reason. And the ' momentous truths ' he can discover are evident to everyone ! In fact, his friends even now will not trust him alone, unless he promises to write treatises like the *Tale*, ' for the universal benefit of human kind.'[79]

Swift can go no farther than this in his brilliantly humorous condemnation of modern abuses of religion and learning. The author displays a host of the excesses found among the moderns. He illustrates some of these excesses in his style, and he praises others in his extravagant panegyric. He has at his command a wealth of learning and a fondness for philosophical argument. But his learning is misapplied, and his reasonings have been put to the service of his love of delusion and proselytizing. Such a person, Swift says (and the author would proudly agree), is mad.

FOOTNOTES TO CHAPTER III

[1] Guthkelch-Nichol Smith, p. 55.   For Swift's opinion on the misuse of classical quotations, see *The Poems of Jonathan Swift*, ed. Harold Williams (Oxford, 1937), II, 572:

> But laugh'd to hear an Idiot quote,
> A verse from *Horace*, learn'd by Rote.

[2] Guthkelch-Nichol Smith, pp. 60, 100.

[3] Ch. II, n. 28, above.

[4] Guthkelch-Nichol Smith, p. 50, and note.

[5] *De Rerum Natura*, bk. I, l. 934.

[6] Guthkelch-Nichol Smith, p. 142, and note.

[7] *Ibid.*, p. 56, and note.   Cf. *The Clouds*, ll. 218 ff.   (In *Aristophanes* (tr. B. B. Rogers, Cambridge, Mass., and London, 1938), I, 283, ff.)

[8] Guthkelch-Nichol Smith, p. 51.

[9] *Ibid.*, pp. 163–4.   Cf. *De Rerum Natura*, bk. IV, ll. 1048, 1055, 1065.

[10] Guthkelch-Nichol Smith, p. 95.

[11] *Ibid.*, p. 154.   Cf. *Description of Greece*, VIII, xxxvi, 6.

[12] Guthkelch-Nichol Smith, p. 111.

[13] *Ibid.*, p. 57.   Cf. Horace, *Satires*, I, i, 31.   Swift uses the same phrase, with a more appropriate application, in writing to Bolingbroke, December 19, 1719. (*Correspondence*, III, 40).

[14] Guthkelch-Nichol Smith, p. 55.

[15] *Ibid.*, p. 200.   Cf. Horace, *Satires*, II, iii, 71, where the line refers to the futility of trying to collect a debt from an insolvent person.

[16] Guthkelch-Nichol Smith, p. 168, and note.   As the editors point out, Cicero wrote to Trebatius in Gaul, warning him against the charioteers in Britain (*Letters to his Friends* [tr. W. G. Williams, 1931], book VII, letter 6).   The quotation in the text is from Cicero's tenth letter to Trebatius, who has still not gone to Britain.

[17] Guthkelch-Nichol Smith, pp. 145–9.

[18] *Ibid.*, p. 187, note.

[19] *Ibid.*, pp. 143–4.

[20] *Ibid.*, pp. 94–5.

[21] *Ibid.*, pp. 101–2.

[22] *Ibid.*, p. 144.

[23] *Ibid.*, pp. 33–5.

[24] *Ibid.*, p. 101.

[25] *Ibid.*, p. 95.

[26] *Ibid.*, p. 101.

[27] *Ibid.*, pp. 53–4.

[28] Huntington Brown (*op. cit.*, p. 158) says that Swift's description of the Aeolists is inspired by Rabelais's account of the Isle de Ruach.   There the people live entirely on wind; they have weathercocks, but no houses.   (*The Works of Francis Rabelais* [ed. Albert J. Nock and Catherine Rose Wilson, 1931], II, 711–12).   On the Aeolists see Starkman, *op. cit.*, pp. 45–9.

[29] Guthkelch-Nichol Smith, p. 151.

[30] *Ibid.*, pp. 150–3.

[31] *Ibid.*, pp. 155–61.

[32] *Diodorus of Sicily* (tr. C. H. Oldfather, 1933), book I, section 96.

[33] Guthkelch-Nichol Smith, pp. 158–60.

[34] *Ibid.*, p. 161.

[35] *Ibid.*, p. 148.

[36] Guthkelch-Nichol Smith, pp. 48–54.   For a discussion of the similarities between Swift and Aristophanes in this respect, see Starkman, *op. cit.*, pp. 124–8.

[37] Guthkelch-Nichol Smith, pp. 36–7.
[38] Ibid., pp. 183, 186.
[39] Ibid., p. 94. The author of the Tritical Essay distinguishes between the 'carping Momuses' whom authors worship and the 'judicious few, a Rymer, a Dennis'. (Works, I, 293–4).
[40] Guthkelch-Nichol Smith, p. 96.
[41] Ibid., pp. 128–9.
[42] As Émile Pons says, Swift attacks the moderns for 'l'orgueil épanoui de leur sottise'. (Op. cit., p. 288).
[43] Guthkelch-Nichol Smith, p. 185.
[44] Ibid., p. 47.
[45] Ibid., pp. 131–2.
[46] Ibid., p. 124.
[47] Ibid., p. 49. Cf. Horace, Epistles, II, i, 208–9, and Pope, 'Epistle to Augustus', ll. 338–9.
[48] See Starkman, op. cit., p. 33, on the relation between neo-Epicureanism and materialism.
[49] Works, III, 180.
[50] Guthkelch-Nichol Smith, pp. 46–7.
[51] Ibid., p. 185.
[52] Ibid., p. 123. Swift substitutes 'perferre' for Lucretius's 'sufferre' (De Rerum Natura, bk. I, ll. 141–2), but the meaning is unchanged.
[53] De Rerum Natura, bk. I, ll. 54–61.
[54] Guthkelch-Nichol Smith, p. 349, note.
[55] Ibid., p. 347, note.
[56] Starkman, op. cit., p. 64.
[57] Guthkelch-Nichol Smith, pp. 1, 180, 184.
[58] Ibid., pp. 267–8.
[59] Works, IV, 198.
[60] Guthkelch-Nichol Smith, p. 55.
[61] 'Methods in Books about Swift,' Studies in Philology, XXXV (1938), 650–1.
[62] Op. cit., pp. 36–7.
[63] Guthkelch-Nichol Smith, p. 56.
[64] Ibid., pp. 61–3.
[65] Ibid., pp. 162–6.
[66] Ibid., p. 170.
[67] Ibid., p. 166. Cf. Swift's ironical statement, in Mr. Collins's Discourse of Free-thinking, that a man's sense is proportionate to the extent of his departure from common opinions. (In Works, III, 191).
[68] Guthkelch-Nichol Smith, p. 169. The author of the Mechanical Operation of the Spirit praises enthusiasm, which has produced the greatest revolutions in history. (Ibid., p. 268).
[69] Guthkelch-Nichol Smith, pp. 166, 169.
[70] Swift's approval of the 'common forms' does not mean, as Basil Willey says, that Swift, in the Argument Against Abolishing Christianity, prefers 'our present schemes of wealth and power' to a truly 'primitive' Christianity (The Eighteenth Century Background [1941], p. 103). Also, this passage and the one on surfaces do not indicate, as Mr. Leavis says, that Swift fought with 'insane egoism' for 'a skin, a surface, and an outward show', and that he had no deep belief in the Church ('The Irony of Swift', Scrutiny, II [1934], 376–7).
[71] Guthkelch-Nichol Smith, p. 171. The author of the Mechanical Operation shows how, in the sacred rites of the enthusiasts, reason is suspended and imagination has full power. (Ibid., pp. 273–5). Dr. Starkman (op. cit., p. 40) argues that Swift's condemnation of the imagination is an attack on Hobbes, who said imagination could work harmoniously with reason and the emotions.
[72] Guthkelch-Nichol Smith, pp. 171–2. Despite certain similarities, the following

passage does not contradict the one in the 'Introduction' (*ibid.*, p. 66) in which the author deplores the modern reader's failure to go beneath the surface of a piece of literature. The early passage is an expression of a commonplace idea, which has an immediate application only to methods of reading. The later one is a philosophical statement on the much more extensive question of reason and delusion.

[73] *Ibid.*, pp. 173–4. For an analysis of this passage based on the idea that Swift, writing ironically, 'traps' the reader, see F. R. Leavis, *op. cit.*, 372–5. The author's interest in observing and performing anatomical dissections is a characteristic which remains undeveloped in the *Tale* and which does not fit very convincingly the sort of *persona* Swift has set up.

[74] Mr. Leavis says that the energy of Swift's irony results from a tension between his matter-of-fact tone, which impels consent, and his actual meaning, which impels rejection. *Op. cit.*, 368. But this is more properly the tension between the 'author's' and Swift's evaluation of a certain fact.

[75] Guthkelch-Nichol Smith, p. 176. Dr. Davis notes the irony in the fact that Swift—a Whig in 1704—urges the Tory leaders in the House of Commons to advocate that public offices be filled by madmen, who would soon excel in their work. (*Op. cit.*, p. 41).

[76] Guthkelch-Nichol Smith, pp. 176–9.

[77] A similar parallelism occurs in the *Mechanical Operation* as the author says that the English are 'the undoubted posterity of that refined people', the Scythians (*ibid.*, p. 270), and that it is the admirable ass 'by whom I take human nature to be most admirably held forth in all its qualities' (*ibid.*, p. 266). Swift would agree with the author in both instances, but upon the basis of a different system of values.

[78] Guthkelch-Nichol Smith, p. 176.

[79] *Ibid.*, p. 180.

IV

THREE WRITERS ON CHURCH AND STATE

The ' author ' of *A Tale of a Tub* is a symbolic character through whom Swift could attack a multitude of abuses of philosophy and learning. But he also found it useful to use impersonation when dealing with more immediate problems. In the years 1704–09 Swift the Anglican clergyman, in his thirties and early forties, living in both Ireland (1704–07) and England (1707–09), shows an intense interest in certain practical questions of church and state. In three pamphlets on these questions he plays three separate rôles, each with a purpose. These *personae*—if all three deserve the name—can be distinguished primarily by their habits of mind ; in contrast to the method of the *Tale*, Swift gives us relatively few biographical details about them. This fact brings up problems about the first two ' authors '. The first one, in fact, is so indistinctly portrayed that one may well feel that Swift has merely adopted a rhetorical pose rather than created a character. The second may also not be a true ' author ; ' one's conclusions depend upon an analysis of Swift's irony. There is no question, however, about the third.

(*a*) THE SENTIMENTS OF A CHURCH OF ENGLAND MAN

The ' author ' of *The Sentiments of a Church of England Man, with respect to Religion and Government* (probably written in 1704, though Swift dated it 1708)[1] speaks as a conceivably ' real ' person. Any reasonably perceptive eighteenth century reader must have doubted that a Grub Street modern wrote the *Tale*, so extensively is the mask exploited for ironical purposes. But one would have had no reason to doubt that the *Sentiments* was written by a genuine Church of England Man. He is, in fact, Swift in a thin disguise, but the disguise is significant. An objective, rational layman, who would ' readily comply ' with changes in Church rites if the clergy should direct him to, he shows more interest in temporal than in spiritual religious problems, which—like the problem of schism—he is willing to leave to divines.[2] He is, however, not ashamed of the theological knowledge he has. He can confidently use ' the phrase of divines ' to speak about those who ' practically deny ' their religious beliefs by the immorality of their lives. He can speak as one on the level of the clergy when he asks how they can be sure that compliance to the demands of non-conformists will reduce the danger of dissension.

Actually the author exhibits a decided amount of self-confidence, though this never becomes pride :

> I believe, I am no bigot in religion ; and I am sure, I am none in government. I converse in full freedom with many considerable men of both parties ; and if not in equal number, it is purely accidental and personal, as happening to be near the court, and to have made acquaintance there, more under one ministry than another.

From this fair, self-assured position, he can proceed with his task of unbiassing his mind as much as possible, and then endeavouring to moderate between the rival powers.

The essay castigates first the extremes of the Whigs in regard to the church, and then the extremes of the Tories in regard to government. Despite Swift's profession that he is taking up a moderate position, his moderation consists in balancing a violent attack against Whig extremes with an equally violent one against Tory extremes. The result is that the temperate style of the opening paragraph,

> Whoever hath examined the conduct and proceedings of both parties for some years past, whether in or out of power, cannot well conceive it possible to go far towards the extremes of either without offering some violence to his integrity or understanding.[3]

gives way to some of Swift's bitter and trenchant imagery. In the first section, attacking the religious latitudinarians, he can say of the Dutch, in concretely figurative language,

> They are a commonwealth founded on a sudden by a desperate attempt in a desperate condition, not formed or digested into a regular system by mature thought and reason, but huddled up under the pressure of sudden exigencies.

Even more pointedly he calls the Whig writers the ' scribblers on the other side ' and refers to the Whigs' encouraging or conniving at ' this intemperance of speech and virulence of pen, in the worst and most prostitute of their party.'[4]

This invective is, however, more than equalled when the author writes against the Tories, or those who believe in the divine or irre-vocable right of kings. The simple illustrative parallel—that arbitrary power is worse than anarchy, as a savage is happier than a slave at the oar[5]—is less violent than three passages of extended invective in the essay. In the first, the author says that the affirmation that King James II

> had any cause to apprehend the same treatment with his father, is an improbable scandal flung upon the nation by a few bigoted French scribblers, or the invidious assertion of a ruined party at home, in the bitterness of their souls.

The second and third are extended analogies used to support a logical point. The second shows that a prince can be deposed without his own consent, if he is bad enough :

> I will suppose a prince limited by laws like ours, yet running into a thousand caprices of cruelty, like Nero or Caligula. I will suppose him to murder his mother and his wife, to commit incest, to ravish matrons, to blow up the Senate, and burn his metropolis.

The third example buttresses the same idea : a doctor is not answerable only to God, if he ' should manifestly prescribe poison to all his patients, whereof they should immediately die '.[6] These instances of invective cannot be called inconsistent with the original character of the author. He set out candidly to show that the middle course is the only one possible for wise men to follow. These purple passages add colour to our conception of the character, although he still remains a largely undifferentiated type.

Two of the ideas urged in this tract have parallels in the letter[7] Swift wrote to Pope, January 10, 1721–2, outlining his six major political beliefs. One is the opposition to a popish successor to the throne (in the essay : ' the pride, the avarice, the luxury, the ignorance, and superstition of popish times, for a thousand years past ').[8] The second is the advocation of a violent change of government if the present is bad enough. As further evidence that the Church of England Man expresses Swift's sincere judgments, one can cite Swift's remark, in the *Memoirs Relating to the Change in the Queen's Last Ministry*, that when he first began to think about the distinction between Whig and Tory, he became a Whig in politics and a high churchman in religion.[9] There is a final corroboration in his *Sermon on the Martyrdom of King Charles I*, where he writes that he is against absolute tyrannical power, since there is ' no more inward value in the greatest emperor than in the meanest of his subjects.'[10]

It was not Swift's intention, however, merely to stand in the centre and attack the extremists as hard as possible from a vantage point of detached reasonableness. Many of the ideas in the essay are presented with the greatest simplicity and moderation, which, as Professor

Quintana observes,[11] we have come to assume was quite foreign to Swift. There is genuine impartiality in the Church of England Man's saying that

> although he will not determine whether Episcopacy be of divine right, he is sure it is most agreeable to primitive institution. Fittest of all others, for preserving order and purity, and under its present regulations, best calculated for our civil state.

And there is a simple factuality, amounting almost to understatement, in the first requisite for a member of the Church of England, that he ' ought to believe a God and his Providence, together with revealed religion, and the divinity of Christ '.[12] Once these moderate positions are established, Swift can proceed to attack extremists. But the violent and the non-violent passages are both consistent with the character. One can see clearly the value of such a mask. As Swift said at the beginning of *Remarks Upon . . . the Rights of the Christian Church*, ' If a theological subject be well handled by a Layman, it is better received than if it came from a Divine ; and that for Reasons obvious enough, which, although of little Weight in themselves, will ever have a great deal with Mankind.'

The author of the *Sentiments* is quite close to the Swift of some of the anonymous non-mask pamphlets (*The Conduct of the Allies*, for example) who writes with an attitude of directness, rationality, and dignity. In being just one step removed from Swift himself, in being nearly a rhetorical pose, the author of the *Sentiments* is more like the author of the *Letter to a Young Clergyman* than any other of Swift's *personae*. The disguise gives Swift an intelligent layman's position from which to set down certain principles. Here a reader can see that behind Swift's biting hatreds rests a fundamental moderation and common sense.

(b) A Project for the Advancement of Religion

There is even more of a question about the amount of impersonation—and, in addition, irony—Swift intended in *A Project for the Advancement of Religion and the Reformation of Manners* (1709), which he wrote as a projector, with a grand scheme which quickly and easily could sweepingly reform English moral behaviour. Many of the author's views and much of his plan do seem plausible. In many ways he does speak for Swift. Yet one who has read the description of Lord Peter's projects in *A Tale of a Tub* and the satire on projectors in *Gulliver's Travels* (to say nothing of the ' project ' of the ' author ' of

A Modest Proposal) might well wonder whether Jonathan Swift could go all the way with his ' author ' in believing that the English people could speedily be made better by a system.

A project ordinarily consists of two parts : a critical view of certain existing conditions and a proposal for improvement. The author of the *Project* certainly voices Swift's criticisms of existing conditions in society in a ' short view of the general depravities among us '. No one acts by religious principles, he says. He repeatedly attacks gambling ; the fraudulence of merchants and lawyers ; immorality in the army and navy ; the want of discipline in the universities and the Inns of Court ; the failure of the clergy to mix with the laity and their vulnerability to charges of immorality (a misbehaving clergyman can always be distinguished by his robe) ; the corruption of the magistrates ; the indecencies of the stage ; lewdness in taverns ; books against religion ; the scarcity of church buildings ; and the present profligates in public office. In short, the essay contains a rapid survey of a multitude of forms of immorality. To present this picture is one of the purposes of the essay.

Swift intensifies the meaning of this picture by presenting the author's broad program for reform. In certain limited reforms, the author continues to represent Swift. For example, the Queen is urged to order the institution of morality at the universities. Such a regulation on a small scale could be quite feasible. It is likewise possible for the clergy to appear more in public as the author urges them, in order to break down the barriers between clergy and laity. It would be good for the clergy not to wear their habits until they had received a preferment in the church : this would prevent young disgracers of the clergy from being singled out by their dress. Equally plausible are the proposals to turn out the corrupt magistrates and justices of the peace, to reform the stage, to close taverns at midnight, to legislate against fraudulent lawyers, to limit publications against Christianity, and to raise funds for new church buildings. With all these plans Swift would heartily agree.

But the puzzling thing about the essay is its plea for making religious conduct necessary for rewards in public positions. Commissioners on an annual salary of five hundred pounds spend two thousand pounds yearly. The only way to stop such abuses, the author says, is to introduce ' religion as much as possible, to be the turn and fashion of the age.'

Professor Quintana says that the plea is serious and moral, that Swift is not ironical in urging ' stringent uniformity ' of moral conduct; that the only possible irony is peripheral : ' if men only could ! '[13] Dr.

Davis calls Swift's proposal to improve public morals ' dignified, sensible, and practical'; he points out that Swift also intended to ' uphold the authority of the Established Church, and in particular to appeal to the Queen to exert all the influence of the Court against its enemies' and employ in the government ' only orthodox members of the Church party'. But the ' language of morality' which Swift used, he says, led even a good Whig like Steele to praise the tract.[14]

If these conclusions are correct (and they may well be), there could hardly be a fictitious author in the pamphlet. But the project itself is still an unusual one. It is an extremely extravagant scheme. Its aim is to spread faith throughout the whole of England, to raise morality ' to as high a perfection, as numbers are capable of receiving'. This qualification indicates the plausibility of the plan. The author is careful to seem to have thought it through in detail. He relies on the practical expedient of executing the laws now in force, not upon the ' airy imaginations of introducing new laws for the amendment of mankind'. He does not believe that all the existing laws will immediately be executed, so that his scheme will flourish at once. And yet, with all this hard-headed carefulness, the extravagant project is supposed to be capable of an easy success, to be accomplished ' in a short time, and with no very great trouble'. In fact, the method is so easy and so obvious and the present opportunities are so good, that it seems only necessary ' to put those in mind, who by their honour, duty, and interest are chiefly concerned'. After repeatedly assuring the reader that this is not a wild speculative project, but such as could be easily made workable, the author confidently outlines the system. The Queen is supposed to require morality among her domestics and as a requisite for preferment at court. The domestics are required to take an oath of morality upon entering the royal service. The bishops are to report on the morality of high-ranking officials. Then the system will spread throughout the kingdom. For if piety and virtue are once considered qualifications necessary to preferment, every distributor of offices will imitate the Queen. Also, the nobility and principal gentry will be influenced. Censors—itinerant commissioners—can report on the conduct of public officials.

Thus the great revolution can be quickly effected. But there is one drawback. The author does not claim that he expects a genuine system of morality to result from his scheme. Only the appearance will occur. The censors are to judge only the conduct of the public officers. For if religion were the way to preferment, all men would affect it; the proud man would pretend to be humble, the morose man would become a flatterer, the lazy man would counterfeit activity. In the army, gambling and swearing would be eliminated, and the men would show ' at least some external decorum ' in their conduct. If a young person of quality should want to be admitted to the Queen, he would have to subdue his vice of drinking to excess, or ' at least endeavour to disguise it '. In short, if religion were necessary to preferment, ' our duty by becoming our interest, would take root in our natures, and mix with the very genius of the people.'

Swift is not really optimistic when the author says that perhaps in time the appearance may change into reality by force of habit. The project reflects Swift's awareness of the limitations of human virtue. The only way to make men, he says ironically, even dissemble virtue is to make it to their interest to do so. There is the same cynicism in the author's countering the objection that for some employments piety may disqualify a man with the argument that even now men are seldom selected for their fitness for positions. But just as the reader is about to accuse Swift of encouraging hypocrisy, the author himself forestalls the attack by saying that of course the result of his system would be hypocrisy, but even hypocrisy would be far better than what we have now ; it would be closer to genuine perfection than our present ' open infidelity and vice ' are.[15] This assertion emphatically shows the connection between the serious criticisms of existing conditions and the grand project. To propose to turn a nation into a race of hypocrites in order to improve them is to criticize their faults with vicious satire.

This author is much more like Swift than his ' projectors ' usually are. The *Project* contains none of the extreme irony of the *Modest Proposal*. Yet one still suspects that Swift could not have had entire faith in this ingenious and ' easy ' scheme for ' practical ' advancement. His is a ' moral realism ' which sees that the fundamental nature of man is eternally the same. But the question of how far Swift is making fun of the author's confidence is of far less significance in this tract than the things which Swift obviously can accomplish using the rôle of a projector. He displays a broad panorama of existing vices ; suggests a number of workable remedies ; sets up, in his project, a moral ideal, for which it would be good to strive ; indicates the general depravity of man, who can probably be improved in appearances only ; and shows that, realistically, men are so vicious that even a race of hypocrites would be better than that of the present rogues. Particularly at the end of the essay, Swift tends to identify non-religious people with the free-thinkers, and those who attack the High Church point of view. And if one substitutes 'Anglican Religion' for 'religion' generally, one can see a meaning which no doubt is implied in what the author says. Thus, as Dr. Davis observes, Swift is to some extent urging the grant of offices to members of the High Church party.[16] But if this is an end of the essay, it is, as he also says, only one of a number.

(c) On The Abolishing of Christianity

Whatever Swift thought of the author of the *Project*, there is no question that he had little sympathy with the author of *An Argument to Prove that the Abolishing of Christianity in England May, as Things Now Stand, be Attended with Some Inconveniences* (1708). This *persona* belongs to a type which reappears in the *Letter to a Young Poet* and the *Vindication of Lord Carteret* : he defends an idea Swift believes in, but he uses an argument which Swift would reject. Like *A Tale of a Tub* the *Argument* contains humour, much of which results from the fact that the supposed author expresses confidently a surface meaning of Swift's irony without being aware of the true meaning which lies beneath it. And the *Argument*, like the *Tale*, has not a single, but a multiple purpose. Professor Quintana says that it aims to defend true Christianity against free thinking and deism. Professor Landa emphasizes its more specific function as a defence of the Sacramental Test Act,[17] the law which barred from military and civil office anyone who refused to take the sacrament in the Church of England. Dr. Herbert Davis includes both these purposes, which easily co-exist, in his comments on the tract.[18] These and several other results Swift accomplishes through using as his spokesman the character of a ' nominal Christian '.

This is a man who has had some education (witness his apt references to Horace and Tacitus, and to history)[19] and whose main concern is with practical affairs, not religion. Unlike Swift, he views the age he lives in as ' wise and paradoxical ', sees those who would abolish Christianity as ' that great and profound majority which is of another sentiment ',[20] and refers tolerantly to two atheists as ' young men of real hopes, bright wit, profound judgment ', natural abilities, and no learning. This indifference usually leads the author to speak superficially of subjects which Swift considered serious. The author finds real Christianity inconsistent ' with our present schemes of wealth and power '. He is at the same time against abolishing established Christianity ' in the present posture of our affairs at home or abroad '.[21] Such a change, he warns, could cause the Bank and East India Stock to fall at least one per cent.[22]

A devout believer might consider such a materialist an atheist. But the author would be surprised to be put in that class : he is defending Christianity, at least the sort he thinks is worth preserving. Yet he occasionally falls into accepting some attitudes which would appeal more to an anti-Christian than to a thoroughgoing churchman. He is sure that the system of the Gospel is antiquated and exploded, and that the common people are as much ashamed of it as their betters. He acknowledges the ' many plausible objections ' which the anti-Christians advance against the system of Christianity.[23] He contrasts the practices of the Turks, who strictly follow their religion and, ' what is worse, believe a God ', with the less binding requirements of nominal Christianity. And in addition to submitting his opinion to that wise majority which is always right, he can humbly say that if it is necessary to repeal Christianity, he favours an amendment : substituting ' religion in general ' for ' Christianity ', since it is religion in general which is the great enemy to free thought and action.[24] This is by no means the best defence Christianity could have ! Humorously Swift is satirizing both the atheist (indirectly) and the lukewarm Christian.

When the author writes with amoral matter-of-factness about serious matters, Swift can attack the immorality of his day. The author feels that it is terrible to break an officer only for blasphemy, since blasphemy is spoken wherever good company meet. Although Swift would of course agree that there is irreligious talk in polite gatherings, the author's attitude points it up ironically. Likewise there is a message behind the frivolousness of the author's entertaining the possibility that money spent on over ten thousand parsons and bishops might maintain two hundred young wits, who would be enemies to religion and priestcraft, and ornaments to the court and town.

The author also speaks for Swift in certain facts which he uses to support his reasonings. For example, he opposes using the revenues of the church to support two hundred young wits—because the revenues would not properly support even one hundred young men. It is not necessary to abolish the institution of Sunday, he says, since men of pleasure can game at home, taverns and coffeehouses are open as usual, and church is a fine place for gallantry and sleep.[25] Similarly, it is not necessary to abolish Christianity in order to eliminate virtues, for they have already been effectually eliminated by modern innovations in education.[26] Passages like these enable Swift to present, with a great deal of emotional control, trenchant facts (and, as in the last example, his opinions, which pass for facts) about the contemporary apathy toward religion and morals. These facts are part of the main substance of Swift's satiric message. But it is the humorous method of presenting them which awakens the reader to their significance.

The author often takes a sound Christian argument and uses its surface meaning for his own purposes, while he rejects the substance behind the argument. With a brittle attitude of superiority (like that in the passage where he says that ideas descend from the upper classes to the vulgar),[27] he comes out against atheism with the complacent argument that ' scattered notions of a superior power ' are good for the common people. Swift's purpose here is to point out the emptiness of both the nominal Christian and the anti-Christian positions. The nominal Christian exhibits an obviously hollow and superficial attitude. The anti-Christian is attacked through the actual truth of what the nominal Christian says : Swift would of course agree that the idea of God is good for the common people, and indeed for all people ; but when the idea is expressed by the supercilious author, in what amounts to an ironical understatement, it comes home with all the more force.

In the same way, the author does not want to abolish preaching against vice, because vice is more enjoyable if forbidden.[28] God should be allowed to remain, because He is needed for great wits to revile.[29] Protestants should not be united because harmless factionalism is necessary to prevent a serious disturbance of the peace : ' Let the mastiffs amuse themselves about a sheep's skin stuffed with hay, provided it will keep them from worrying the flock '. Swift would vote with the author on each of these issues, but for diametrically opposite reasons.

Swift seldom lapses into obvious inconsistency in this tract. Perhaps he neglects his pose when the author refers to the ' trumpery ' of the deist writers, because he later praises their ' wonderful productions of wit ' ; when he speaks of the ' scrofulous, consumptive ' offspring of ' our men of wit and pleasure ', because he later includes some of them among the ' wise reformers ' opposed to Christianity. It is rather inconsistent with the amoral character of the author for him to answer the argument that abolishing Christianity would eliminate factionalism by asking whether if the words ' whoring ', ' drinking ', ' cheating ', ' lying ', and ' stealing ' were eliminated from the English language, we should all awake ' chaste and temperate, honest and just, and lovers of the truth ? '[30] The parallel here makes it unmistakably clear that the author regards whoring and drinking as evils comparable to factionalism. He seems for once to support a

E

conclusion with an argument Swift would consider serious. But if this is an inconsistency, it is a minor one. Furthermore, it does remind the reader that there are stronger arguments against anti-Christianity than those the polite author makes.

The essay gives a thorough picture of the viciousness of non-religious English wits and materialistic pleasure-seekers. It is most trenchant where Swift attacks the degeneracy of the English breed, the

> scrofulous, consumptive productions, furnished by our men of wit and pleasure, when, having squandered away their vigour, health, and estates, they are forced by some disagreeable marriage to piece up their broken fortunes, and entail rottenness and politeness on their posterity.[31]

In contrast to this negative satirical picture there stands the ideal of true, primitive Christianity cleverly worked into the author's argument. Any anti-Christian would of course oppose it, as does the nominal Christian, who with conventional horror feels that to adopt such a sincere religion

> would be to dig up foundations ; to destroy at one blow all the wit, and half the learning of the kingdom ; to break the entire frame and constitution of things ; to ruin trade, extinguish arts and sciences with the professors of them ; in short, to turn our courts, exchanges, and shops into deserts.[32]

This fact, announced near the very beginning of the essay, is the key to the irony which follows. Here Swift does imply that there are values beyond those of his contemporary world, with its pettiness, pretentiousness, and immorality. Yet this passage has a different meaning for the author, who in his horror exaggerates ; and it lies in a context of superficial qualifications, as he says he is against this ' wild project ', which is fully as absurd as Horace's proposal that all the Romans leave Rome to mend their manners.

One must not forget that it is probably true, as Professor Landa says, that Swift's immediate objective was to attack the people who opposed the Test, by implying that they are opposed to Christianity. Certainly in 1708 the abolition of the Test was a more pressing issue than the abolition of Christianity. And if one substitutes the term ' Sacramental Test ' for ' Christianity ' throughout the pamphlet, one can see clearly one meaning the work must have had for contemporary readers. This is particularly true when the author cites the argument that abolition ' will very much contribute to the uniting of Protestants, by enlarging the terms of communion so as to take in all sorts of dissenters '. On the other hand, from Swift's point of view one is not only upholding the Test and the Church of England, but also—equally important—defending Christianity against its free-thinking enemies, if one sets up true Christianity as a goal worth striving for. In fairness the essay must be said to accomplish at least six results, all of them interrelated. It attacks the position of the anti-Christian, of the nominal Christian, and of opponents of the Test. It presents facts on the present state of immorality. And it contrasts real Christianity with both the present world of hollow religion and the world of no religion. In doing all this, it continually surprises and delights the reader.

NOTES TO CHAPTER IV

[1] On the dating of the three pamphlets discussed in this chapter, see : Herbert Davis, ed., *The Prose Works of Jonathan Swift* (Oxford, 1939–), II, ' Introduction ' ; and Irvin Ehrenpreis ,' The Date of Swift's " Sentiments ",' *Review of English Studies*, III (July, 1952), 272–4.

[2] *Works*, III, 55, 61–2.

[3] *Works*, III, 51–6.

[4] *Ibid.*, 57–9.

[5] *Ibid.*, 65–6.

[6] *Ibid.*, 70–2.

[7] *Correspondence*, III, 120.

[8] *Works*, III, 60.

[9] *Ibid.*, V, 380.

[10] *Ibid.*, IV, 199.

[11] *The Mind and Art of Jonathan Swift* (1936), p. 136.

[12] *Works*, III, 54–5.

[13] *The Mind and Art of Jonathan Swift*, p. 53.

[14] *The Satire of Jonathan Swift*, p. 51 ; *Prose Works*, II, xx–xxi.

[15] *Works*, III, 28–35, 40–5.

[10] The tract, according to Dr. Davis, was evidently a revision of a paper mentioned by Swift in October, 1708 ; it was probably printed in April, 1709. (*Prose Works*, II, xx). He calls it a ' Tory tract ', evidence, as Swift said, that he had written against the Whigs before 1710. (*The Satire of Jonathan Swift*, p. 51).

[17] Louis A. Landa, review of Ricardo Quintana's *Mind and Art of Jonathan Swift*, *Modern Philology*, XXXV (1937), 203. See also Professor Quintana's suggestion that a multiplicity of voices are involved in the tract. (' Swift as a Situational Satirist ', 135–6).

[18] *Prose Works*, II, xix.

[19] *Works*, III, 5–7, 8, 13. The author misquotes '*Deorum iniurias dis curae* ' as ' *Deorum offensa diis curae* '. The sense—that offences against the Gods are to be avenged by them—remains essentially unchanged. The quotation is appropriate to the author's argument that there would be far more ' pernicious ' consequences from attacks on political groups than on religion.

[20] *Ibid.*, 6.

[21] *Ibid.*, 5–7.

[22] *Ibid.*, 19. An interesting parallel, which for contemporary readers would establish the author as a concrete character, occurs in *The Conduct of the Allies*, where

Swift mentions that the city coffee-houses have for some years been filled with people whose fortunes depend upon the Bank, East India, or some other stock. (*Works*, V, 111).

[23] *Ibid.*, III, 6, 7.
[24] *Ibid.*, III, 18–19.
[25] *Ibid.*, 8–11.
[26] *Ibid.*, 14.
[27] *Ibid.*, 6.
[28] *Ibid.*, 13–15.
[29] *Ibid.*, 7–8.
[30] *Ibid.*, 9–17.
[31] *Ibid.*, 10–11.
[32] *Ibid.*, 6.

V

THE MEMBER OF THE IRISH PARLIAMENT

Swift was born in Ireland of English parents. Although he spent much of his early career in England, and although his feelings for Ireland were by no means unmixed, he was well aware, long before he wrote the *Drapier's Letters* and the *Modest Proposal*, that the Irish were suffering from certain injustices of English rule. Probably as early as 1707 he had written the *Story of an Injured Lady*,[1] a monologue in which the wretched Lady (a *persona* allegorically symbolizing Ireland) protests against the unkind persecutions of her faithless lover (England), who is about to marry (Act of Union) her tall, lean, sluttish rival (Scotland) ; in *An Answer*, her friend gives her helpful advice on managing her household (measures similar to those Swift would urge later, on bettering Ireland's economic and political status). These two short pieces were never printed in Swift's lifetime. But in December, 1708, there appeared in Dublin and London a tract supposedly written by a Member of the Irish Parliament to a member of Parliament (controlled at the time by the Whigs) in England, a *Letter Concerning the Sacramental Test*. It was Swift in a new disguise, arguing against an extreme Whig plan to repeal the Test in Ireland before repealing it in England. The disguise was necessary : Swift was at this time on good terms with the Whigs in Parliament, from whom he hoped to get certain benefits for the Irish Church, and he did not wish to alienate them. But, more important, the mask was a tool of ironical argument. For Swift—in order to deal with repeal and (incidentally) certain Irish grievances— becomes an Irish spokesman whose most obvious characteristic, like that of the Drapier, is humility.

This humility takes two primary forms ; an extreme, self-debasing affection for England, so that he expresses the exact opposite of what Swift felt ; and a mild deference toward the English, so that he seems to be voicing Swift's own ideas in an unusually polite manner. The two attitudes of the author coincide rather closely with the two main divisions of the essay. As the author moves from one to the other, his attributes change to serve Swift's satiric purpose.

In the first part of the essay the author protests against the false reports current in England that Presbyterians in Ireland are suffering injustices. He expresses his great love for England and states his main case : that the Sacramental Test is not unjust. In the second part of the essay he argues politely in favour of the Test. This argument includes his opinions that repeal would cause Presbyterianism to spread, and that repeal probably could not be made workable in Ireland.

The first section is for the most part diffuse in organization, containing long paragraphs and a certain amount of what appears to be irony; this section contains only a few striking metaphors. The second section is more straightforwardly organized. Main topics are announced with such a phrase as 'Now I would consider . . .' With perhaps one exception—a digression on persecution—the topics follow a clear outline form. Yet in this later part Swift relies heavily upon vivid metaphors and analogies. To understand the difference between the two sections it is necessary to examine the character of the author as he is presented in each.

The first is designed to inspire the Irish people to stand for their rights. The tract begins with an unusually long first paragraph, in which the author straightforwardly lists certain falsehoods that have been circulated in England about Ireland:

> I received your letter, wherein you tell me of the strange representations made of us on your side of the water . . . But it is easy to observe, how mighty industrious some people have been for three or four years past, to hand about stories of the hardships, the merits, the number, and the power of the Presbyterians in Ireland, to raise formidable ideas of the dangers of Popery there, and to transmit all for England, improved by great additions, and with special care to have them inserted with comments in those infamous weekly papers that infest your coffee-houses.

Here and there he interjects remarks consciously using the irony of inverted values. Lies about Ireland, he says, were ' printed with shrewd remarks by your worthy scribblers '. For bad qualities he ranks Tutchin above Defoe:

> The Observator is much the brisker of the two, and I think farther gone of late in lies and impudence than his Presbyterian brother.

As the author criticizes the English coffee-house view of Ireland, the reader feels that this is the true indignant Swift himself arguing as he might if he were an actual member of the Irish Parliament. But even in this first paragraph there are hints of the humble character of the author, which are later to be developed. He prefaces his remarks on the papers against the Test by saying apologetically, ' I know it may be reckoned a weakness to say anything of such trifles as are below a serious man's notice'. Fitting his powerfully abusive point perfectly with this mild attitude, and combining humility with invective, he goes on to say about the 'wretches' who wrote them, 'Much less would I disparage the understanding of any party to think they would choose the vilest and most ignorant among mankind, to employ them for assertors of a cause.' He then disparages one of the 'weekly libellers', Defoe :

> One of these authors (the fellow that was pilloried, I have forgot his name) is indeed so grave, sententious, dogmatical a rogue, that there is no enduring him.

It is a mistake to conclude that here Jonathan Swift has (perhaps ironically) forgotten Defoe's name. Rather Swift attacks Defoe by writing as an Irishman of no more than average information. After all, who could be expected to know Defoe's name outside England ?

The *persona* is still only slightly developed. But as Swift proceeds to the most powerful section of the whole essay, in which he violently attacks the way England has treated Ireland, he wages his campaign purely by exploiting the humility of the author, so fondly infatuated with England. In the first paragraph he had said that the repeal of the Test is 'a matter purely national, that cannot possibly interfere with the trade and interest of England '.[2] More explicitly, he tells the English parliamentarian that he will give his opinion freely on the Test :

> only, whereas you desire my thoughts as a friend, and not as I am a member of parliament, I must assure you they are exactly the same in both capacities.

This affirmation of friendship leads to an unusually effective passage. The author speaks both for himself and for the Irish people :

> We are generally surprised at your wonderful kindness to us on this occasion, in being so very industrious to teach us to see our interest, in a point where we are so unable to see it ourselves.

Then he says that the English attitude has made the Irish people in general suspicious :

> Though, in my own particular, I am hugely bent to believe, that whenever you concern yourselves in our affairs, it is certainly for our good ; yet I have the misfortune to be something singular in this belief, and therefore I never attempt to justify it but content myself to possess my own opinion in private, for fear of encountering men of more wit, or words than I have to spare.[3]

Swift's use of the *persona* here is extremely adroit. For the author speaks not for the English, for the Irish, or for Swift, but simply for himself. In standing alone in his affection for England he is shown to be foolish, afraid of encountering someone of more wit and words who dislikes the English treatment of Ireland. Such a passage is so extreme in itself as to be ridiculous. It shows the weakness and folly of anyone who holds the author's views. And it gives Swift a chance to show the true strong resentment the vast majority of Irish feel against the English, for behind the foolish protestation of the author is the insistent suspicion of his countrymen.

By continuing to exploit the author's character, Swift makes the most strongly emotional point of the whole essay, and one of the strongest in all his works. He introduces this by the ironical, yet sobering factual statement of the author that ' we at this distance, who see nothing of the spring of actions, are forced by mere conjecture, to assign two reasons for your desiring us to repeal the Sacramental Test ' : one, repeal would be a step toward the ' like good work ' in England ; and two, it would permit a way to reward the ' worthies ' who cannot now hold office. He is still firm in his inverted affection for the English and in his inverted praise of repeal and dissenters ; but the two reasons are facts which hit home. Then the author, a practical parliamentarian (who only once cites classical history, and who uses only two common Latin phrases),[4] apologizes that ' I do not frequently quote poets, especially English, but I remember there is in some of Mr. Cowley's love verses a strain which I thought extraordinary at fifteen '. In his phrase ' especially English ' there is a mild jab at England, though not one inconsistent with the character of the speaker, who sees poetry mainly as a pastime for adolescents. These lines, he goes on, he has often since imagined to be spoken by Ireland :

> Forbid it Heaven my Life should be
> Weigh'd with her least conveniency.

This phrase leads to the climax, in which the author speaks for all the Irish. He urges the English to say plainly what advantage they expect by repealing the Test,

> for we value your interest much more than our own : If your little finger be sore, and you think a poultice made of our vitals will give it any ease, speak the word and it shall be done.

The infatuated feeling is amplified : the interest of all Ireland is less important than that of one of England's poorest fishing towns ; the author would be willing to blow up his house to protect a metaphorical English stable from fire, but he should not be required to come next morning to thank the Englishman. The extremeness of the humility, and this final undercutting remark, may indicate that the author is aware of the irony of what he is saying. If so, he is only consciously exaggerating his own recurrent habit (which Swift in either case intends to ridicule) of being obsequious toward the English and of not attacking their policies toward Ireland.

Throughout the second part of the essay, the author replaces this extreme humility with mild deference. He treats the member of the English Parliament simply as a friend. There are no extreme expressions of love for England. The style is well-mannered and informative. After the passage about how Broderick told the Bishop of Kilaloe he hoped there would soon be no bishops in Ireland, the author politely says, ' These last lines, perhaps you think a Digression ; therefore to return . . . ' In discussing the clergy the author can begin : 'And I must let you know, that we of Ireland . . . generally love and esteem our clergy.' Such an Irishman can express Swift's ideas with persuasive reasonableness. With clear, straightforward logic based upon his own extensive observations, the author decides first that the repeal would not be likely to succeed because (1) there are very few dissenters in Parliament ; (2) most members of Parliament are moderate Whigs, opposed to the Presbyterians ; (3) the bishops in the House of Lords are Whigs, against repealing the Test ; and, lastly, (4) the whole clergy are against repeal, being Whigs and devoted to the Queen. He argues in the second place that repeal should not be introduced to prevent the rise of popery, since the Irish papists are as powerless as women and children. Lastly he says repeal would not unite Anglicans and dissenters against the common enemy, popery, since it is no aid to friendship to confer a right on a faction which never had this right, and since there is no guarantee that, if in power, the dissenters would grant even toleration to Anglicans.[5]

Polite and friendly, the author finds it difficult to speak harshly even about people Swift disliked. Though the author says the real reason the Irish people oppose repeal is that it would encourage the spread of Scottish Presbyterianism, he does not denounce the Scots with forceful directness. In fact, he admires their bravery, industry, devotion to their religion, and love of each other. They are a ' noble nation ', he says, going on to praise their ' extreme parsimony, wonderful dexterity in dealing, and firm adherence to one another '. Yet this politeness merely leads to the point that the Scots—because of these good qualities—are not quick to assimilate members of the native Irish population. They force the Irish to move. Even worse, they are the deadly enemies of the Anglican religion, since ' they bring along with them from Scotland a most formidable notion of our church, which they look upon at least three degrees worse than Popery '. And, he adds, ' It is natural it should be so, since they come over full fraught with that spirit which taught them to abolish Episcopacy at home '. Thus the passage which began 'And, pray, observe, how we reason here in Ireland upon this matter ' concludes, still perfectly consistently, with a deadly thrust. As an example of the speaker's point of view, it is perfectly convincing.

Swift can manage well to hold back his genuine feelings while he expresses merely the facts supporting his ideas. But this quality can break down in passages in which temporarily the author, like Swift himself, speaks in bitter direct statement and consciously uses the irony of inverted values. Pointing out that some people want to abolish the Church, he refers to ' an honest bellwether of our house ' who ' had the impudence some years ago, in Parliament time, to shake my Lord Bishop of Kilaloe by his lawn sleeve ', and tell him that he hoped to see the clergy abolished. The word ' impudence ', as well as the parenthetical remark, ' You have him now in England, I wish you could keep him there ', reflects Swift's true feeling, and intensifies the irony of the praise for the ' honest bellwether '. Yet Swift holds his indignation in check as the author apologetically begins the next paragraph with ' These last lines perhaps you think a digression '.

Another value of the *persona* in this essay is that details of his life can be used to illustrate his argument. Except for the passage on poetry, the autobiographical references in the essay all occur in the latter part; they add concreteness, interest, weight and distinction, to Swift's argument, and increase the credibility of what he is saying. The author casually mentions, for example, the fact that ' when I was last in England, I told the King, that the highest Tories we had with us would make tolerable Whigs there ' ;[6] what an Irish parliamentarian said to the King must be important. As a member of Parliament he can strengthen his argument by telling how he and several other parliamentarians asked the clergy their opinions with regard to the repeal, and found out that all were against it ; there was ' but one divine, that we could hear of, in the whole kingdom, who appeared of a contrary sentiment '.[7]

The author, however, refers to himself less often as a public figure than as a private individual. Reinforcing the argument that the dissenters would never grant the Anglicans toleration, he says, ' I have been so very idle, as to read above fifty pamphlets, written by as many Presbyterian divines, loudly disclaiming this idol toleration'. He continues with an even more vivid picture substantiating his argument, of how ' I should be loathe to . . . steal to prayers in a back room, as my grandfather used in those times when the Church of England was malignant '.[8] Equally concrete is his complaint that he cannot maintain English farmers on his land when there are Scots in the neighbourhood, even though one English farmer became a Presbyterian in the hopes of joining with them.[9] Elsewhere an illustration can add a sense of deceptive wonder : ' when I was a boy, I often heard the Presbyterians complain, that they were not permitted to serve God in their own way.' The author's boyhood reminiscence, about the time when the dissenters lacked even toleration, brings the argument to life.

The author's character governs even his metaphors. It is due to Swift's ingenuity that the author can make a smooth transition to these from a reasonable statement of an argument or from frank and reasonable reminiscences about his own past. Such a transition occurs as he rejects the arguments that repeal would unite Irish Protestants against a common enemy, popery : ' I have been tired in history with the perpetual folly of those states who call in foreigners to assist them against a common enemy.' In the irritated statement ' I have been tired ' and the term ' perpetual folly ', the author begins to show some impatience with his opponent's argument. This anger finds its outlet in a vivid metaphor :

> 'Tis agreed among naturalists that a lion is a larger, a stronger, and more dangerous enemy than a cat ; yet if a man were to have his choice, either a lion at his foot, bound fast with three or four chains, his teeth drawn out, and his claws pared to the quick, or an angry cat in full liberty at his throat ; he would take no long time to determine.

The metaphor is vivid, but, more important, it is reasonable. Beginning with the universal principle, Swift proceeds to point out the exception to the rule. The metaphor is kept in check by the same control that characterizes the author's direct arguments. The same thing is true of the author's discussion of the increasing demands of the dissenters, whom he compares to a lover complaining of cruelty as long as his lady denies him anything :

> And when the Lady ceases to be cruel, she is from the next moment at his mercy : So persecution, it seems, is everything that will not leave it in men's power to persecute others.

While this metaphor is less logical than the first, it is contained by the same spirit of rationality and (in the undogmatic 'it seems') unaggressiveness. There is more apparent anger in a third metaphor, which makes concrete the distinction between toleration and repeal: 'For, to say the truth, we make a mighty difference here between suffering thistles to grow among us, and wearing them for posies.' This metaphor suggests only in part the outright anger which follows: 'we shall always tolerate them' though it is uncertain that 'they will always tolerate us'; then comes one of the few outbursts of pride and power in the essay: 'and we are the majority, and we are in possession.'[10]

Also near the end of the tract, there is intensity in the author's ironical use of a mocking epithet, as in 'Miserable condition! Woeful dilemma!', to describe the consternation of the dissenters, who cannot fight in self-defence because they cannot take the Test in order to enter the army; and in his mocking retort: 'they had rather lose their estates, liberties, religion, and lives, than the pleasure of governing'. However much one may hear the voice of Swift in scattered passages like these throughout the essay, one must recognize that they do not really contradict the author's essential humility. He can become angry, when it serves Swift's purpose for him to do so. He can himself employ bitter irony to state his case. Yet always we return to his humility. This may be mild, as when he makes his case against repeal, or it may be extreme, when he offers the vitals of Ireland as a poultice for England's little finger. Such a passage as this is not so extended as in *A Modest Proposal*, but it does for a moment take the reader into a world of bitter irony where the author seems hardly to be a real person.

The varied way in which Swift handles the quality of humility should be a sufficient answer to any righteous objection that he was simply trying to mislead people by presenting a specious argument as though it were the sincere product of a genuine Irish parliamentarian. Such trickery is not a primary aim of Swift's *personae*. Although Swift certainly conceals his own identity, it is hard to believe that any careful reader could have examined the extreme irony in the first part of the pamphlet without at least some suspicion about its 'authorship'. This suspicion could not have been wholly explained away by the less likely hypothesis that the author—really an Irish parliamentarian—was consciously indulging in a brilliantly ironical exaggeration of his and Ireland's humility. Yet even when one has these doubts (or when one knows Swift to be the author), the argument is still a powerful one. By recklessly exploiting the supposed humility of a *persona* (in other words, by not writing the entire essay in the more subdued tone of the second section) Swift was able to add immeasurably to the passionate intensity of what he wanted to say. Without this intensity he might have succeeded in fooling a few more of his readers. But much of the effective excellence of the pamphlet would have been sacrificed. These facts should remind us that for Swift the creation of a *persona* was a means to an end, usually satire, and not an end in itself.

NOTES TO CHAPTER V

[1] Herbert Davis, ed., *Prose Works*, IX, ix–x.
[2] *Works*, IV, 5–8.
[3] *Ibid.*, 9–10.
[4] *Ibid.*, 18, 20.
[5] *Ibid.*, 14–8.
[6] *Ibid.*, 12–5.
[7] *Ibid.*, 16. In the first edition of 1709 but not in the 1711 *Miscellanies* printed by Morphew, two paragraphs follow this statement. (*Works*, XII, 120, note). These are what Swift refers to when, not admitting authorship of the pamphlet, he writes to Archbishop King, January 6, 1708–9: 'The author has gone out of his way to reflect on me as a person likely to write for repealing the test, which I am sure is very unfair treatment. This is all I am likely to get by the company I keep. . . . I have told the ministry, with great frankness, my opinion, that they would never be able to repeal it, unless such changes should happen as I could not foresee; and they all believe I differ from them in that point.'

As Swift at this time was on good terms with the Whigs, it would probably not have been expedient for him to have admitted writing the pamphlet; in fact, it was doubtless prudent for him to include this 'suggestion' that he is in favour of repeal, though he reassures King that the suggestion is groundless. King, writing to Swift on February 10, realizes that Swift is the author.

[8] *Ibid.*, IV, 18. Temple Scott (*ibid.*, note) says that the reference is to Thomas Swift, Jonathan Swift's grandfather. Thomas Swift was a staunch Royalist, but the 'grandfather' of the essay must be regarded as equally fictitious as the 'grandson', who is certainly not Swift.
[9] *Ibid.*, 13.
[10] *Ibid.*, 18–21.

VI

BICKERSTAFF AND THE REPORTER

Swift's *personae* often had serious, practical, or fighting work to do in the world. But for him the creation of a mask was more than an exercise of grim calculation. It was a matter of imagination and high humour. These qualities abound even when, as in *Gulliver* and *A Modest Proposal*, Swift feels most intensely the agonies of a mordant indignation. One is reminded frequently of the heroic humour of Beethoven—playful but rough. Yet there were times when Swift could create characters out of a sheer love of fun, with no more important purpose than to amuse a reader. This is the Swift who frequently appears in the *Poems*, including ' Mrs. Frances Harris's Petition ', where he writes in the breathless manner of a servant girl who has had several misfortunes :

> Well ; I thought I should have swoon'd ; Lord, said I, what
> shall I do ?
> I have lost my money, and shall lose my True-Love too.

It is also the Swift of the *Meditation upon a Broomstick*, the imitation (written as a joke on Lady Berkeley) of Robert Boyle's *Occasional Reflections*, with its solemn observation, ' Surely man is a broomstick '.[1]

Among his other pursuits in London in 1708 Swift with high spirits conducted a campaign against a well-known maker of astrological almanacs, John Partridge. Swift doubtless was angered by Partridge's abusing the Anglican clergy, and his ulterior motive may well have been to strike back.[2] But Swift's weapon of attack was by no means a direct or sober defense of the clergy. It was the Bickerstaff Papers, a series of pamphlets which for sheer fun-making he never surpassed.

Early in 1708 there appeared in London a pamphlet entitled *Predictions for the Year 1708*, by ' Isaac Bickerstaff '. The ' author ' is a grave and meticulous astrologer, full of a proud and exaggerated admiration for his noble art and full of contempt for its defilers.[3] And he condemns in particular one astrological fraud, John Partridge.

In violent language Bickerstaff censures the ' gross abuses of astrology ' carried on by those ' gross impostors, who set up to be the artists '. Piling one indignant term on another, he reports that these impostors have led some to think ' it is absurd and ridiculous ' that ' stars can have any influence at all on human actions, thoughts, or inclinations.' In exposing the astrologers' fraudulent practice—of

making predictions which will ' suit any age or country in the world '
—Bickerstaff sees them as Swift does. 'A few mean, illiterate traders
. . . import a yearly stock of nonsense, lies, folly, and impertinence ' ;
these men—for example, Partridge—Bickerstaff regards ' with the
utmost scorn and contempt '.

But if the essay were merely a lampoon against Partridge, half the
fun would be lost. For even in the foregoing passages, Swift is careful
to maintain the character of Bickerstaff. It is not merely the mis-
representations of Partridge that bother him ; more important, Partridge has degraded a ' noble art '. A false trader ' between us and the
stars ', he offers lies to the world ' as genuine from the planets '.
Furthermore, Bickerstaff announces his intention ' in a short time, to
publish a large and rational defence of the art', which has ' been in all
ages defended by many learned men '. Swift adds further humorous
interest to the character of Bickerstaff through his constant appeals to
reason and his citation of Socrates (' the wisest of uninspired mortals ')
as a defender of astrology.

After condemning the carelessness of Partridge and other fakes,
Bickerstaff proudly proceeds to describe his own methods. These
involve the most scrupulous care : he will offer none of his findings
to the world unless he is fully sure of them. Limiting himself with
scientific meticulousness, he announces he will publish no secrets of
state, but rather confine himself to minor events at home ; he will,
however, predict major foreign events (by the Old Style Calendar).
Astrology, he honestly admits, has limitations : a man may by reason
oppose the influence of the stars, though it is unlikely that great
numbers of men—on which major events depend—will join in opposing the stars. Though his satisfaction with his system is undeniable,
he proceeds with what he would consider modesty. He frankly admits
mistakes he has made in his past calculations, and he says that ' any
man who reads this paper will look upon me to be at least a person of
as much honesty and understanding, as a common maker of Almanacks.'

His minute carefulness merely makes him more ludicrous as he
goes on to say that he began to calculate his predictions ' from the
time that the sun enters into Aries. And this I take to be properly
the beginning of the natural year ' ; and when he points out his
successful predictions in the past—of the miscarriage at Toulon, and
of the loss of Admiral Shovel—though he modestly adds, in the
interests of truth, that he did miscalculate the exact time of the latter
by about thirty-six hours. This section of the essay contains incidental
satire against Partridge : Bickerstaff invites the reader to compare the

manner of Partridge ' and the rest of his clan ' with the scrupulous
exactness of Bickerstaff, who does not ' lurk in the dark '.[4]

Aware of the true nature of both these ' experts ', the reader arrives
at the really important part of the essay, in which Bickerstaff outlines
events to come. In this section the satire continues to operate against
both Bickerstaff and Partridge, but its content permits Swift to indulge
also in a good many playful irrelevancies. Bickerstaff mentions, for
example, an insurrection in Dauphiné on April 7, a violent storm on the
south-east coast of France, the death of the Dauphin on May 7, and the
fact that on May 9 a Mareschal of France will break his leg by falling
from his horse.

Such details merely give Swift a chance to indulge in some straight-
faced humour: Bickerstaff can't foresee whether the broken leg will
cause the Mareschal's death. He can remark that on May 23 ' a famous
buffoon of the playhouse will die a ridiculous death, suitable to his
vocation '. And he can finish his predictions with one ' in mystical
terms ': a verse from Virgil,

> *Alter erit jam Tethys, et altera, quae vehat, Argo,*
> *Delectos heroas,*

the meaning of which will be clear to everyone on September 25. That
another Tethys and another Argos bearing chosen heroes could be
significant in 1708 is indeed a deep mystery. But the details in this
catalogue of predictions are also important in the satire, for they do
bear out what Bickerstaff said earlier, that his predictions are not of
the false sort that would fit any time and any age. His mind, the
reader must agree, is nothing if not exact. And his conclusions, he
says, are reinforced by ' eighteen years diligent study and application '.

Bickerstaff continues mercilessly to expose the mistakes of Partridge.
He cannot bear the ignorance of ' those sottish pretenders to astrology '
who ' with an old paltry cant, and a few pot-hooks for planets to
amuse the vulgar, have, in my opinion, too long been suffered to abuse
the world '. But Partridge's days are numbered. For Bickerstaff
predicts that he ' will infallibly die upon the 29th of March next, about
eleven at night, of a raging fever '.[5] This fact, of course, is ' but a
trifle '; Bickerstaff mentions it among more important predictions
(such as that of the death of a playhouse buffoon, for example) only to
show how ignorant the astrological impostors are when it comes to
their own affairs. This is the point for which the whole essay was
written. Bickerstaff had predicted the event. The London audience
would wait to see what happened.

In the next pamphlet[6] Swift shifts his rôle. From an astrologer he becomes an intelligent, self-effacing, and observant reporter, a former employee in the Revenue Office, who carefully records, in obedience to the commands of a noble lord, an *Account of the Death of Partridge*. Bickerstaff was right! Moreover, in Partridge's last hours several things had happened which would make one doubt the validity of his astrology—though not that of Bickerstaff's, of course !

It is no small compliment to Bickerstaff that the reporter, as well as his noble friend, shows a genuine, though critical, curiosity about the validity of his predictions. Objectively and accurately the reporter sets down the facts about his own acquaintance with Partridge and about the circumstances of his death. He recalls that Partridge used to present him and others in the Revenue Office with a copy of his almanac, ' upon the score of some little gratuity we gave him '. Ten days before Partridge died the reporter saw him appear to droop and languish—but, he adds, ' his friends did not seem to apprehend him in any danger '.

Although the friends at the death-bed said Partridge had been delirious, the reporter notes that ' when I saw him he had his understanding as well as ever I knew '. Two famous quacks, the author observes, Dr. Case and Mrs. Kirleus, were sent for to tend to Partridge in his dying hours, and on his death-bed Partridge ' declared himself a non-conformist, and had a fanatic preacher to be his spiritual guide '. There is an attitude of aristocratic, detached superiority towards so base a creature as Partridge in the author's saying that he went to see Partridge on his death-bed ' partly . . . out of curiosity ' ; in his report that Partridge ' seemed surprised ' at this show of condescension ; and in his saying that he could not stay with Partridge to the end, for ' after half an hour's conversation ' he was ' almost stifled with the closeness of the room '. But he still feels commiseration for ' poor Partridge '.

But the author came not merely to observe, but also to question. As he talks with Partridge, he guides the conversation politely, yet with a pertinacious interest in getting at the facts. As the answers to his questions come out, we recognize the second character Swift has brought to life in this three-page pamphlet, Partridge himself. There is a distinct contrast between the cool, objective, transparent style of the author and the violent piling up of terms, the expressions of strong contempt, and the use of concrete detail in what Partridge says. With thoroughgoing repentance, he harshly condemns himself and astrologers generally. Bickerstaff, he feels sure, was merely guessing about the future, about which he knew no more than Partridge himself.

F

At this, the reporter shows surprise : intelligently he wishes Partridge could ' tell me what reason he had to be convinced of Mr. Bickerstaff's ignorance '. Partridge replies that although he himself is a ' poor ignorant fellow, born to a mean trade ', he has sense enough to see that ' all pretenses of foretelling by astrology are deceits ', because the wise and learned universally ' laugh at and despise ' the pseudo-science. One hears Swift's voice (though these frauds are not worth his anger) in the appeal to the judgment of the wise as later in the scorn for the ' poor ignorant vulgar ' who, according to Partridge, believe the ' word of such silly wretches as I and my fellows who can hardly write or read '.

Swift thus cleverly puts the respectable, sceptical reporter as well as Bickerstaff in the wrong, while it is the repentant Partridge who comes closest to the truth. When the reporter seriously asks Partridge whether he has ' calculated his own nativity, to see whether it agreed with Bickerstaff's prediction', Partridge bursts out impatiently, ' Oh! sir, this is no time for jesting, but for repenting those follies, as I do now from the very bottom of my heart '. All astrologers, he admits, follow a ' common form ' and largely invent their predictions. He is momentarily pitiful as he says that he carried on this false art only to support a wife, since he had ' no other way to get . . . bread ', and ' mending old shoes is a poor livelihood '. This mournfulness carries into his last repentance (prefaced by a sigh) that he hopes he has done no more harm by his dabbling in medicine than by his astrology ; in medicine he depended upon ' some good receipts from my grand-mother ' and such compositions of his own ' as I thought could at least do no hurt '. This satire is all the more effective for drawing the reader into sympathy with the quack who, nearing the end of life, has nothing to look back to but a series of hoaxes he has perpetrated on the innocent. Before Partridge has finished repenting his fraudulent ways, the author has come to his serious and objective conclusion : ' By what I can gather from you, the observations and predictions you printed with your almanacks, were mere impositions on the people '.

Through this whole scene the reporter's respect for Partridge has been declining. But his respect for Bickerstaff, though never without reservation, mounts steadily. The author leaves the house and tells a servant to come to a nearby coffee-house and report the exact minute of Partridge's death, so that the author can check exactly on Bickerstaff. It turns out that the actual time of Partridge's death is almost four hours from the time Bickerstaff predicted. But, the author adds fairly, ' in the other circumstances he was exact enough '. Objectively, though somewhat critically of the results of Bickerstaff's work, he says, 'whether he hath not been the cause of this poor man's death, as well as the predictor, may be very reasonably disputed'. But at the end of the essay the author, still carefully weighing the evidence, and still a sceptic, is just about to admit belief in Bickerstaff. ' The matter is odd enough,' he says, ' whether we should endeavour to account for it by chance or the effect of imagination.' He concludes, that though no one has ' less faith in these matters ', yet he will wait, not without expectation, for the second death Bickerstaff predicted, that of the Cardinal de Noailles on April 4. If that should be verified, ' I must own I should be wholly surprised, and at a loss, and infallibly expect the accomplishment of all the rest '. All that Bickerstaff could say about himself would add nothing to the dignity of his reputation when it is attested to by such an intelligent, sceptical, and eminent observer.

Partridge, for many people, was indisputably dead. 'An Elegy on Mr. Partridge, the Almanack-Maker' appeared, a broadside written by Swift with an epitaph at the end. Stationers' Hall took Partridge's name off its rolls,[7] and obtained the right to continue his almanac after his death '.[8] It was in vain that in *Squire Bickerstaff Detected* (probably written by Swift and Congreve, and, through a trick, published by the unsuspecting Partridge in his own defence) and in his almanac for the following year he argued that he was still alive. For Isaac Bickerstaff was ready, in *A Vindication of Isaac Bickerstaff Esq.*, to prove once and for all that Partridge was, to all logic, dead.

Bickerstaff rises to the defence of the integrity of his art with all the dignity of which he is capable. He is still interested in ' the discovery of truth, which ought to be the great end in all disputes of the learned '. He modestly censures the roughness of Partridge's attack on him, since, though ' philosophers have differed in all ages, . . . the discreetest among them have always differed as became philosophers '. But he has a selfless concern for ' the republic of letters, which Mr. Partridge hath endeavoured to wound through my sides '. He exhibits his old amusing scrupulousness, in saying that ' few men are readier to own their errors than I ', and the same moderation, in designing to handle all questions with ' brevity, perspicuity, and calmness '. His high regard for his noble art remains undiminished. These matters are ' too serious to be trifled with '. Lamenting that these things ' of the greatest importance ' are turned into ridicule, he grieves to see his labours, 'which had cost me so much thought and watching, bawled about by the common hawkers of Grub Street '. He regrets that it was reported that he miscalculated Partridge's death by four hours, whereas in reality he missed it by only a half-hour ; he humbly qualifies even this statement by his ' private opinion ' that this was an error of no great magnitude. Throughout he shows the same serene confidence : he had no doubt that his prediction about Partridge's death would be verified, and at the end of the essay he reaffirms that he has proved ' by invincible demonstration ' that Partridge really has died.

It is the quality of this demonstration which provides the best satire of the essay and which distinguishes the character of Bickerstaff here from that in the *Predictions*. Bickerstaff now writes not as an opponent of Partridge, piling up abusive terms against his enemy. Rather he takes up a position so lofty that he can only look down with pity upon poor Partridge :

> I wish Mr. Partridge knew the thoughts which foreign universities have conceived of his ungenerous proceeding with me : but I am too tender of his reputation to publish them to the world.

Even a vivid scene is handled with detached humour : Bickerstaff says that ' the said carcass '—Partridge—had no right ' to beat the poor boy, who happened to pass by it in the street, crying, "A full and true account of Dr. Partridge's death " '.

With such an attitude established, Bickerstaff can patiently give his arguments ' proving ' Partridge is really dead. The first is that people reading Partridge's almanacs continually say, ' " they were sure no man alive ever writ such damned stuff as this " ' ; so it follows that Partridge must either disown his almanac or admit that he is no man alive. Second, Partridge must be dead, since death is defined by philosophy as a separation of soul and body, and Partridge's wife has frequently sworn that he had ' neither life nor soul in him '. Third, in order to tell fortunes and recover stolen goods, Partridge, according to all the parish, must converse with the devil ; he could do this only after death. Fourth, Partridge says he is alive now, and was also alive last March 29 ; but the sophistry of this argument is clear, since he does not dare to assert he has been alive in the meantime. Fifth, it would be improbable that Bickerstaff should begin his predictions ' with the only falsehood that ever was pretended to be in them '. Last, the fact that Partridge continues to write almanacs is no proof of his being alive, since many men long dead still continue to publish their almanacs.

Swift must have enjoyed working out these ' logical proofs '. But to Bickerstaff they are wholly convincing. Rejecting a Frenchman's claim that the Cardinal de Noailles did not die, as Bickerstaff had predicted, he answers, ' how far a Frenchman, a Papist, and an enemy is to be believed in his own case, against an English Protestant, who is true to the government, I shall leave to the candid and impartial reader '. As Bickerstaff scorns Partridge, his pride in his reasonings becomes ludicrous. This is true also as he lists expressions of praise he has received from Leibnitz, Le Clerc, Magliabecchi, and other renowned professors—in a parody of the manner of Swift's old enemy Richard Bentley. As Bickerstaff thus sets himself up as a person far above the level of Partridge, showing Bickerstaff up as illogical (as well as proud) is a means of further debasing Partridge. Bickerstaff can confidently and effortlessly overcome the best of Partridge's reasonings.[9] It is unthinkable that Partridge should be alive !

Bickerstaff had dealt effectively with Partridge, and he was too good and popular a *persona* to be forgotten. In the *Tatler* papers he reappears. The free use Steele made of him has already been mentioned. In the numbers probably written by Swift[10] (including two of William Harrison's *Tatler* papers, which appeared after Steele gave up the enterprise, January 2, 1710–11) Bickerstaff appears less distinctly— reporting a dream, criticizing manners[11]—than in his attacks on Partridge. In other papers attributed to Swift or ' containing hints furnished by him ' (including four of Harrison's), Bickerstaff—still occasionally presented as old, and humorously pompous—acquires not only a sister, Jenny, but other new characteristics. He can express his indignation at being called ' honest Isaac ' by a lord, who in his insolence thus insulted a man of wit and learning ;[12] he can refer to ' the awe and reverence due to the character I was vested with ', and in an inflated manner inform his fair correspondent Sylvia : ' there was formerly such a philosopher as Pythagoras '. Bickerstaff, in accepting Pythagoras' doctrine of the transmigration of souls, thinks that since the days of the Emperor Trajan his own Bickerstaff-soul has passed quickly from one body to another, always scourging the follies of the world.[13]

Moreover, he becomes a projector. He would like to set up a system of ' rural censors ' who would report all instances of offensive conduct to him, as ' Censor of Great Britain '.[14] He also has a ludicrously exaggerated plan for a Chamber of Fame, in which all men will be ranked according to the opinion other people have of them.[15] Swift could later write great satire (*A Modest Proposal*) by impersonating a projector, but such a scheme as Bickerstaff's seems, by comparison, to be mere careless play. And the fine subtlety of the former portrayal of the astrologer is gone.

Swift never again returns to Isaac, as he never returns to any other of his *personae* after they have served their purpose. But he was later to use characters similar to those which appear in the Bickerstaff papers. Du Baudrier, the Frenchman who ' writes ' *A New Journey to Paris*, is, with a great difference, a ' reporter '. So is Gulliver, especially as he recalls the conversations with the King of Brobdingnag and the Houyhnhnm master. Among Swift's masks the closest relation of Bickerstaff himself is Simon Wagstaff, who reveals himself best in the ' Introduction ' to *Polite Conversation*, published in 1738. For even in his later years Swift could handle a Bickerstaffian character. The grand humour and imagination that went into the creation of the serious astrologer were never really lost. But for the most part Swift found it necessary to use them for more significant purposes.[16]

NOTES TO CHAPTER VI

[1] *Works*, I, 333–4.

[2] Herbert Davis, ed., *Prose Works*, II, x.

[3] Professor W. A. Eddy shows that in Tom Brown's cruder attack on Partridge, *Sylvester Partridge's Prophesie* (1700), Sylvester, like Bickerstaff, has a high concept of astrology, a scorn of charlatans, and a willingness to acknowledge his miscalculations. But Sylvester specializes in domestic rather than foreign news and attacks Partridge more for medical quackery than astrology. (' Tom Brown and Partridge the Astrologer ', *Modern Philology*, XXVIII [1930–1], 163–8).

[4] *Works*, I, 301–5.

[5] *Ibid.*, 305–10.

[6] *Ibid.*, 313–5.

[7] *Poems*, I, 97–101, and note.

[8] Eddy, ' The Wits vs. John Partridge, Astrologer ', *Studies in Philology*, XXIX (Jan., 1932), 37–8.

[9] *Works*, I, 319–24.

[10] On the authorship of these contributions to the *Tatler* see the ' Introduction ' of Dr. Herbert Davis to *Prose Works*, II, xxv–xxxvi.

[11] Harrison's No. 5 (*ibid.*, 178–83) ; and his No. 20 (*ibid.*, 184–7).

[12] Harrison's No. 1 (*ibid.*, 249) ; and his No. 8 (*ibid.*, 258).

[13] Harrison's No. 28 (*Prose Works*, II, 261–3).

[14] Harrison's No. 2 (*ibid.*, 255–6).

[15] No. 67 (*ibid.*, 239–40).

[16] To the Bickerstaff papers should be added the *Famous Prediction of Merlin* of 1709. (*Works*, I, 329). The ' author ', T. N. Philomath, says his notes on Merlin's prophecy do not force Merlin's words ' into any other sense than what they will naturally bear ' ; yet every note contains an impossible distortion of a simple meaning. Professor Eddy shows that this pamphlet, like Tom Brown's *Prophecies out of Merlin's Carmen*, is a parody on Partridge's *Merlinus Liberatus*. (' The Wits vs. John Partridge, Astrologer,' 34). Swift shows the author to be ridiculous by exaggeration.

VII

THE EXAMINER AND DU BAUDRIER

(a) THE EXAMINER

Swift had disappointed the Whig leaders by opposing repeal of the Test. They had disappointed him by failing to have certain tithes remitted to the Church of Ireland. Late in 1710 Swift shifted his political allegiance and began working for the Tories, who had recently come into power and who willingly granted the funds to the church. One of his first duties was to take over the writing of a three months old weekly paper, the *Examiner*, the purpose of which was to defend the policies of the Tory government, headed by Harley and St. John. Swift found it advantageous not to make an obvious and straightforward partisan defence. Instead, giving his *persona* a more definite character than it had under the previous writers of the paper, Swift wrote as an ' Examiner ', an impartial[1] observer who expresses his own independent views[2] and takes a middle course between Whigs and Tories.[3] To him the division of the nation into parties is unfortunate, since the only disagreement between them is over means—both professing a mighty zeal for religion and government.[4] Parties, he thinks, divide not only a nation but also an individual's wit, honesty, and good nature.[5] As the Examiner speaks—a representative of the moderate group between the extremes which are equally far from the truth[6]—one may well hear the voice of the fair-minded Swift of the *Sentiments of a Church of England Man*. One may also find something admirable in the Examiner's humility. He says he is a ' bashful and unexperienced ' writer,[7] a mere examiner, not a reformer.[8] Another paper, he finds, is better in style and spirit than his own.[9] And he can say that if he does not treat a particular subject well, he desires to be excused, as ' talking out of my trade '.[10] But one should recognize that the objectivity and humility of the *persona* often conceal a purposeful irony.

The Examiner is Swift's main contribution to the group of more or less clearly defined *personae* (see Chapter I) who were the supposed authors of a number of the periodicals of his day. The journalistic nature of the Examiner—the fact that he writes not one work, but a series—tends to distinguish him from Swift's other masks. Swift is less careful to make him literally consistent.[11] Also, like the Church of England Man, he is more of a generalized type and not so much of an individual as Swift's authors usually are. We know less about him than, for example, the nominal Christian and far less than we know about the Irish parliamentarian or the author of *A Tale of a Tub*.

But the satire of the *Examiner* depends in large part upon the exploitation of the author's characteristics. Dr. Herbert Davis[12] notes the irony in *Examiner* XXXV, where the Examiner says that only the unthinking would call his writings satire. If the Whigs should regain power, he says, they would honour the Examiner and boast of the very things he accuses them of—such as ' intending great alterations in religion and government ' and designing against Harley's life. For the truth is praise to one side and satire to another.[13] The point here depends upon the assumptions that what has been said about the enemy is true, and that his sense of values is so inverted that he delights in evil. But the method also reflects the character of the author : the affectation of harmless objectivity is basic.

Since the Examiner claims to have an entirely detached view of the world, he can present a satiric message (frequently an exaggeration) under the guise of fact. For example, he quite frankly says he is resolved to report any bad government in the Tory administration, but that he has never found any.[14] He summarizes fairly the charges that Tories and Whigs throw at each other, cites the reasons behind the Tory charges, but humbly adds that he can find no justification for the Whig attacks.[15] To present the facts is his aim, not to please one side and oppose another. And he finds himself, because of his moderate attitude, criticized by both Whigs and Tories, for being at once too severe and too gentle.[16]

In connection with this type of satire—over thirty issues were written by Swift—it is not surprising to find inconsistencies in the characterization of the author. Although at first he claims to write as an independent, it soon becomes clear that he considers himself a member of one ' faction '—which includes the Queen, the Tory Ministry, and nine-tenths of the people ;[17] that he writes as a volunteer in the service of a ' flourishing ministry ', though without being officially recognized by the Tories for his efforts ; and finally that he frankly writes ' to expose the gross impositions of the fallen party '.[18] And with this breakdown of the actual attributes of his mask goes a partial breakdown of his characteristics of humility and objectivity. He can straightforwardly inform the people that his purpose is to show how they have been ' abused ' by the men of ' new-fangled moderation ',[19] or, even more bitterly, say that as long as ' that faction ' —the Whigs—remain in their ' frantic ' state, he will treat them as they deserve, ' as the inveterate, irreconcilable enemies to our country and its constitution '. This is invective, and it reminds one that when Swift abandons his pose he can frequently go to an extreme of direct attack which is also a distortion—by exaggeration—of what he considered the literal truth.[20] But even here the frontal assault is not so violent as it might be. The first quotation is qualified by the protestation that he will state the facts, but with ' due regard to truth, discretion, and the safety of my person from the men of the new-fangled moderation '. The second is qualified by the statement that the Whigs will receive frank treatment only while in their present frantic state.

Swift subdues even his satiric metaphors and figures in keeping with his mask. He asks the Whigs, for example, why they consider it no disrepute to them to have a ' whole herd ' of Presbyterians, Independents, and atheists under their banner. The uncomplimentary term ' herd ' is concealed by the Examiner's ' genuine ' interest in the Whig policy. Likewise, when he illustrates the purpose of satire by saying that it is a supplement to law, and by adding the analogy that next to taming or binding a savage animal, the best service one can do is to warn the neighbourhood, he only states colourlessly the analogy between the Whig party and the ' savage animal ' without developing it into a powerful comparison.

Even in the instances where the mask of humble objectivity is forgotten, so that the Examiner becomes frankly superior to his enemies, the victory is restrained. He leaves the question of whether he has written only of things, not of persons, to his ' little antagonists, who may want a topic for criticism.'[21] The triumph goes no further than this single phrase of name-calling. Likewise, in the final paper, when he parallels his operation to that of a victorious general—sending out ' small bodies, in order to take in petty castles and forts, and beat little straggling parties, which are otherwise, apt to make head and infest the neighbourhood '—he does not entirely crush his opponents. They are not that important. In fact, he hardly seems angry : he counts the Whigs ' entirely subdued ; at least until they appear with new reinforcements I shall reckon them as such ', and therefore he has the leisure to examine other abuses.[22] He speaks of his enemies with condescension, not anger, when he says that they print ridiculous replies to him only in order to get him to answer ; for once the quarrel became a matter of attack and reply, he says, he and they would be on a single level, and this equality is what the Whigs want.[23]

The most serious inconsistencies in the mask come when the author flatly contradicts himself about details of his own life. For example, showing himself to be different from Swift, he says that he does not understand ecclesiastical affairs well enough to comment on the convocation of the clergy and the message from the Queen urging them to avoid disputes. Yet in the discussion which follows, the Examiner comprehends quite adequately the disagreements between the low-church bishops and the high-church lower clergy.[24] In a more noticeable contradiction, the Examiner says that the subject of soldiers and armies is out of his trade, and that therefore he must proceed cautiously. He then writes an entire *Examiner* showing a surefooted knowledge of the history of military activity since the time of ancient Greece and Rome, and a clear idea of what the duties and discipline of soldiers should be.[25]

This free use of the author's character would not have bothered many eighteenth century readers : it was not common practice for a writer to be primarily concerned with creating and maintaining a sharply delineated individual character as the supposed author of a serial publication. Indeed, the Examiner is so slightly individualized that one could argue that he is, in his fair attitude, really Swift, and that the irony in the papers is merely Swift's irony, not the exploitation of a genuine *persona*. The Examiner, it is true, is a case on the border-line between the steadily ironical pose (to be discussed later) and the clearly defined mask. Nevertheless, under the name of the Examiner, and using objectivity and humility to ironical advantage, Swift was able to succeed in his purpose : to satirize the late Whig ministry gently (for the most part), factually (though he at times exaggerates), and without excessive malice, and to avoid being drawn into protracted wrangles with the writers on the other side.

(b) DU BAUDRIER

Although Swift could on occasion ridicule his enemies by writing as the Pretender or as an atheistic member of the Kit-Cat Club, the demands of the Tory ministry did not ordinarily call forth Swift's full powers of creating distinct, humorous, or imaginative *personae*. In the summer of 1711, however, there was an occasion which gave him a chance to use again a technique which had appeared first in the Bickerstaff papers. In July, 1711, the ministry sent Swift's friend, Matthew Prior, to France in order to negotiate secretly for an end to the War of the Spanish Succession. In England many felt strongly, supporting Marlborough and other Whig leaders, that England should fight on until the Spanish throne was given to Charles of Austria instead of to the grandson of Louis XIV. Among England and her allies there was an agreement that no nation should make a separate peace. News of Prior's trip leaked out.[26] In an ingenious effort to confuse or laugh down protest against the illegal procedure and to undermine the position of those who wanted no peace without Spain, Swift in September wrote *A New Journey to Paris*. This was a piece which necessarily required the true author's identity to be kept secret. It is a brilliantly fictitious account of Prior's journey to Paris, ' written ' by a French ' reporter ', du Baudrier, who accompanied him, and ' translated ' into English.

One of the most striking things about the *New Journey* is the number of observed details which add verisimilitude and interest to the story. Two typical examples of the minuteness of Baudrier's description are his recording that on the journey the axletree of the chaise broke, requiring two hours to mend, and that Prior's group arrived at Paris on Tuesday, July 20, ' in the cool of the evening '.[27]

Such careful observations are important in establishing the character of Baudrier, who is portrayed with considerable distinctness. These details, as well as the author's own later admission,[28] establish him as a frequent and willing talker. His social status is less clearly defined. In ' The Translator to the Reader ', we are warned that he is a menial servant who takes on the airs of a secretary. The ' translator ' regrets that the author was not a person of more importance, who knew more about the details of Prior's negotiations; on the other hand, the ' translator ' says, Baudrier does give details which a more distinguished author would have omitted, ' and by his not pretending to know more, we cannot doubt the truth of what he relates.'[29] Thus Swift carefully prepares the reader to believe Baudrier's account.

The equivocal social status of the author is a source of subtle, playful humour. He says he was called upon originally to act as Mr. Prior's secretary, the day after Prior's secret arrival in Boulogne from England, because he understood English, ' wrote a tolerable hand, had been conversant with persons of quality, and formerly trusted with secrets of importance.' Actually, however, Baudrier attends Prior as a servant, since Prior has very little need for a secretary.

Throughout the essay Baudrier emphasizes the regard Prior has for him. Prior, at their first meeting, ' accosted me with great civility ' and soon said that ' I had fully answered the character Monsieur de Marais had given me '. During the next few days of the negotiations, Prior sends Baudrier meat and wine from his own table. On the trip from Boulogne to Paris, the diplomats ride in a chaise, while Baudrier accompanies them on horseback, carrying a small valise for Prior.

Once when two cavaliers, armed with pistols, stop the chaise, Baudrier rides on ahead to ' wait the event ' at the next small village because he suspects the contents of the valise are important. The cavaliers, who turn out to be only joking, twit Baudrier for his cowardice, but Prior praises his discretion.[30] Baudrier, after having a long discourse with Prior in Paris, carries the valise on Prior's trip to Versailles ; on their arrival there Prior asks for the valise and takes out a small box of important writings.[31] Yet it is unmistakable that the author is merely a servant. Baudrier ' offers ' his services to Prior at the table ; Prior accepts ' with abundance of apologies '. And the translator, in a foot-note, adds that this is a clear indication of what kind of ' secretary ' Baudrier is.[32] As a reward for ' discretion ' Prior allows Baudrier to see the palace at Versailles, warning him to tell no one of the occasion that brought him to Versailles ; Baudrier adds in his own favour, ' though he did not suppose I needed ' this caution.[33]

Besides being a source of humour, this combination of qualities makes Baudrier, as Sir Walter Scott pointed out,[34] the ideal person to report this intended imperfect story. He must know English, in order to be able to converse with Prior. Yet he must not know too much about the negotiations, since Swift, whatever he knew about them, was not trying to publicize his information. Thus Baudrier, going in and out of the dining room as he serves Prior and the other negotiators, can catch only snatches of the conversation.[35] Such snatches, such slight facts as Baudrier notes, serve one major purpose—to make the illegal secret negotiations of Prior appear as honourable as possible, to add dignity to the character of Prior himself, and, wherever possible, to satirize the Whig opposition.

Baudrier's facts, unlike those of the reporter of Partridge's death, are intended to praise, not ridicule, his subject. Baudrier begins the essay with a dry, factual résumé of Prior's career which shows him as a truly illustrious person, distinguished at Paris ; a friend of the King of France ; a good poet ; a man of business ; a valuable servant of King William ; an excellent diplomat ; and a professor at Cambridge. (The last distinction is corrected by the translator in a footnote : Prior is a fellow, not a professor, of Cambridge.)[36] When Prior sees the King, Baudrier overhears, they talk of two friends they have in common, Newton and Boileau. Prior, praised by Baudrier for his ' wit and vivacity ',[37] is a man who has such a great reputation that a French ' secretary ' is willing to accompany him from Boulogne in any capacity, even as a menial.

Other, purely fictitious, details add something to the reader's

conception of Prior as a patriot. After a long ride in the rain from
Calais to Boulogne, Prior is shut up in a room with the French nego-
tiant, de Torcy, without refreshment.[38] After the negotiations, on the
return from Paris to Calais, Baudrier notes that Prior, tender of
constitution, has caught cold, so that speaking is difficult for him.
More serious is the instance when Baudrier overhears Prior, leaving
Versailles, say firmly to the King and Madame de Maintenon, ' Sir, all
or none, as I have had the honour to tell your Majesty before.'[39]
Prior appears as an excellent and firm diplomat, with the interest of
his country fully at heart. Baudrier reinforces this presentation by
listing as a reason for the choice of Prior as diplomat (in addition to his
known abilities) the fact that King William had formerly sent him to
negotiate the Peace of Ryswick.[40] This clever reference to the negotiations of 1699, which were also secret, and which by 1711 would
probably have been regarded as respectable, adds greatly to Prior's
prestige.

But cleverest of all is the report of a brief bit of conversation
between the negotiants. Baudrier overhears Monsieur de la Bastide
say :

> Good God ! Were ever such demands made to a great monarch
> unless you were at the gates of his metropolis ? . . . It is not
> enough that our king will abandon his grandson, but he must
> lend his own arm to pull him out of the throne ?[41]

Swift here shows Prior making the same impossible demand of the
French that the Whig leaders had made at the Hague in 1709, and which
had caused the French to fight on stubbornly—the demand that King
Louis join the allies in forcing his own grandson off the Spanish
throne. It is significant that in Prior's actual requests, this impossible
demand was forgotten; the English insisted only that the union of
the French and Spanish crowns should be prevented.[42] Swift, in
having Prior fictitiously voice the Whigs' interest, turns the tables on
them. One of the chief Whig gains from continuing the war, the
Tories said, was to enrich Marlborough. De la Bastide seems to be
trying to make Prior change his mind when he begs him to

> consider which is to be more preferred, the good of your country,
> or the particular advantage of your general ; for he will be the
> only gainer among your subjects.[43]

Here is Prior, through the keyhole reports of Baudrier, becoming
the firm, witty, honourable defender of the purposes of the Whigs and
the ambition of Marlborough! But as in the *Account* Swift speaks

through the remarks of Partridge, so here Swift primarily speaks in the
reported conversation of Prior. Baudrier writes that he is surprised
to hear Prior wondering at the misery he observed during the journey,
and

> at the scarcity and poverty of the inhabitants. . . . He seemed to value
> himself very much on the happiness of his own island, which as
> he pretended, had felt no effects, like these, upon trade or agri-
> culture.[44]

It is quite true that France was suffering in 1711. Marlborough,
among others, reported on the high rate of mortality and disease
among the people.[45] Swift, in order to discourage the prolongation
of the war, could not pretend that France was not suffering. The
point in Prior's statement is his claim (' pretend ' means ' claim ' here)
that no such effects had occurred in England. Of course the extent of
the hardships in England was certainly not equivalent to that in
France. But Swift knew that England, and particularly the landed
interest, was undergoing difficulties. He was to write *The Conduct of
the Allies* in large part to show how much England was losing by
continuing the war, which was fought to ruin the public interest and
advance a private ; to enrich Marlborough, the Whig faction and
profiteers ; to destroy the interest of the landed people, who were
having to pay England's debts. Furthermore, England was suffering
from piratical attacks of the French, as well as from the discourage-
ment of trade which these attacks caused. Swift therefore hated to
hear people proudly counter the fact of the lamentable ' heavy debts
and poverty of the nation ' by pointing to the power, courage, and
' inexhaustible riches of England '.[46] He intended Prior's brief reference
to the much greater French suffering to make the English more conscious of their own troubles ; his innocent remark was a reminder that
still more suffering awaited them unless the war were brought to an
end. And the fact of French suffering would seem to make peace
possible.

But Swift had also to warn the English against making impossible
claims as a result of underrating the French. In *The History of the
Four Last Years of the Queen* he says that the French, thought by the
English to be exhausted, were driven in 1709—by the harsh demand
that the French King should with arms help drive his grandson out of
Spain—to finance the war further through three following campaigns,
and finally to defeat the allies at Denain in 1712.[47] In more detail
Swift writes in *The Conduct of the Allies* that even after the battle of

Ramillies in 1706 the French were so discouraged and exhausted that they would have agreed to reasonable terms, but that the exorbitant demands of the allies made them fight on. As a result, Swift summarizes in the *Conduct* (several months after the appearance of Baudrier's pamphlet), the French King has been able to fight a thrifty defensive war, paying his troops with his receipts from the Spanish West Indies and spending his money in his own country ; furthermore, his subjects carry on a piratical war at their own expense, and the King shares in the profits! These facts, he says, show the King ' to be not so sunk in his affairs, as we have imagined, and have long flattered ourselves with the hopes of.'[48]

Details like these are behind Baudrier's confident answer, to Prior's observation on French poverty, that in France only the magnificence and power of the sovereign are considered. The King's grandeur, as evidenced by Versailles, exceeds that of any other Monarch in Europe, Baudrier says, and so what Prior calls poverty is rather the effect of policy in the court, than any real want or necessity.[49] Similarly, the realistic statement of the French King in April, 1711, that he was in a condition of continuing the war ' with honour '[50] finds an extravagant echo in his subject Baudrier's confident announcement that ' our king ' was resolved

> once more to give peace to Europe, notwithstanding the flourishing condition of his fleets and armies, the good posture of his finances, that his grandson was almost entirely settled in the quiet possession of Spain, and that the affairs of the north were changing every day to his advantage.[51]

There is of course humour in this excessive praise, as there is when Baudrier on the ride back to Calais loquaciously entertains Prior, who can't speak because of a cold, with

> the praises of our great monarch, the magnificence of his court, the number of his attendants, the awe and veneration paid him by his generals and ministers, and the immense riches of the kingdom.[52]

But behind this excessive and rather foolish adulation of the monarch —which resembles that of the patriotic English who, Swift says in *The Conduct of the Allies*, can't see the losses in the war for the ' inexhaustible riches ' of the country—there is a definite warning that peace was a desirable thing, and that some kind of intelligent compromise would have to be made, in view of the French strength. This warning is similar to that which concludes the section on the French King's power in *The Conduct* : 'An absolute government may endure a long war, but it hath generally been ruinous to free countries.'[53]

Into the discussion about the French King's great wealth of power, Swift weaves a powerful satiric fact. Baudrier contrasts the distribution of wealth in France with that in England, where, ' it was confidently told (though hardly believed in France) that some subjects had palaces more magnificent than Queen Anne herself.'[54] This reference to Marlborough's Blenheim Palace, introduced as an illustration in an economic discussion, struck home in the mind of a contemporary reader. The cost of the Palace had been originally estimated at one hundred thousand pounds, but by June, 1710, one hundred and thirty-four thousand had been spent, and the work was only half finished.[55] Prior, however, in keeping with his honourable and somewhat Whiggish character in this essay, does not refer further to Marlborough's extravagance. In fact, he disagrees gently with Baudrier, saying that, though he understands the maxims whereby the French are governed, yet, ' for his part, he thought those countries were happier, where the productions of it were more equally divided '. With this humble and intelligent attitude is contrasted the self-assertive statement of Baudrier that Prior ' had no better answer to make me ', and Baudrier's proud exclamation, ' such unaccountable notions is the prejudice of education apt to give '[56] The conversation reminds the reader that Prior, in spite of his Whiggish peace terms, has Swift's approval in his manner, his observations on France, and his ideas. It also reminds the reader that the reporter, Baudrier, is in the main a humorously pretentious, talkative, and opinionated French servant.

As in the *Account of the Death of Partridge*, the reporter is a foil to the character reported on, whose ideas often reflect Swift's. Baudrier is a source of amusement in not realizing the significance of the events he so carefully describes and in not seeing himself as the reader does. Moreover, like the Church of England Man and the observer of Partridge's death, he is among the *personae* who are most like real-life people. These characters are not extreme ironical symbols, having a distorted sense of values, or possessing a quality, such as humility, which is used for a wide variety of satiric purposes. They do not convey Swift's most intense satiric expressions. But Swift was a writer who knew how to control his materials in order to reach a goal. He could create an excellently lifelike *persona* when he found it necessary to do so; when, for example, his party urgently needed *A New Journey to Paris*, a ' pure bite ', ' a formal grave lie, from the beginning to the end '.[57]

(c) IRONY WITHOUT THE MASK

It would be a mistake to give the impression that Swift's writings are the works of one fictitious author after another. In fact, as has been said, only roughly one-third of his works are written behind a clear mask. In general Swift's irony results from the contrast between the surface meaning expressed by the ' author ' and a true meaning underneath. But in the tracts in which Swift creates no fictitious mask, there is also irony. The nature of this irony throws light on a habit of his mind which is clearly related to that which produced the ' authors ' of most of his greatest works.

Frequently in Swift's works one can see him, for rhetorical effect, temporarily adopting attitudes which cover, superficially, his sincere feelings. One may instance his calm, detached attitude toward the Whigs in *The Conduct of the Allies* (1711) and the *History of the Four Last Years of the Queen*, his impersonal view of the *Character of Wharton* (1710):

> Whoever were to describe the nature of a serpent, a wolf, or a crocodile, or a fox, must be understood to do it for the sake of others, without any personal love or hatred for the animals themselves. [58]

and his controlled reference to Walpole :

> I am no more angry with [Walpole] than I was with the kite that last week flew away with one of my chickens ; and yet I was pleased when one of my servants shot him two days after.[59]

In taking on these poses Swift, superficially for a brief instant, pretends in a sense to be someone else.

But a *persona* involves much more. In 1713 Swift wrote, among other things, two pamphlets in which an ironical attitude predominates; yet in neither can he be said to have created a mask. *A Preface to the Bishop of Sarum's Introduction* is an explication of a text written by the Whiggish Bishop Burnet, whom Swift disliked. He enjoyed making fun of the Bishop's style : to Burnet's remark that *Paradise Lost* was the ' perfectest poem . . . in our language ', Swift once added the marginal note : 'A mistake, for it is in English '.[60] In the *Preface* Swift humbly tries to make out His Lordship's meanings, ' translating ' where necessary.[61] He is falsely humble in his amazement at some of Burnet's ideas and in his urging him to mend his style and to ' examine a little into the nature of truth and sometimes hear what she says '.[62] He even falsely praises the ' right reverend historian ' for the ' spirit of

G

candour, charity, and good nature, generosity, and truth' shining through his story.[63] But when necessary for satire, the submissive pose and the false elevation can be overturned : in an imaginative burlesque picture of Burnet as the ' champion' who comes ' armed only with a pocket pistol, before his great blunderbuss could be got ready, his old rusty breastplate scoured, and his cracked headpiece mended ';[64] or in savage invective against his Whiggishness :

> There let the enemies of the Queen, and monarchy and the church, lie, and mourn, and lick the dust, like serpents, till they are truly sensible of their ingratitude, falsehood, disobedience, slander, blasphemy, sedition, and every evil work.[65]

In *The Importance of the Guardian Considered* Swift again is an explicator, this time of Richard Steele's *The Importance of Dunkirk Considered*. Steele had been sent to Parliament ; Swift (on the title-page the 'author' is supposedly ' a friend of Mr. Steele') undertakes patiently and objectively to explain Steele's text to the Bailiff of Stockbridge and Steele's constituents. People outside London, Swift says, might not understand that the real aim of *The Importance of Dunkirk* is to show the importance of Mr. Steele.[66] With objectivity, he shows the resemblances between the Whigs and the French King.[67] Refusing to talk about Steele's early life, ' because I owe him no malice ', Swift can admire his humour, 'for after the first bottle he is no disagreeable companion '. Though Swift ' never knew him taxed with ill nature ', he wonders ' how ingratitude came to be his prevailing vice '.[68] Some people may believe Steele is ungrateful for the favours of Queen Anne, but Swift refuses to share this view : Steele had already accepted his salary from the government and spent the money at least a week before he would insult his prince.[69]

With praise for Steele's ' great eloquence ',[70] genuine concern for Steele's promise to vote in Parliament according to his conscience (this, Swift feels, would make him useless to the Whigs),[71] and modest objectivity, Swift makes one of the most bitter of his personal attacks. At times he abandons the pose : ' What shadow of a pretence has he to offer his crude thoughts in matters of state ? To print and publish them ? '[72] But for the most part the irony is essential. Perhaps the most severe blow comes by way of a mere offhand illustration to show that it is better to insult a minority out of power than a majority in power : ' What bailiff would venture to arrest Mr. Steele, now he has the honour to be your representative ? And what bailiff ever scrupled it before ? '[73]

In both these pamphlets the irony can be said to make the Swift of the surface statement different from the real Swift underneath. He carries the pose further than he ordinarily does. Yet the ' authors ' remain undefined. These works remind us how close the process of irony is to that of creating characters. But they should also remind us that, for Swift at least, the difference between the processes is important: he does his very greatest work not through mere irony but through a mask.

With carefully controlled logic and rhetorical devices (*The Conduct of the Allies*), with irony, and with created characters Swift had served the Tory cause well. Even during these years of serious political responsibilities, however, Swift remains a man of playful and energetic humour. It finds an outlet not only in the immediately political pamphlets which he wrote for Harley and St. John (Oxford and Bolingbroke). It also appears in *Mr. Collins's Discourse of Freethinking*; *Put into Plain English, By Way of Abstract, For the Use of the Poor* (1713), ' written ' by ' a friend of the author '. In the ' Introduction ' the abstract-maker announces his reasons for turning the ' sublime ' deistical writer's *Discourse* into a digest : ' several well-willers to infidelity ' might be frightened away from the original by its ' show of logic, and . . . multiplicity of quotations, . . . which to understandings of that size, might carry an appearance of something like book-learning ' ; further, ' these great discoveries ' should be brought down to the level of the (Whig) frequenters of White's, Tom's, the Kit-Cat, and Hanover Clubs. Finally, these doctrines, if given to the people, will greatly help prolong the war and put the Whigs back in power.[74] In the abstract itself (the parody remotely recalls the *Tale of a Tub* and the *Tritical Essay*) Swift mimics in a mock-logical way the argument of Collins in favour of free-thinking :

> How can a man think at all, if he does not think freely ? A man who does not eat and drink freely, does not eat and drink at all. Why may not I be denied the liberty of free-seeing as well as free-thinking ? Yet nobody pretends the first is unlawful, for a cat may look on a king . . .[75]

The abstract ends with a long list of the greatest freethinkers of history ; Socrates, Plato, Epicurus, Plutarch, Varro, Cato the Censor, Cicero, Seneca, Solomon, the Old Testament prophets, Josephus, Origen, Minutius Felix, Synesius, Bacon, Hobbes, and—finally—

Archbishop Tillotson ! The tract had a religious and political purpose. But it was also a good joke.

There is humorous vitality also in the *Journal to Stella*, in which he sees himself in the playful rôle of ' Pdfr ' (changed by Deane Swift to ' Presto ') ;[76] and in such a ' bite ' as the ' sham subscription for a book ' which, he tells Stella, he composed (at Arbuthnot's instigation) as a jest at the expense of the maids of honour.[77]

These amusements belonged to the days when Swift and the Tory party rode at the top of their power and of fortune's wheel. Yet after he became Dean of St. Patrick's Cathedral in Dublin in 1713 (a move which gave him financial troubles) he could write verses imaginatively and half-humorously portraying himself as miserable, arriving at Harley's gate

> . . . so dirty, pale, and thin,
> Old *Read* would hardly let him in.
> Said Harley, Welcome Rev'rend Dean!
> What makes your Worship look so lean ?
> Why sure you won't appear in Town,
> In that old Wig and Rusty Gown!

Before he met Harley, the Swift of the poem

> Look'd with an easie, careless Mien,
> A perfect Stranger to the Spleen.

But now, fed up with his misfortunes, he begs :

> Then since you now have done your worst,
> Pray leave me where you found me first.[78]

One must not take the character of the Dean in this poem with any more literal seriousness than Swift himself appears to have taken it. But the request in the poem was not to be granted. With a split between Oxford and Bolingbroke the Tory power had been irreparably weakened. Swift despaired of the situation's improving :

> By Faction tir'd, with Grief he waits a while,
> His great contending Friends to reconcile.
> Performs what Friendship, Justice, Truth require :
> What could he more, but decently retire ?[79]

In June, 1714, he left London. In August Queen Anne died and the Tory ministry fell. Swift was, whether he liked it or not, to be Dean of St. Patrick's. But he was also to be Drapier and Gulliver.

NOTES TO CHAPTER VII

[1] *Works*, IX, 270. [5] *Ibid.*, 202. [8] *Ibid.*, 176.
[2] *Ibid.*, 258-9. [6] *Ibid.*, 86. [9] *Ibid.*, 262.
[3] *Ibid.*, 187. [7] *Ibid.*, 108. [10] *Ibid.*, 164.
[4] *Ibid.*, 84.

[11] Because the *Examiner* papers are a group rather than a single work, there are a great many more devices used in them which are not really dependent upon the main point of view established. In the way that Swift uses ironical devices in anonymous non-mask pamphlets—to make a point at a particular moment—the *Examiner* uses the same devices : of undercutting humility with fact, as when he says humbly he is sorry to have said Wharton defiled Gloucester Cathedral, for it was another church (*Works*, IX, 157) ; of ' impartially ' showing that princes are discouraged from appointing Tories to public office—because Tories are not made more loyal by such appointments, as Whigs are (*ibid.*, 232-3) ; and of mock praise, as when he praises the Whigs for the ' admirable expedients ' which enabled them to escape punishment for their bad government (*ibid.*, 251). These devices are treated more fully later in this chapter. *Examiner* XXIII contains a parody of a Whig author, who unabashedly admits his bad practices. In *Examiner* XVII (*Works*, IX, 96-7), the author makes ' objective ' statistical computations years before *A Modest Proposal.*

[12] *The Satire of Jonathan Swift,* pp. 59-60. [13] *Works*, IX, 223-4.
[14] *Ibid.*, 270. [16] *Ibid.*, 116-21. [18] *Ibid.*, 298-9.
[15] *Ibid.*, 255-61. [17] *Ibid.*, 102. [19] *Ibid.*, 110.

[20] *Ibid.*, 254. For an interpretation of the Examiner as a Tory partisan, see Kelling, *op. cit.*, p. 192.

[21] *Ibid.*, 100, 190, 253. [28] *Ibid.*, 204. [35] *Ibid.*, 202.
[22] *Ibid.*, 298. [29] *Ibid.*, 193-4. [36] *Ibid.*, 196.
[23] *Ibid.*, 183. [30] *Ibid.*, 197-9. [37] *Ibid.*, 202.
[24] *Ibid.*, 135-6. [31] *Ibid.*, 201. [38] *Ibid.*, 198, 196.
[25] *Ibid.*, 122-8. [32] *Ibid.*, 202, and note. [39] *Ibid.*, 204.
[26] *Ibid.*, V, 188-9, note. [33] *Ibid.*, 203. [40] *Ibid.*, 197.
[27] *Works*, V, 198-9. [34] *Ibid.*, 190, note. [41] *Ibid.*, 201.

[42] *The History of the Four Last Years of the Queen,* in *Works*, X, 51-2, 62-3.
[43] *Ibid.*, V, 202.

[44] *Ibid.*, 200. There are two reasons for omitting mention of the incident (*ibid.*, 205) of the beggar who approaches Prior and turns out to be a *marquis*. First, although Swift wrote to Stella (September 11, 1711) that he had written ' all but about the last page ', which he dictated, he later wrote (September 13) that the printer got someone else to add the ' two last pages ', which ' are so romantick, they spoil all the rest ' (*Journal to Stella,* ed. Harold Williams [Oxford, 1948], I, 357, 359). The authorship of the section must therefore be in some doubt. Second, the incident follows the pattern usual in the essay : Prior is shocked that a marquis should be a beggar, and Baudrier answers patriotically that many marquises have an income of ten thousand pounds in a year, adding that the ' wisest men have the prejudices of their country about them ! '

[45] Coxe, *Marlborough,* Chapter 88, cited in W. E. H. Lecky's *History of England in the Eighteenth Century* (1892), I, 122.

[46] *Works*, V, 116-8. [48] *Ibid.*, V, 117-8. [50] *Ibid.*, X, 56.
[47] *Ibid.*, X, 52. [49] *Ibid.*, 200. [51] *Ibid.*, V, 196.

[52] *Ibid.*, 204. Not all French subjects shared this feeling of excessive devotion to Louis. Madame de Maintenon wrote to the Duke of Noailles on June 9, 1709, for example, that when it was known that the King had refused the shameful terms of peace, ' everyone cheered and called for war '. This impulse, she adds, did not last : soon were heard insistent murmurs that before the nobles gave up their plate, the

King should first begin economizing by giving up his horses, dogs, and servants.
(*Lettres de Madame de Maintenon* (1758), V, 120. Quoted in Winston S. Churchill's
Marlborough, His Life and Times [1933–8], VI, 95).

[53] *Works*, V, 118.   [55] Churchill, *op. cit.*, VI, 317.   [57] *Journal to Stella*, I, 357–8.
[54] *Ibid.*, 200.   [56] *Works*, V, 200.   [58] *Works*, V, 8.
[59] *Correspondence*, III, 293 (Swift to Pope, November 26, 1725).
[60] *Works*, X, 336.
[61] *Ibid.*, III, 146, 149, 151. Swift is careful not to write as a clergyman (*Ibid.*,
141, 143).

[62] *Ibid.*, 160–2.   [67] *Ibid.*, 292.   [72] *Ibid.*, 298.
[63] *Ibid.*, 136.   [68] *Ibid.*, 287–9.   [73] *Ibid.*, 297.
[64] *Ibid.*, 132.   [69] *Ibid.*, 293–4.   [74] *Ibid.*, III, 170.
[65] *Ibid.*, 160.   [70] *Ibid.*, 292.   [75] *Ibid.*, 171–2.
[66] *Ibid.*, V, 286.   [71] *Ibid.*, 298.

[76] Deane Swift adopted the name which the Italian Duchess of Shrewsbury
once used for Jonathan Swift. (Harold Williams, ' Deane Swift, Hawkesworth, and
The Journal to Stella ', in *Essays on the Eighteenth Century Presented to David Nichol
Smith*, pp. 41–3).

[77] *Journal to Stella*, I, 363.

[78] ' Part of the Seventh Epistle of the First Book of Horace Imitated,' *Poems*, I,
169–75.

[79] ' The Author Upon Himself,' *ibid.*, 196.

VIII

TWO ADVISERS ON STYLE

The years 1714 to 1720 were for Swift a period of relative silence. In a well-known letter to Pope (June 28, 1715) he grumblingly (though amusingly) described his life in Dublin :

> You are to understand that I live in the corner of a vast unfurnished house. My family consists of a steward, a groom, a helper in the stables, a footman, and an old maid, who are all at board wages, and when I do not dine abroad, or make an entertainment, which last is very rare, I eat a mutton-pie, and drink half a pint of wine. My amusements are defending my small dominions against the Archbishop, and endeavouring to reduce my rebellious choir. *Perditur haec inter misero lux*.[1]

But he could not permanently stay out of political activity. In 1720 he wrote *A Proposal for the Universal Use of Irish Manufacture in Cloaths and Furniture of Houses. Utterly Rejecting and Renouncing Everything Wearable that Comes from England*. This was the first of a large number of tracts which he was to write in an attempt to improve economic conditions in Ireland. It was obviously dangerous to be the author of such a pamphlet—the printer was prosecuted for his part in it—and so Swift was careful to conceal the fact that he was a clergyman.[2] Moreover, he uses repeated ironical expressions, as he had in the *Preface to the Bishop of Sarum's Introduction* and *The Importance of the Guardian*. Sometimes he pretends to have an inverted sense of values and praises stupidity :

> It is the peculiar felicity and prudence of the people in this Kingdom that whatever commodities, or productions, lie under the greatest discouragements from England, those are what we are sure to be most industrious in cultivating and spreading.

He can refer to ' some wonderful laws and customs ' of the past thirty years, and praise the ' politic gentlemen ' who continue to use ' vast tracts ' of land for sheep despite England's restrictions on Ireland's exports of wool.[3] At other times he admits humbly that he, like most Irish people, has a bias in favour of anything that comes from England :

> I have somewhat of a tendency that way myself ; and upon hearing a coxcomb from thence displaying himself with great

volubility upon the park, the playhouse, the opera, the gaming ordinaries, it was apt to beget in me a kind of veneration for his parts and accomplishments.[4]

Although it is in a mild tone that he says, ' I hope, and believe, nothing could please his Majesty better than to hear that his loyal subjects of both sexes in this Kingdom celebrated his birthday (now approaching) universally clad in their own manufacture ', he can ask with bitterness, ' Is there virtue enough left in this deluded people to save them from the brink of ruin ? '[5] and wish, with powerful feeling, ' that oppression would, in time, teach a little wisdom to fools '.[6] Direct statement and irony remain independent. They do not reinforce one another, making a satiric pattern, as they had in the *Preface to the Bishop of Sarum's Introduction*. Swift does not even maintain a pose through the *Proposal*.

In the period 1720–3 one should mention the brief *A Letter to the King at Arms* (probably by Swift), ' written ' by one 'A. B., Esquire ', a subscriber to the proposed Bank of Ireland who, somewhat like Baudrier, presses his claims to being a genuine Squire : Swift intends to discredit what he considers the unsound scheme for a Bank by ridiculing the group of ' Esquires ' who were supporting it. Another minor work is *The Last Speech and Dying Words of Ebenezer Elliston* (1722), an Irish criminal who, about to be executed, ' confesses ' realistically the vices of which he and other law-breakers are guilty.

(*a*) ON THE ART OF PREACHING

But for *personae* of any real significance[7] one must turn to several ' letters of advice ', examples of a type of essay popular since the seventeenth century. Of the three most famous advisory letters attributed to Swift, one—the *Letter to a Young Lady, on her Marriage* (written 1722–3) —involves no mask : Swift speaks in a tone that is direct, frequently gruff though affectionate, and didactic. The *Letter to a Young Clergyman* (1719–20), however, does have a *persona*. Unlike some clergymen who within the past fifty years had written tracts of advice to ministers, particularly on preparing and delivering sermons,[8] Swift chose to write not as a divine but as a layman who signs the tract as 'A. B.' The title-page of the first Dublin edition (1720) designates him as ' a lay patron ' writing to ' a gentleman designing for holy orders ', though in the text the author does not appear as the patron of this particular young man, who has already entered the ministry. More consistently the

London edition (1721) names the author ' a person of quality ' writing to a young man ' lately entered into holy orders '.

Like the Church of England Man, the 'author' of the *Letter* is one of Swift's less vivid, non-ironical *personae*. Dr. Patrick Delany reported that Swift, listening to another clergyman preaching in St. Patrick's, used pencil and paper to list carefully

> every wrong pronunciation or expression, that fell from him. Whether too hard, or scholastic (and of consequence, not sufficiently intelligible to a vulgar hearer) or such as he deemed, in any degree, improper, indecent, slovenly, or mean ;

for these errors he admonished the preacher, ' as soon as he came into the chapter-house '.[9] In the *Letter* Swift goes a step further and becomes a member of the congregation in order to review the technique of preaching in terms of the practical effect that sermons have upon an intelligent listener. Because this point of view is so carefully and consistently maintained throughout the whole tract, one must be very careful not to say that the views expressed in it are flatly Swift's ; rather they are Swift's views as modified by the nature of the *persona* he has clearly established.

Several qualities of this *persona* are at once apparent. First, the author is a layman who has an active non-professional interest in the technique of preaching and in the general circumstances of the clergy. He is quite well educated. He knows, for instance, that Demosthenes was a less moving orator than Cicero, and that one cannot say that before the Reformation the clergy were the only learned people while all the rest were uneducated and superstitious. He can quote Hobbes, and he has even read slightly in the church fathers.[10] Furthermore, he is aware that the books which clergymen bring from college are ' usually not the most numerous, or judiciously chosen '. He can urge the young clergyman not to condemn heathen moralists, but rather to use their wisdom.

It may at once be objected that in these instances Swift himself is speaking, or that he gives his *persona* a professional inside information and interests. The author knows, for example, that young divines are afraid of being thought pedants. Somehow he realizes that the second purpose of a sermon, to convince the people of their duty, is not so difficult to accomplish as the first part—to tell them what their duty is. Preachers, he says, tend to write their sermons in too small a hand and to finish them just before church begins.[11] The bad habit among preachers of keeping commonplace books concerns him. And he is confident that every clergyman is now ready to admit that he does not know the ' mysteries ' of religion.[12] But not one of these facts is such as could not be known to an intelligent layman, if he were sufficiently interested. The question of whether a layman could be so much interested in preaching is insoluble, but one must remember that the eighteenth century was a more religious period than ours.

There is also evidence that Swift did intend the ideas in the essay to represent a layman's view. For example, he scrupulously accounts for every piece of technical information the author has. When the author talks about the use of ' hard words ' in sermons, he is careful to say that he has been ' curious enough to take a list of several hundred words in the sermon of a new beginner '. When he says that Dr. Tillotson preached in a popular manner to city congregations, he is using general knowledge. From listening to an orator of the ' florid ' species for a half hour, he knows such orators are incomprehensible.[13] The valuable piece of information about writing sermons out in a large hand was given to him by a clergyman whose excellence of preaching he has always admired.[14]

The author is intelligent, but his intelligence is of a very practical sort. Though he has tried to read the church fathers, he has found the going difficult ; in some he has made ' very little progress, in others none at all '. He has perused only such as have fallen into his hands, and now really he hasn't time to read them.[15] Since he is no theologian, he has trouble understanding such terms as ' omniscience, omnipresence, ubiquity, attribute, and beatific vision '. And many of the terms used by St. Paul could, as far as he is concerned, be well ' changed into plainer speech '. But the clearest example of his practicality is his belief that a farmer can make one understand that his foot is injured, whereas a doctor would phrase his diagnosis in incomprehensible jargon.

The author's sound sense more than anything else conditions what Swift has to say to the young preacher. For the author is given to using a flat, unadorned statement in expressing his very pronounced, though limited, views. The famous dictum that ' proper words in proper places make the true definition of a style '[16] has been taken to be Swift's final pronouncement on the subject.[17] But just as Milton's statement that poetry is ' simple, sensuous, and passionate ' must be read in the context that it has these qualities more than logic has, so Swift's statement must be read in its context, as the utterance of a specific character. Swift's pronouncement, if one defines ' proper ' sufficiently broadly, is quite an adequate definition of style. But as it occurs here, it is probably meant to be rather more limited, being descriptive of the plain style of Swift's own sermons, or of the unadorned style of the Brobdingnagians. That it is certainly not Swift's whole stylistic ideal can be seen abundantly from his practice. It is likewise true that when the author says that ' we your hearers ' prefer that a clergyman should be theologically less correct than be perpetually stammering,[18] he is speaking less from the Dean's point of view than from that of a layman. In both instances the purpose is the same: to state the case for clarity and simplicity in preaching, since these qualities appeal to the listeners. Dr. Herbert Davis thus justly says that Swift is not objecting to a technical vocabulary, but to the use of ' hard words ' in the pulpit.[19] Any *dictum* in this essay has a bearing only upon the practical preacher-listener relationship, and no more.

To give advice to a young clergyman is certainly the major aim of the essay. But there is a subsidiary aim, and other characteristics of the author contribute to it. That aim is to censure the present faults of the clergy. To do so, Swift gives the author an elevated position from which he can both talk down didactically to the young man, and at the same time pronounce *ex cathedra* on present clerical practices. That the author does not consider himself humble, or even one of the generality, is seen from his statement that he is apt to put himself ' in the place of the vulgar and think many words difficult or obscure ' which his friends the clergymen do not consider so, because they are obvious to scholars. From this elevated viewpoint he takes a kindly attitude toward the young man, prefacing his remarks with phrases of a suggestive tone such as ' I could heartily wish ', ' and you will do well ', ' the principal thing to be remembered is ', ' I therefore entreat you '. But there is no indecision about what he has to say. The essay begins with a blunt paternalistic reproval of the young man for entering the ministry in its present state. The advice which follows is given to him only because it is now too late for him to back down from his decision. Such a situation provides an excellent basis for attacking the clergy—their lack of learning, their use of obscure terms, their poor delivery of sermons, their habit of condemning heathen moralists, their habit of condemning atheism, their attempt to make a moving or a witty sermon. Always the author writes downward, as when he suggests that the young man might have applied himself a little more closely to the study of the English language, adding that ' the scholars of this kingdom . . . seem not to have the least conception of a style, but run on in a flat kind of phraseology, often mingled with barbarous terms and expressions, peculiar to the nation '.

It is notable that the style of the author of this essay is in keeping with his character. He does not make use of vivid metaphorical expressions. Consistently with his advice to his young friend, he never allows the pathetic part of his message to swallow up the rational. He can feel strongly about this point as when he tells the young man ' in God's name ' to offer his arguments in as moving a manner as the nature of the subject will bear, when he expresses ' disgust ' at hearing preachers ' perpetually reading their sermons ', or when he talks against the ' common insufferable cant ' of disparaging heathen philosophers. But these expressions of anger are usually confined to a trenchant, non-metaphorical phrase. The structure of the essay is likewise admirably plain and simple. The author usually announces his topic with such a phrase as ' I would say something concerning quotations ' or 'the mention of quotations puts me in mind of common-place books '. His advice follows succinctly. A typical passage is the one in which the author points out the two primary duties of a clergy-man.[20] First he lays down the principle that the two duties are to instruct and to convince, adding that the topics for both are brought from Scripture and reason. He remarks briefly on the nature of both duties; then he states the two again, pointing out once more that it is within the power of a ' reasonable clergyman ' both to instruct and convince the ' most ignorant man ' in his duty.

Throughout the *Letter*—as in the advice to the young lady—one may well hear the didactic tone of voice characteristic of the Dean who was accustomed to giving plain, blunt instruction to his flock. The disguise, to be sure, is a thin one. But if this is Jonathan Swift, it is Jonathan Swift in the rôle not of a theologian but of an intelligent, observant, and practical man in the congregation who has some useful advice for the clergy.

(b) ON THE ART OF POETRY

The ' author ' who writes to the young clergyman is thoroughly credible. But the ' author ' of *A Letter to a Young Poet* (1721) is not. He is created for ironical purposes, in a way that looks back in the direction of *A Tale of a Tub* and *An Argument Against Abolishing Christianity*, and forward to *A Modest Proposal* and *A Vindication of Carteret*. Dr. Herbert Davis has pointed out the very real difficulty of proving that Swift wrote the *Letter*.[21] But whether he wrote it or not, the handling of the *persona* in it deserves some attention, either as an instance of Swift's own technique or as an example of the work of a contemporary who must have understood and imitated Swift's methods.

Superficially like the adviser of the young clergyman, the 'author' (who signed his initials ' E. F.') writing to the young poet introduces himself as an observer from the outside : he has written no poetry since his schoolday blunders. Consequently he has no love for it, though he regrets his neglect of poets 'in those periods of my life, which were properest for improvements in that ornamental part of learning'. Now, however, with spectacles on, and with a shaking hand, he offers his ' scattered thoughts upon the subject ', gleaned from reading and observation, upon the ' profession and business ' of English poetry.

His amateur status does not prevent his taking an exaggeratedly lofty view of the place of poetry, based mainly on statements from Sir Philip Sidney. There is no person, ancient or modern, the author says, who was eminent in any station without being skilled in poetry. To be a good clergyman, lawyer, or soldier, one must be a good poet. From Sidney also he learns that Socrates and Plato were poets. He admires the idea of Poetical Orders—a hierarchy among the poets corresponding to that in the church.

This extravagant enthusiasm for poetry Swift doubtless did not share. Furthermore, this lofty goal is to be reached by a road which Swift would never have advised anyone to travel. Petronius said the poet should be a *Liber Spiritus* : this, according to the moderns (and the author agrees), means the poet should be a freethinker.[22] The author's idealism begins to look suspicious.

It is equally unlikely that Swift shares the author's views on the technical means of arriving at poetic excellence. He encourages the young poet to leave other unprofitable and severe studies ; with mere luck, he may succeed as a poet. For writing poetry is a matter primarily of surface devices. The author cites the authority of Sidney again to the effect that rhyming is ' the very essential of a good poet '. He deplores the fact that the present age is less good at it than the past generation was, though he takes comfort in the fact that a young poet is now busy turning *Paradise Lost* into rhyme ; its blank verse had been its only defect. The author recommends the game of pictures and mottoes, to give the young poet's imagination a ' great store of images and suitable devices ', and the game of ' What is it like ? ' which will ' supply the fancy with variety of similes for all subjects '. The ability to ' bring things to a likeness which have not the least imaginable conformity in nature ' is the true creative process for a poet. To write as ordinary people speak is a mistake :[23] a great preacher once delivered a sermon in blank verse.

These and other recommendations are for the most part a description of contemporary poetic practice. The poet should frequent the coffee-house (to learn about wit, religion, and politics) and the theatre. He should keep up with all the latest modern miscellanies and plays, and record in a commonplace book much of what he reads. Like other poets, he should wear his worst clothes. By attacking others' reputations in satire he can successfully launch his career. His pen should serve a political faction. That Swift himself had done some of these things need not mean that he considered them universally good practice, particularly if their purpose were merely to enable a writer to rise in the world.

The ' reasons ' the author gives for his advice also show how different he is from Swift. His arguments are supported frequently by metaphors. Advising the young man to dress in rags, he says that an author, like a limbeck, yields better if a rag is tied around him ; a gardener cuts the outside rind of a tree to make it bear well ; and the richest minerals are always discovered ' under the most ragged and withered surface of earth '. Urging the young man to write satire, he concludes, 'A young robber is usually entered by a murder : a young hound is blooded when he comes first into the field : a young bully begins with killing his man : and a young poet must show his wit, as the other his courage, by cutting and slashing, and laying about him, and banging mankind '. The author urges political partisanship, ' for it no more becomes an author in modesty to have a hand in publishing his own works, than a woman in labour to lay herself '.[24] These are scarcely rationally convincing arguments. They are *ex cathedra* pronouncements backed up by a wealth of figurative parallels. This habit of mind characterized even more clearly the ridiculed author of *A Tale of a Tub*.

In these passages the author, in his reasoning and his conclusions, stands apart from Swift. Like his uncritical and excessive statement of poetic ideals, his exposition of modern practices carries its own force. Through a mere presentation of the contemporary poetic scene, Swift gets part of his satiric message across. It lies in the facts the author uses in his discussion, not in his evaluation of them or in the conclusions he draws from them. But to the author's evaluations and conclusions belongs the wit.

Elsewhere in the essay the author can present a conclusion with which Swift would agree, but for a reason different from the author's. This characteristic of the *persona* links him with the nominal Christian and, later, with the defender of Lord Carteret. For example, the author begins by saying that it is unnecessary for a modern poet to believe in God or to have ' any serious sense of religion '. Religious prejudices defeat poetic wit, as has been found by recent professors of poetry. If a man cannot free himself from these prejudices, he should give up writing poetry. On the other hand, the author concedes, religious ideas are necessary for the common people so that the poet can exercise his wit upon them, as Lucretius did.

If one considers that by ' poetry ' the author means the type in contemporary practice, one can see that Swift would agree that such poetry could not easily co-exist with a sincere Christian belief. (Swift himself, of course, wrote indecent, though not anti-religious, poems.) Swift's implied message is that no sincerely religious person could attempt to write the type of poetry popular at present. The statement is equally appropriate to the author and to Swift, depending upon the value the words have for each of them. Furthermore, Swift would agree that religion is necessary for the common people, though not in order to give wits a butt for satire.

When the author urges the poet to read the scriptures, and to become an entire master of them, he is speaking like Swift. But his reason for the advice is : ' to read them as a piece of necessary furniture for a wit and a poet, which is a very different view from that of a Christian '. The *Bible* becomes a mere source-book for wit, images, allusions, and examples.

Again like Swift, the author advises the poet to read the great humanistic writers of antiquity. Of course, the author does not personally believe that it is necessary for a poet to study humanistic literature, though he recommends it ' in compliance with vulgar opinions '. Indeed, he admires the poets who oppose Horace's dictum, ' *Scribendi recte sapere est et principium et fons* ', and he has contempt for Petronius Arbiter, who says that a poet should have *Mens ingenti literarum flumine inundata*. For, he says, this is a reflection on the modern poets who ' have not as much real learning as would cover a sixpence in the bottom of a basin ', and yet who are none the less poets. Here again Swift speaks to the reader, as in *A Tale of a Tub*, through quotations which the author contemptuously rejects.

Yet, despite these objections, the author believes the ancient humanists, like the Biblical writers, can be used for a purpose. The classics are not to be stolen from but rather improved upon : Swift may have objected to the idea that moderns could ' improve upon the ancients '; he would agree that the ancients should be learned. But the author values original thought far more than the writing that comes from sources outside oneself. The humanists are to be used merely as pump-primers. Furthermore, the poet is to study them not through laborious work, but through abstracts, abridgments, and indexes : ' For authors are to be used like lobsters, you must look for the best meat in the tails, and lay the bodies back again in the dish.'[25] The overtones of the words ' tails ' and ' bodies ' reinforce Swift's meaning. Similarly, the author urges the invocation of the Muse, not, as former writers, to bring a blessing, but to impress the reader and to enable the poet to write at greater length, in Horace's phrase.[26]

Throughout the essay the author uses classical writers in the way he advocates. To buttress his argument that a writer adds stature to his work by trampling upon religion he quotes Lucretius's phrase ' *religio pedibus subiecta* '.[27] In Lucretius the phrase means that those who have conquered religion have progressed spiritually, not in personal reputation. It is equally unilluminating for the author to parallel the satiric genius's riding on mankind with Pyrrhus's riding his elephant (in Justin and Plutarch Pyrrhus uses elephants prominently in battle but actually rides a horse ; the author probably confuses him with Porus),[28] or for him to say that a writer must surrender his works with a mild objection—' *digito male pertinaci* '.[29] This phrase Horace applies to the way in which a young girl coyly allows her lover to take a ribbon or a ring from her.[30] Similarly, where Horace applies to some of his contemporaries the phrase ' *genus irritabile vatum* ',[31] the author uses it to characterize poets generally.[32]

These free and somewhat inaccurate uses of classical phrases are merely amusing. Elsewhere the author uses phrases in a way which actually distorts their original meaning. His interpretation of Petronius's ' *liber spiritus* ' has been mentioned. Actually Petronius uses the phrase to ennoble the epic poet, who unlike the merely factual historian—must be able to handle the activities of the gods, myths, and fables.[33] More objectionably, the author says the writer should make generous use of words and epithets (which cost nothing), for Horace has indicated such a practice in his phrase, ' *Os magna sonaturum* '.[34] The phrase probably refers to nobility of utterance or diction ;[35] it certainly has nothing to do with encouraging wasteful fluency. The most obvious example of distortion is the author's use of the famous lines in Horace,

> *Scribendi recte sapere est et principium et fons* :
> *Rem tibi Socraticae poterunt ostendere chartae*
> *Verbaque provisam rem non invita sequentur*[36]

It has been mentioned that the author quotes the first two of these lines to repudiate them. The third line he quotes elsewhere—as ' *Verba non invita sequentur* '. When one has thought thoroughly on a subject, in Horace's hexameter line, the words will follow. The ' author ', however, sees the line as an argument for a lavish fluency. ' Words are but lackeys to sense,' he says, ' and will dance attendance without wages or compulsion.'

When Swift's message comes through to the reader by means of a Latin quotation (like the first two lines of the excerpt from Horace, or the *mens litterarum inundata* of Petronius),[37] the positive message of the phrase is heightened by his *persona's* disregard for it. For the eighteenth-century reader both understood and enjoyed the way the ancient sense was being twisted to fit a modern purpose.

The value of presenting a good conclusion supported by a bad argument is that the part Swift agrees with contrasts clearly with the part he would repudiate. The old truths come to life in a fresh context. There is a converse of this method : the presentation of an argument or facts which Swift would endorse, but accompanied by a conclusion which fits only the author. This device looks forward to those of such later projectors as the ' author ' of *A Modest Proposal* and the *Answer to ' The Craftsman '*. For instance, one reason the author wishes to encourage the writing of facile poetry (which Swift does not wish to do) is that such production will insure a great amount of waste paper, and that can be used in many businesses. The satiric fact supports an insincere argument. Likewise, the author wishes more people would support the theatre in Ireland, since it is an effective school of cursing, swearing and lying. There should be a Corporation of Poets, because although Dublin lacks ' one masterly poet ', the town has plenty of ' performing poets ' as well as ' poetasters, poetitoes , . . . and philo-poets ' who could be organized. He desires an Irish Grub Street because now the wit of the writers is discharged, like vapours, all over Dublin, and the smell is offensive. A Dublin Grub Street would act as a common drain, so that the whole city would not be infected.[38]

These last examples, with their disgusting imagery, seem perhaps inconsistent with the generally distorted values of the author. In fact, the mask is not always consistent. After praising Sidney's sweeping glorification of poetry, the author adds (equivocally, to be sure), ' he argues there as if he really believed himself '. He says that those who have the cure of souls ' ought to be poets and too often are so '; Swift's remark aside is contradictory to the author's viewpoint. So

H

is his praise of Addison for making a good use of his Bible ; this, from Swift's amicable correspondence with Addision and Addison's *Evidences of the Christian Religion*, seems probably to be sincere, not ironical. The equivocal ' Many are too wise to be poets, and others too much poets to be wise '[39] is rather Swift than the author. Milton's example, the author says, has spoiled as many ' reverend rhimers . . . as he has made real poets '. The stage is the school of Wisdom, which there, however, is not always ' sound knowledge '.[40]

These remarks have satiric value, even though they decrease the clarity of our visualization of the ' author'. And Swift's positive views on poetry come through the distortions of his *persona*. They can be inferred from his negative criticism of contemporary bad poetic practices. His attitude is that poetry is not all things to all men, something of equal importance with religion ; on the other hand (witness his frequent expressions of praise for Homer, Virgil, and Milton) he abhors seeing it treated superficially, as a mere wit device, to be learned through mechanical tricks. Finally, he hates to think of it as anti-religious. His own poems, though undeniably worldly, are not blasphemous. On some middle ground bounded by these extremes, he would assign poetry a dignified place among the arts.

All these conclusions about Swift's theory of poetry fall to the ground if he did not write the *Letter*. If he is the author of it, we have not only useful information about his attitude toward poetry but also evidence that he had not lost interest in his earlier ways of using a mask. If Swift is not the author, there was someone else—probably in Dublin —who had not only mastered some of the devices in *A Tale of a Tub* and *An Argument Against Abolishing Christianity*, but who could also anticipate (less skilfully, of course) some of those in *A Modest Proposal*.

NOTES TO CHAPTER VIII

[1] *Correspondence*, II, 288.
[2] *Works*, VII, 20–1, 26, 23.
[3] *Ibid.*, 17.
[4] *Ibid.*, 23.
[5] *Ibid.*, 19.
[6] *Ibid.*, 22.
[7] In 1723 Swift wrote *Some Arguments Against Enlarging the Power of Bishops*. He does not develop a *persona* in the course of his argument, but for rhetorical purposes he addresses ' those among our own party, who are true lovers of the Church ' (*Works*, III, 228). The ' party ' is that of the Whigs. Swift attacks maligners of the clergy who ' do infinite mischief to Our Good Cause, by giving grounds to the unjust reproaches of Tories and Jacobites, who charge us with being enemies to the Church '. He outlines the beliefs that ' can be reasonably demanded of me as a

Whig ' : loyalty to the King, abjuration of the Pretender, veneration of the memory of King William, ' proper indulgence to all dissenters ' ; he rejects those within the party who would undermine the Church (*ibid.*, 234). By pretending to be a genuine Whig Swift is evidently trying to enlist the support of the moderate Whigs against a bill to remove some restrictions on the terms under which the bishops—who, Swift says, are ' almost entirely ' Whigs—could lease their lands. This bill, he feels, would not hurt the present bishops : ironically Swift says he ' cannot well blame them for taking such advantages (considering the nature of human kind) when the question is only, whether the money shall be put into their own or another man's pocket '. But ' they will be never excusable ' if they do not oppose this bill, which will ultimately ruin the Church ' and their own order ' (*ibid.*, 229–30).

⁸ See Herbert Davis, ed., *Prose Works*, IX, xxii–xxiv ; and, for example, *Directions Concerning the Matter and Stile of Sermons, Written to W. S., a Young Deacon, by J. A., D.D.* (London, 1671).

⁹ *Observations Upon Lord Orrery's Remarks* (London, 1754), pp. 206–7.

¹⁰ *Works*, III, 205, 216, 210.

¹¹ *Ibid.*, 200–09.

¹² *Ibid.*, 212–4.

¹³ *Ibid.*, 201–4.

¹⁴ *Ibid.*, 207–8.

¹⁵ *Ibid.*, 210.

¹⁶ *Ibid.*, 200 n.

¹⁷ By W. B. C. Watkins, for one. (*Perilous Balance* [Princeton, 1939], p. 6).

¹⁸ *Works*, III, 208.

¹⁹ ' Swift and the Pedants ', *Oriel Review*, I (1943), 140.

²⁰ *Works*, III, 199–211.

²¹ *Prose Works*, IX, xxiv–xxvii.

²² *Works*, XI, 93–8.

²³ Cf. Horace, Bk. III, Ode I, l. 1, and Petronius, *The Satiricon* (ed. E. T. Sage, 1929), 118, 4.

²⁴ *Works*, XI, 101–6.

²⁵ *Ibid.*, 95–100.

²⁶ *Ibid.*, 104–5.

²⁷ *Ibid.*, 95. Cf. Lucretius, *De Rerum Natura*, I, 78.

²⁸ *Works*, XI, 105. Cf. Justin, *History of the World*, in *Justin, Cornelius Nepos, and Eutropius* (tr. John S. Watson, 1853), XVIII, 1 ; and Plutarch, *Pyrrhus, passim*. Edith S. Krappe has pointed out the fact that in the *Letter* Pyrrhus is probably mistaken for Porus, an elephant-riding Indian king who was defeated by Alexander ; there are references to him in Plutarch and other sources ('A Lapsus Calami of Jonathan Swift,' *MLN*, LIII [February, 1938], 116–7).

²⁹ *Works*, XI, 106.

³⁰ Bk. I, Ode 9, l. 24.

³¹ Bk. II, ep. 2, l. 102.

³² *Works*, XI, 105.

³³ *Op. cit.*, 118, 6.

³⁴ *Works*, XI, 104.

³⁵ Bk. I, sat. 4, l. 43. Cf. E. C. Wickham, ed., *The Works of Horace* (Oxford, 1891), II, 53, note ; and H. R. Fairclough, tr., *Horace's Satires, Epistles, and Ars Poetica* (Cambridge, 1942), p. 53.

³⁶ *Ars Poetica*, ll. 309–11.

³⁷ *Op. cit.*, 118, 3–4.

³⁸ *Works*, XI, 104–11.

³⁹ *Ibid.*, 94–8.

⁴⁰ *Ibid.*, 101, 109.

IX

M. B., DRAPIER

(a) INSTRUCTION AND EXHORTATION

In 1724, after ten years of residence as Dean, Swift assumed his most notable rôle in defence of Irish liberty. The English government had in 1722 granted William Wood, an English iron merchant, a patent to make copper money for Ireland to remedy the shortage of small coins there. A protest arose in Ireland against what was considered the introduction of a debased coinage into the country. Early in 1724 Swift entered the scene and wrote eight major tracts against Wood's coin, letters addressed to the people of Ireland (Letters I and IV), Harding the printer (II), the Irish nobility and gentry (III), Lord Viscount Molesworth (V), Lord Chancellor Midleton (VI), the Irish Parliament (VII), and the Grand Jury which was to examine the case against Harding after his printing the allegedly seditious Letter IV (*Seasonable Advice to the Grand Jury*). The last was published anonymously, and to Letter VI (this and Letter VII were first published in 1735) Swift signed his initials. But the ' author ' of the other Letters was not the Dean but one ' M. B., Drapier ' (frequently called ' the Drapier '), a humble but resolute Irish patriot.

Like the humble Member of the Irish Parliament, whom he recalls but whom he surpasses as an ironical device, the Drapier is not an invariably uniform character. For the Drapier's various attributes to a large extent result from the situation in which he plays a part. As spokesman for Swift he has a number of functions. Not only must he conceal superficially the identity of the true author of this dangerous set of tracts (though the authorship became an open secret). But also he must inform the uneducated as well as the educated Irish people about the nature of this coinage and the dangers it holds for Ireland. He must exhort them not to accept it. He must heap abuse on the head of Wood, who stands to profit at Ireland's expense. He must inform government officials in England and their representatives in Ireland that the Irish people will not accept the coin, and that it would be dangerous to try to introduce it. Finally, he must show both the Prime Minister, Robert Walpole, and King George I that the Irish opposition to their measure is not in any way treasonable. To accomplish all these ends Swift has to use the character of his *persona* in a number of ways.[1]

Although Swift often considered himself an Anglo-Irishman, as when he says that the low opinion the English have of the Irish brogue

> affects those among us who are not the least liable to such reproaches, farther than the misfortune of being born in Ireland, although of English parents, and whose education has been chiefly in that kingdom,[2]

it is fairly clear that the Drapier is interested in the welfare of Ireland as a whole. A possibly more reliable indication of Swift's whole attitude toward the Irish is found in *The Intelligencer*, XIX (1728), where Swift, writing as an Irish country gentleman and Member of Parliament, complains that the great scarcity of silver is a hardship for him. He continues :

> But the sufferings of me, and those of my rank, are trifles, in comparison of what the meaner sort undergo ; such as the buyers and sellers, at fairs, and markets ; the shopkeepers in every town, the farmers in general. All those who travel with fish, poultry, pedlary-ware, and other conveniences to sell.[3]

This passage would seem to indicate that when Swift spoke of the sufferings of the whole people of Ireland, he perhaps meant the poor as well as the more well-to-do. Swift usually wrote with a definite purpose in mind. And so when Lord Orrery said,

> The papist, the fanatic, the Tory, the Whig all listed themselves volunteers under the banners of M. B. Drapier, and were all equally zealous to serve the common cause.[4]

it probably indicated that Swift clearly intended to speak for the whole country, not just his own group. But, of course, one cannot at this time know with absolute certainty what his attitude was.[5]

' M. B. ', the Drapier, like the Member of the Irish Parliament, is basically a humble person. He is a simple tradesman, who has done some reading and thinking, who has a general intellectual alertness, but who nevertheless remains a small businessman ; he enters into the serious controversy against Wood only because of his great patriotism, not because he is skilled in the intricacies of political affairs. This characterization is suggested in Letter I, as the Drapier gives extravagant examples of what could happen if Wood's inflationary coin were brought into Ireland : if a lady comes to ' our shops ' in a coach, ' it must be followed by a car loaden with Mr. Wood's money ' ;[6] he will not sell a yard of ten penny stuff for under two hundred of Wood's coins, and he will not count them but rather weigh them in a lump.[7] Here the *persona* makes the argument concrete. Elsewhere the Drapier speaks confidentially to his fellow tradesmen : ' They say Squire Conolly has sixteen thousand pounds a year ; now if he sends for his rent to town . . . he must have two hundred and forty horses to bring up his half year's rent.' And the Drapier has been ' assured ' that ' some great bankers ' keep forty thousand pounds by them in ready cash, a sum which, to carry it in Wood's coin, would require twelve hundred horses. How should a tradesman behave in such a situation ? The Drapier can say for himself :

> For my own part, I am already resolved what to do. I have a pretty good shop of Irish stuffs and silks, and instead of taking Mr. Wood's bad copper, I intend to truck with my neighbours the butchers, and bakers, and brewers, and the rest, goods for goods, and the little gold and silver I have, I will keep by me like my heart's blood till better times, or till I am just ready to starve, and then I will buy Mr. Wood's money as my father did the brass money in K. James's time, who could buy ten pound of it with a guinea, and I hope to get as much for a pistole, and so purchase bread from those who will be such fools as to sell it me.

Such an occasional long breathless sentence should probably remind the reader that the writer (like Mrs. Frances Harris ?) is not a stylistic expert.[8]

But the Drapier is not the humblest of tradesmen. He can, in showing how landlords will be forced to discharge their tenants and farmers, look down upon the ' few miserable cottiers ' whom the landlords will subsequently keep on. The farmers, shopkeepers and handicraftsmen, the Drapier adds, will be merely forced to starve ;[9] in this latter, higher, group the Drapier includes himself. This distinction, which gives the Drapier a certain eminence, is developed further in Letter II, where he says that he has no worry for himself, since he has a good shop, but that he has the public good at heart.[10] By saying he is ' no inconsiderable shopkeeper ', that he has talked with other tradesmen, with gentlemen of city and country, and with many farmers, cottagers and labourers,[11] he backs up his argument that Ireland does not need small copper. In Letter III he introduces an anecdote as one told to him when he was in England many years ago,[12] and in Letter VII he refers to the absentee landlords whom he knew well enough when he resided in England.[13] Such instances show that Swift had to temper the Drapier's humility with enough eminence to make him able to carry on a convincing argument.[14]

Thus when in Letter I the Drapier, consistently with his character, writes urgently in a structure and style designed to present the most elementary facts about Wood's halfpence to the least-informed minds, he helps the common people along with specific directions :

> I will therefore first tell you the plain story of the fact; and then I will lay before you how you ought to act in common prudence, and according to the laws of your country.

He continually addresses his hearers as ' you ', and like a teacher he admonishes them, ' even the wisest ' among them, for not reading the works written to do them political good. To him Wood is ' a mean ordinary man, a hardware dealer ';[15] the well-to-do merchant can share this view with the Dean of St. Patrick's ,who, in the sermon *Doing Good*, constantly refers to Wood as a ' mean man ' and calls him ' one obscure ill-designing projector '.[16]

Not only is Letter I ' in a style pitched studiously in the lowest key ';[17] it is likely also that, as Dr. Herbert Davis says, readers could hear in it the voice from the pulpit of St. Patrick's Cathedral.[18] In first explaining and then exhorting, Swift is following the advice in the *Letter to a Young Clergyman* as well as the practice of his own sermons. In *Doing Good*, for example, Swift writes :

> I therefore undertake to shew you three things. First: That there are few people so weak or mean, who have it not sometimes in their power to be useful to the public. Secondly: That it is often in the power of the meanest among mankind to do mischief to the public. And, lastly: That all wilful injuries done to the public are very great and aggravated sins in the sight of God.

He then takes up each point in order.[19] In the sermon *On the Martyrdom of King Charles I* he follows the same plan,[20] and in the sermon *On the Poor Man's Contentment* he frankly addresses ' you of the meaner sort '.[21]

This style, frequent in the sermons, occurs also in Swift's secular works. In *The Conduct of the Allies*, which at least in its informative purpose is similar to the *Drapier's Letters*, Swift talks down to his audience :

> Now, to give the most ignorant reader some idea of our present circumstances, without troubling him or myself with computations in form. . .[22]

More extensively Swift assumes the same strict didactic attitude as he instructs the young lady approaching marriage; he will indicate ' how you are to act, and what you ought to avoid '.[23] At the end of the essay he says, ' I desire you will keep this letter in your cabinet, and often examine impartially your whole conduct by it.'[24] This advice is like the Drapier's to the Irish at the end of Letter I :

> I desire all persons may keep this paper carefully by them to refresh their memories whenever they shall have farther notice of Mr. Wood's halfpence, or any other the like imposture.[25]

But this is the Drapier, not just Swift. Although the Drapier teaches as one who has an amount of legal and historical learning and inside facts about contemporary life far more extensive than that of his audience, he is still a simple tradesman. Occasionally he forgets to list a source for his information, as when he tells the people about how the French government calls in its money and re-coins it at a higher value. But usually he is at some pains to cover up his superior knowledge. ' I will now go on to tell you the judgments of some great lawyers in this matter ', he says, ' whom I fee'd on purpose for your sakes ' in order to be sure about the legal grounds.[26] That a linen draper (who admits, in Letter VII, to more reading ' than is usual to men of my inferior calling ')[27] should know the *Bible* is understandable ; so without qualification the Drapier can compare the halfpence to ' the accursed thing which the children of Israel were forbidden to touch '. But a reference to Phalaris's story of the eastern king who put a man into a bull of brass, the Drapier must excuse by saying he had ' heard scholars talk ' of it.[28] In Letter VII, he refers easily to Alexander the Great and Phidias,[29] quotes ' the wise Lord Bacon ',[30] and paraphrases Luther briefly and aptly, ' poor Ireland maketh many rich '.[31] Yet even in this last letter, where one suspects Swift was being less cautious about the attributes of his *persona*, the Drapier can claim he has been ' told by scholars that Caesar said, he would rather be the first man, in I know not what village, than the second in Rome.'[32] One must accept a linen draper's talking with scholars as one must accept his reports of conversations with members of the nobility, eminent lawyers, and poor papist cottiers. For this draper, by his own account, is not just an average member of his humble profession.

Thus throughout Letter I, the Drapier reveals qualities of both the Dean and the shopkeeper. At times the Drapier shifts from one to the other. He can quote from the ' famous law-book, called *The Mirror of Justice* ', since he has obtained the advice of ' great lawyers '. He can quote the ' Statute Concerning the Passing of Pence ' as he ' got it translated into English, for some of our laws at that time, were, as I am told writ in Latin '. Yet he proceeds to discuss law sure-footedly, citing Parliamentary Acts to prove his points, and using such legalistic phrasing as ' pursuant to this opinion ' and ' this is further manifest from the statute of the ninth year of Edward the 3d. chap. 3 '. This legalistic discussion would impress the more simple people in the audience by reference to things over their heads, as well as convince the more intelligent. Even so, the Drapier is careful to summarize the results in very simple terms :

> I will now, my dear friends to save you the trouble, set before you in short, what the law obliges you to do, and what it does not oblige you to.[33]

This method occurs again in Letter IV, addressed to ' the whole people of Ireland '. Early in the essay the Drapier offers ' to explain to those who are ignorant, what the meaning of that word " pre-rogative " is '. But Swift takes his usual care to emphasize the author's humility ; he explains the prerogative ' as far as a tradesman can be thought capable of explaining it '. He concludes with ' the opinion of the great Lord Bacon ' that as God governs the world by the laws of nature, so the best kings govern by the laws of the kingdom and seldom make use of their prerogative.[34] This ' quotation ' (which has not been found specifically in Bacon's works) adds impressiveness to the argument of the simple unscholarly man.

The didactic method is somewhat different in the other Letters. In Letter II, intended—like I—' for all my countrymen '[35] and addressed ' to people of my own level and condition ',[36] the Drapier can still inform his hearers that ' N. B. ' means ' nota bene ' or ' mark well '.[37] He can, in a simple analogy, explain that Newton's test of Wood's coins does not prove they are good ; while the Drapier admits that a gentleman buys material from him on the basis of a sample, yet he says that if he, the Drapier, were to buy a hundred sheep, he wouldn't evaluate the whole flock by a single wether. The test of Wood's coin reminds the Drapier of a man who wanted to sell his house and so carried a brick about in his pocket as a sample.[38] It is clear, however, that this letter, unlike Letter I, is intended mainly for the Drapier's equals, not his inferiors. He urges his readers to warn ' the poor innocent people not to receive ' Wood's coins. And at the end of the essay he writes up a long petition, in competent legalistic language, to be signed by several hundred of the principal men of Ireland. This petition, like the legal discussions in Letter I, is curiously prefaced by the remark that it should be drawn up by ' some skilful judicious pen '.[39]

When the Drapier, in Letter III, addresses the Irish nobility and gentry, his humility serves a different purpose from that in I and IV. Through much of the tract Swift seems to have forgotten that he is pretending to be a simple tradesman, in his effort to make a full and convincing argument to his educated audience. He produces facts to prove the low character of Wood's three witnesses—Coleby, Browne, and Finley—who testified that Ireland needed small currency ; he shows a detailed knowledge of the many types of small coins circulating in Ireland ;[40] and he knows that there would be a difference between English and Irish halfpence—because the profit to be allowed Wood for his coinage is much greater than that allowed in England. Wood's coin, contrary to Wood's claims, he proves to be no better than its predecessors.[41] He exhibits a detailed knowledge of the history of Irish coinage since before the time of Tyrone's rebellion,[42] and accurately discusses the difference between Wood's patents and those issued earlier to Lord Dartmouth (1680), Knox (1685), and Moore (1694). And without hesitation he quotes St. Paul's distinction between things lawful and things expedient, as well as the High Priest's judgment that ' it was expedient that one Man should die for the people '.[43]

For the most part the Drapier presents this information without citing his source as he does in the earlier letters. Only occasionally does he modestly give his authority, as when he says he has ' been told by persons eminent in the law ' that the worst criminal actions may be justified by precedent, or when he says he has checked the Custom House books for details on the importation of coin into Ireland.[44] An important purpose of the *persona's* humility in this essay is to enable Swift to present his arguments with quiet rationality, punctuated by occasional forceful understatements. Whereas in Letter II the Drapier opposed Newton's report on the value of Wood's halfpence with vivid analogies drawn from his experience as a tradesman ; in Letter III, by contrast, he says persuasively that it was ' possible enough ' to find Wood's coin good ' in the pieces upon which the assay was made ; but Wood must have failed very much in point of dexterity ' if he couldn't provide good coins especially for the test.[45]

But most important, the Drapier's modesty in this third essay is connected cleverly with the detailed knowledge he does show. He is a simple shopkeeper, requesting the nobility for a declaration against Wood's coin. He apologizes for his ' long, undigested ', repetitious paper. He is an unlearned champion, with only ' some

informations from an eminent person.' Even these were not a great
help :

I am afraid I have spoiled a few by endeavouring to make them
of a piece with my own productions, and the rest I was not able to
manage : I was in the case of David who could not move in the
armour of Saul, and therefore I rather chose to attack this ' un-
circumcised Philistine (Wood I mean) with a sling and a stone '.

He continues the analogy between Wood and Goliath : both are armed
in brass. And cleverly Swift ends the passage with the Drapier as
hero, yet consistently a tradesman :

But if it happens that I prevail over him, . . . he shall never be a
servant of mine, for I do not think him fit to be trusted in any
honest man's shop.[46]

The use of such humility with competent, detailed argument implies
that the case of the enemy is so weak that any man of sound rationality
can overcome it. ' A poor ignorant shopkeeper, utterly unskilled
in law ' wins his case ' by plain reason, unassisted by art, cunning, or
eloquence ' :[47] ' there was no great skill required to detect the many
mistakes ' in Newton's report.[48]

In various ways the tradesman has informed his countrymen of
Wood's vicious scheme ; next, as in the sermons, he must exhort them
to action. Occasionally, as in Letter II, he stands apart from his
hearers and scolds them for not following his instructions :

It is my chief endeavour to keep up your spirits and resentments.
If I tell you there is a precipice under you, and that if you go for-
wards you will certainly break your necks, . . . must I be at the
trouble of repeating it every morning ? Are our people's ' hearts
waxed gross ' ? Are ' their ears dull of hearing ', and have ' they
closed their eyes ' ?[49]

His eloquence (with the powerful use of Biblical quotations) would
again remind some readers of the preaching of the Dean, who believed
that a strong argument ought to be presented ' in as moving a manner
as the nature of the subject will properly admit '.[50] Yet even eloquent
exhortation can be introduced in keeping with the mask of a tradesman.
In Letter IV the Drapier points out factually and mildly (in the manner
of Letter III) that it doesn't matter whether rumours claim that the
Irish will be forced by England to accept Wood's coin :

For in this point we have nothing to do with English ministers,
and I should be sorry to lay it in their power to redress this
grievance.

Then comes the most forceful sentence on liberty in all the *Letters* :

> The remedy is wholly in your own hands, and therefore I have
> digressed a little in order to refresh and continue that spirit so
> seasonably raised amongst you, and to let you see that by the laws
> of God, of Nature, of Nations, and of your own Country,
> you are and ought to be as free a people as your brethren in
> England.[51]

In another type of exhortation the Drapier, with none of the characteristics of the Dean, is presented as a heroic individual whom Swift sets
up to lead the people by his brave example :

> Mr. Wood will *oblige* me to take fivepence halfpenny of his brass
> in every payment ! And I will shoot Mr. Wood and his deputies
> through the head, like highwaymen or housebreakers, if they dare
> to force one farthing of their coin upon me in the payment of an
> hundred pounds.[52]

Such a passage could serve only to rouse the Irish people to resolute
action.

In writing against Wood himself, the Drapier has an aim similar to
that of exhortation : to give the Irish people an object upon which to
vent their anger. Since Letter I is mainly controlled and didactic,
Wood is insulted only in passing, as a ' hardware dealer ', while he
and his supporters are called ' blood-suckers '.[53] This is also largely
the method of Letter IV, likewise primarily didactic in purpose. Invective against Wood is limited to such phrases as ' this impostor and
his crew ', ' the vile accusation of Wood and his accomplices,'[54] ' the
unsupportable villainy and impudence of that incorrigible wretch '.[55]
Letter II, however, which followed Newton's report, is much more
violent. The first paragraph contains a direct and savage outburst
against Wood for his claim that Ireland needs small coin :

> What then ? If a physician prescribes to a patient a dram of physic,
> shall a rascal apothecary cram him with a pound, and mix it up
> with poison ?

Such an onslaught, based on a medical metaphor, is frequent in the
Letters. In Letter II again, Wood's remedy for Ireland's ills is ' to cure
a scratch on the finger by cutting off the arm ',[56] and in Letter IV his
recent threats are ' the last howls of a dog dissected alive '.[57] The
Drapier often piles up one fertile term of abuse after another. Wood,
in Letter II, is ' one single, diminutive, insignificant mechanic '. His

coin the Irish ' detest, abhor, and reject . . . as corrupt, fraudulent,
mingled with dirt and trash '.[58] If it were received in Ireland, the
Drapier says in Letter VII, the kingdom would be ' wholly un-
done, destroyed, sunk, depopulated, made a scene of misery and desola-
tion.'[59]

Such angry outbursts, designed to overwhelm Wood by their
extremeness, though they may remind us of an angry Dean, are
perfectly consistent with the character of the Drapier. ' Good God !
Who are his supporters, abettors, encouragers, or sharers ? ' he asks.
Immediately afterwards, the Drapier threatens to ' shoot Wood and his
deputies through the head ' if they try to ' oblige ' him to take their
coin. There is no doubt that this is an angry shopkeeper speaking as he
warns his fellows :

> Shopkeepers look to yourselves. Woods will *oblige* and force
> you to take fivepence halfpenny of his trash in every payment. . . .
> If any of you be content to deal with Mr. Woods on such conditions
> they may. But for my own particular, ' let his money perish with
> him '.

The wrath is perfectly sustained. Wood is debased, and the Drapier,
consistently a shopkeeper, is much superior to him : ' It is no loss of
honour to submit to the lion, but who, with the figure of a man, can
think with patience of being devoured alive by a rat '. One value of
having Wood overwhelmed by the Drapier instead of by Swift is
obvious. To be crushed by a simple tradesman is more humiliating
than to be crushed by a prominent Anglican divine. And there is
added power from the humour of the shopkeeper who can (when it
serves Swift's purposes) lose control of his sentences and in the first
two Letters spell Wood's name ' Woods '.

The intensity of the Drapier's anger causes him to use against
Wood the converse of this device : Wood and his friends are, by an
inversion of values, raised to a false eminence. The Irish merchants
and traders who betrayed their country by testifying that Ireland
needed Wood's coin are called ' excellent witnesses ' ; Wood becomes
' this honest liberal hardwareman '. The Drapier says he chooses
' rather to be hanged than have all my substance taxed at seventeen
shillings in the pound, at the arbitrary will and pleasure of the venerable
Mr. Wood '.[60] Of Wood's plan not to drain Ireland of its gold and
silver the Drapier declares, ' This little arbitrary mock-monarch most
graciously offers to " take our manufactures in exchange " '.[61] And as
in direct statement the Drapier says that the struggle is between Wood

on the one hand and the rights of a whole free country on the other, so in irony he says :

> But he must be surely a man of some wonderful merit. Hath he saved any other kingdom at his own expense to give him a title of reimbursing himself by the destruction of ours ? Hath he discovered the longitude or the universal medicine ? No.[62]

Indeed, the Drapier claims he has been

> sometimes tempted to wish that this project of Wood might succeed, because I reflected with some pleasure what a jolly crew it would bring over among us of lords and squires, and pensioners of both sexes, and officers civil and military, where we should live together as merry and sociable as beggars, only with this one abatement, that we should neither have meat to feed, nor manufactures to clothe us, unless we could be content to prance about in coats of mail, or eat brass as ostriches do iron.[63]

His ironic device, with its undercuts such as ' hardwareman ' and ' little ', is of the sort that Swift uses constantly throughout his works. Here (there is a similar use in the Irish parliamentarian's letter), it temporarily becomes a weapon in the hand of the Drapier, without modifying his character as a tradesman.

In Letter III there are fewer of these extremes of anger. Quite often the Drapier, writing to the Irish nobility, is content to present merely factual evidence against Wood : he lost a collectorship in Shropshire ; six years previously, when several bids on coinage were accepted, he made a bad offer ; his coins are not milled, and so they can be ' more easily counterfeited by himself as well as others '. Wood becomes an object of burlesque humour rather than of hatred :

> Let Wood and his accomplices travel about the country with cartloads of their ware, and see who will take it off their hands, there will be no fear of his being robbed, for a highwayman would scorn to touch it.

The Drapier, too, abandons his attitude of proud scorn and as a tradesman contends with Wood, for the King has left the field open between Wood and the Irish people :

> Wood hath liberty to offer his coin, and we have law, reason, liberty and necessity to refuse it. . . . I hope the words ' voluntary ' and ' willing ' to receive it will be understood, and applied in their true natural meaning, as commonly understood by Protestants. For if a fierce captain comes to my shop to buy six yards

of scarlet cloth, followed by a porter laden with a sack of Wood's coin upon his shoulders . . . and thereupon seizes my cloth, leaving me the price in his odious copper . . . : In this case I shall hardly be brought to think I am left to my own will.[64]

This is humility of another sort. This Drapier is not a triumphant hero but an Irish shopkeeper facing a serious problem, which all his fellow tradesmen will face, in his battle against the enemy. Like the humble David, the Drapier has gone out to meet Wood in his armour. Wood here is no mean and insignificant mechanic. And the outcome of the battle is by no means certain.

After Swift came under the fire of the authorities for some of his remarks in Letter IV, the Drapier uses this self-debasing method of attacking Wood more than his earlier methods. In Letter VI the Drapier says he has been told by lawyers that the first person to strike a blow in a quarrel should be punished first ; therefore the Drapier humbly desires that Wood be hanged and ' his dross thrown into the sea ' ; afterwards the Drapier would stand his own trial.[65] In Letter VII the lowly Drapier appears as a brave, though obscure, person, who would suffer the most ignominious and torturing death rather than accept Wood's coin.[66] Such a statement sounds very unlike the Drapier's angry promise to shoot Wood and his deputies. Yet both statements follow from the character of the humble tradesman that Swift has created.

(b) The Drapier on Walpole, the King, and Himself

Wood was the one object of all the Drapier's anger. The problem for Swift throughout the *Letters* was to distinguish between Wood's evil practices and the policy of the King and his ministers. Any reference to Walpole had to be extremely careful. But these references which in their restraint superficially show that the Irish have no quarrel with Walpole, at the same time carry a great deal of subtle ironical power. In Letter III, for example, Walpole is attacked only indirectly. In the Drapier's humble opinion the committee set up to evaluate Wood's coin prejudged the case by calling ' the united sense of both Houses of Parliament in Ireland " an universal clamour " '. Then he adds : ' I never heard of a wise minister who despised the universal clamour of a people '.[67] In Letter IV the attacks on Walpole are much more direct. Walpole could not have said he would force the Irish to accept Wood's coin or eat their brogues, the Drapier, ' defending ' him, says, for Walpole ' never heard of a brogue in his whole life '. Such a cutting remark occurs in the midst of fluent declarations of esteem for the integrity of the Prime Minister, a ' wise man, an able minister, and in all his proceedings pursuing the true interest of the King his master '.[68] In Letter VII also the Drapier reiterates that he ' never had the least intention ' to reflect upon the King or his ministers and that the King and his ministers intended only to benefit the Irish people.[69] Such passages of praise supply a background of flattery which Swift can puncture by satire.

With this flattery usually goes a remark gently critical of Wood, as Swift tries to restrict the quarrel to one between a drapier and a hardware dealer. How could Walpole be on Wood's side ? The Drapier knows he is not :

> I must beg leave in all humility to tell Mr. Wood that he is guilty of great indiscretion by causing so honourable a name as that of Mr. Walpole to be mentioned.

Wood should never have reported that the Prime Minister had threatened to make the Irish swallow the coins in fire-balls. The Drapier carefully computes the number of Wood's coins, the number of people in Ireland, and the number of administrators necessary to force the Irish to swallow the coins ; he ' concludes ' that the scheme couldn't possibly work. Wood's audacity shocks the simple tradesman :

> If Mr. Wood hath no better a manner of representing his patrons, when I come to be a great man, he shall never be suffered to attend at my levee.

In the final sentence of the Letter Swift completes his oblique remarks on Walpole's policies :

> as his integrity is above all corruption, so is his fortune above all temptation. I reckon therefore we are perfectly safe from that corner, and shall . . . be left to possess our brogues and potatoes in peace as remote from thunder as we are from Jupiter.[70]

In irony similar to this against Walpole, when Swift time and again professes the Irish loyalty to the crown and says that the English Protestants in Ireland love their brethren across the Channel,[71] he sets these attitudes against satirical comments on English indifference to the Irish people—that the English know little more of Ireland than they do of Mexico, that Irish affairs are a topic of coffee-house conversation when there is nothing better to talk about,[72] and that the English,

crowding about an Irishman newly arrived in a country town, won-
dered ' to see him look so much better than themselves '.[73] The Drapier
says he is sorry the English people have a false report of ' us ', the
Irish,[74] but behind this friendliness is a definite warning. In Letter I
he says it would be bad if Ireland were placed in one scale and Wood in
another, and Wood should weigh down

> this whole kingdom, by which England gets above a million of
> good money every year clear into their pockets, and that is more
> than the English do by all the world besides.[75]

In Letter II he reminds the English that Wood's money will reduce
their income, as well as that of the absentees.[76]

But sometimes the Drapier lashes out at the English with earnest-
ness which is savage. As he attacked Wood with irony based on an
inverted sense of values, so in Letter IV he says of the Irish-English
relationship (speaking apparently as an Anglo-Irishman) :

> One great merit I am sure we have, which those of English
> birth can have no pretence to, that our ancestors reduced this
> kingdom to the obedience of England, for which we have been
> rewarded with a worse climate, the privilege of being governed
> by laws to which we do not consent, a ruined trade, a House of
> Peers without jurisdiction, almost an incapacity for all employ-
> ments ; and the dread of Wood's halfpence.[77]

In an even harsher passage, in Letter VII, representing all the unfortunate people of Ireland, he argues that Ireland deserves some indulgence
from England ' not only upon the score of Christianity, natural equity,
and the general rights of mankind ; but chiefly on account of that
immense profit they receive from us '.[78] Everything the Drapier has
said about English selfishness and ignorance of Irish affairs is out-
stripped in the one ironical word ' chiefly ', which sets economic
values above those of religion and morality. Here, as in the *Modest
Proposal*, Swift is talking the cynical language of his enemies ; they
may not be moved to help out of decency, but even they can be aroused
at once if they see they may lose a share of their income from Ireland.
These passages show the Drapier, identified with the Irish people, in
humble submission before the mighty English.[79]

It was even more necessary for Swift to be extremely cautious in
remarks about the King. When the Drapier writes about him, he speaks
as he does about the English, as an unassuming representative Irishman, not as an individual tradesman. As in his attacks on Walpole, the

I

irony is subtle. It can come in a concealed reference to the fact that the Duchess of Kendal, the King's mistress, obtained Wood's patent, as when the Drapier says in Letter III that Wood was selected 'by favour, or *something else*, or by the pretence of merit and honesty '.[80] Or the irony can be open but so clever that the King could hardly take offence at it. For instance, the Drapier says that increasing the number of pure gold coins with the King's image upon them cannot increase the Irish veneration for the King, which is already great, but it can ' very much enliven it with a mixture of comfort and satisfaction '.[81] Such a passage emphasizes the sincerity of the Drapier's protestations that the Irish honour their King. But these protestations can be vitiated by the sort of turn used against Walpole. The Drapier observes that the King said at the end of his address to the House of Lords

> that ' he will do everything in his power for the satisfaction of his people '. It should seem therefore that the recalling of the patent is not to be understood as a thing in his power.[82]

For the most part, however, the Drapier does not rely on irony in his remarks on the King. Rather he expresses the rights of the Irish people in polite but firm terms. As in references to Walpole, the Drapier is careful not to identify the King with Wood's interests. The teacher of Letter I informs his fellow countrymen that he is sure that if the King knew the dangers of Wood's coin he would immediately recall it.[83] At the same time, he adds, ' the laws have not given the crown a power of forcing the subject to take what money the King pleases '; for then ' if ever we should happen to live under an ill prince ', he might soon manage to get all the gold and silver into his own hands.[84] Letter II strikes angrily at Wood as the base minion who is insulting the King his master by ' raking up so much filthy dross and stamping it with His Majesty's image '. The loyal Irish who, the Drapier recalls, set up a copper statue to George I, are ashamed to see his image on Wood's coins. The King gave Wood the patent in good faith, to alleviate the troubles of Ireland; only Wood is to be blamed ' if his representation be false, and the execution of his patent be fraudulent and corrupt '.[85]

In these passages from Letters I and II the Drapier speaks meekly for all his countrymen. When in Letter III he refers to the King's treatment of the Irish, he does so as an individual of rather slow intelligence. He is ' under some doubt ' whether the gain of eight hundred pounds a year is equal to the ruin of a kingdom. He does not understand that Poyning's Act (which concerns the King's authority

over Irish parliaments) deprived the Irish of their liberty. When the
report of the Privy Council says that Wood's patent is obligatory,
'After long thinking, I am not able to find out what can possibly be
meant here by this word " obligatory " '. Again, in tentative understatement, when the report says that the patent does not invade the
rights of the 'King's subjects of Ireland', the Drapier answers that
in singling out 'Ireland' the report 'would seem to insinuate that we
are not upon the same foot with our fellow-subjects in England'. And
since no one would be 'so bold as to affirm' that in common law rights
the Irish and English are not equal, 'in my humble opinion, the word
" Ireland " standing in that proposition, was, in the mildest interpretation, *a lapse of the pen* '.[86]

But the Drapier of this Letter is not all mildness. He says that the
common people will never accept Wood's coin, 'I hope, and am almost
confident'.[87] In anger at the beginning of the essay he asks frankly
whether, if the English Parliament and all the English people should
ask the King to recall a patent for coinage, the King would debate
one half-hour on what he had to do. Then follows a barrage of eleven
questions about Irish equality, ending with 'Am I a freeman in England,
and do I become a slave in six hours by crossing the Channel ? '[88]
Bluntly he concludes,

> Let England be satisfied . . . they . . . may keep their adulterate
> copper at home, for we are determined not to purchase it with our
> manufactures.[89]

The fourth Letter continues this direct rejection of the threats that
the King may compel the Irish to take Wood's coin. Along with every
one of these rejections, however, the Drapier emphasizes his loyalty
and humility. He and the other Irish people certainly have no intention
at all of disputing the King's right to issue a patent for Wood to produce
coins ; but there is 'one small limitation' : 'nobody alive is obliged
to take them'.[90] In an unusual instance of the Drapier's writing on this
subject as an individual, not a representative Irishman, he stands up
heroically to say that

> I, M. B. Drapier, . . . next under God . . . *depend* only on the King
> my sovereign, and on the laws of my own country ; and I am so
> far from *depending* upon the people of England, that if they should
> ever rebel against my sovereign . . . I would be ready at the first
> command from His Majesty to take arms against them.[91]

The shopkeeper at one stroke reaffirms both his loyalty to the King and his stubborn resolve not to let him force Wood's coin on the Irish people.[92]

But such *bravado* is less frequent in this Letter than in the first two. Primarily the Drapier uses in the fourth Letter the cringing method of the third. After a discussion of the great difference between Wood's patent and those issued earlier, the Drapier concludes,

> in my private thoughts I have sometimes made a query, whether the penner of those words in His Majesty's most gracious answer . . . had maturely considered the several circumstances, which, in my poor opinion seem to make a difference.[93]

And in the midst of an argument that the Irish are a free people, the Drapier humbly recognizes the helplessness of his position and that of his country. For although ' in reason all government without the consent of the governed is the very definition of slavery ', in fact

> eleven men well armed will certainly subdue one single man in his shirt. But I have done. For those who have used power to cramp liberty have gone so far as to resent even the liberty of complaining, although a man upon the rack was never known to be refused the liberty of roaring as loud as he thought fit .[94]

The Drapier has no intention of giving up the struggle, however ; for it is in the next paragraph that he makes his most eloquent plea for Irish liberty.

(c) Results

The Drapier's insistence on Irish freedom, as well as his barbed esteem of Walpole and the King, got him and his printer, Harding, into trouble. Letter VI is written privately (though it antedates Letter V, it was not published until 1735) to Lord Chancellor Midleton, who opposed Wood's patent but who also signed the proclamation of the Lord Lieutenant and the Irish Privy Council offering a reward to whoever discovered the author of the Fourth Letter.[95] Swift therefore writes Letter VI in his own name, defending the Drapier against a charge of treason. He still pretends to think of the Drapier as a real person, and some of his vindication is such as the Drapier himself might have made. Does not the Drapier, Swift notes, clear Walpole ' by very strong arguments ' and speak of him ' with civility ' ? But Swift has heard others claim that Walpole favours Wood's patent.

Besides, the Prime Minister always gets blamed for anything that goes wrong ; this was true even of Harley (Walpole would not like the praise of the Tory leader), ' the greatest, the wisest, and the most uncorrupt minister, I ever conversed with '. Swift feels that the Drapier always ' meant well ', though perhaps he doesn't always express himself well ;[96] the humble tradesman would never have mentioned the King's prerogative but for Wood's claims, and, in addition, his ' invincible arguments (wherever he picked them up) ' furnished proof the Irish were not obliged to take the coin. His own abilities, Swift confesses, are simply not enough to enable him to pick out the treasonable parts in Letter IV. Furthermore, Swift, like the Drapier, asks humbly ' whether it is utterly unlawful in any writer so much as to mention the prerogative ' ; for do not Coke and ' other eminent lawyers ' frequently refer to it ?[97]

Swift was aware, however, that Midleton knew the true identity of the Drapier. This fact is revealed as Swift says he sent ' these papers ' (the *Drapier's Letters*) to an ' eminent lawyer ', who assured him they were not treasonable.[98] And Swift frankly tells Midleton that he will continue to urge the people to reject Wood's coin by lawful means.[99] Although he will be careful to incur no criminal charges in his future writing and would certainly submit if there were a law against opposing Wood's coin, he says he has ' not yet learned to pay active obedience against my conscience, and the public safety '.[100]

Such a policy of cautious opposition to Wood is reflected in the next Letter (V) to Lord Molesworth, a distinguished Whig and Irish patriot.[101] In large part the Drapier in this Letter repeats publicly the defense Swift had prepared in Letter VI. Writing once again under a mask, Swift has the Drapier assume an even more exaggerated attitude of humility. The anonymous defence of the Drapier and his printer, the *Seasonable Advice to the Grand Jury*, he says, could not be by the same person as the Letters, because that is the work of ' a more artful hand than that of a common Drapier '.[102] He openly claims never to have written anything for which his printer, Harding, could be prosecuted. By ' engaging in the trade of a writer ', a business out of his calling,[103] he got into difficulty. He defies any man of fifty times his understanding to avoid being trapped[104] when the law is as meticulous as it has been made by the ' commendable acuteness ' of Sir William Scroggs and when he has been pursued with ' laudable zeal and industry ' by my Lord Chief Justice Whitshed.[105] He refuses to try to clear himself of the charge that he would oppose the Pretender, because his defence would be sure to be misinterpreted. In this ironically helpless position, the Drapier pretends to be at the mercy of his enemies :

> There are, my lord, three sorts of persons with whom I am resolved never to dispute : A highway man with a pistol at my breast, a troop of dragoons who come to plunder my house, and a man of law who can make a merit of accusing me. In each of these cases, which are almost the same, the best method is to keep out of the way, and the next best is to deliver your money, surrender your house, and confess nothing.[106]

But, as Swift promised in Letter VI, the Drapier continues the fight against Wood. The attack is, as it had to be, careful. As the Drapier says, he is worried and, on the advice of ' a certain Dean ', is thinking about giving up his cause, since he is in danger while other more able people are afraid to speak out.[107] The Drapier's feeling that he has been repaid for his efforts only by persecution and ingratitude is the basis for two extended autobiographical passages. While the first ostensibly reviews the career of the wretched, unfortunate man who undertook to defend Ireland against Wood, it actually encourages his readers, who recall his former brave entreaties. Swift parallels the draper's trade and the writer's. The Drapier refers to his early ' apprenticeship ' in London, whence he was forced to return to Ireland (in playful allusion to the fall of Harley and the Tory Party) ' by the deaths of some friends and the misfortunes of others '. His first Letter was made of a ' plain coarse stuff ' to defend the Irish poor against ' strong easterly winds ' and the fourth of ' the best Irish wool ', fit to be worn by the noblest lord in the land. But for all his labour, the Drapier has gained naught, for ' of late some great folks complain . . . " that when they had it on, they felt a shuddering in their limbs " ' ; they have therefore condemned the cloth and ' the poor Drapier who invented it '.

Yet in this Letter, where the Drapier seems to be completely overcome, rejected by his own countrymen, Swift makes a powerful ironical appeal for liberty which equals his direct appeal of Letter IV. Though the Drapier sees that his ignorance may have led him to violate legal technicalities, he cannot admit that he actually did wrong. In addition to consulting his own conscience, he has spoken with several well-known divines and assured himself of his innocence in the sight of heaven. He goes beyond the immediate problem of the halfpence as he sees at last how absurd it was to be misled by the idea that freedom consists in government by the consent of the governed :[108] he should

never have appealed to law, liberty, and the common rights of mankind
but rather indulged in ' whining, lamenting, and crying for mercy '.
Why didn't he notice with whom he was yoked ? Why was he not
expedient in his battling ?

The Drapier, in his final autobiographical account, is forced to sell
his nag because snuffing the air around Brackdenstown made him an
unruly lover of freedom ; he himself plans to settle down harmlessly
in the country reading the conservatives Hobbes, Filmer, and Bodin
instead of Locke, Molyneux, and other ' dangerous authors ' who
argued against political slavery. The Drapier is at last completely
subdued, completely humbled. He assures Molesworth at the end of
the essay that

> If you ever see any more of my writings upon this subject, I
> promise you shall find them as innocent, as insipid and without a
> sting as what I have now offered you.[109]

The Drapier has made his final submission.

When Swift, in Letter I, set out to instruct his countrymen about
the dangers of Wood's coin, he created a character who would be
equal to any emergency. Despite a few exceptions, it is with astonishing
consistency that Swift continually fits his arguments to his *persona*.
Even in the instances where it appears that Swift himself is speaking,
using every argument at his disposal, without holding himself back to
keep the Drapier a consistent dramatic character, the humble Drapier
always reappears to reinforce Swift's message. The Drapier is not
intended always to seem ' real ' in order to make readers believe a
tradesman is actually the writer. Like the member of the Irish Parliament, he is a fictitious character whose attributes can be exploited in
extreme ways. He shows his humility in many forms : as a tradesman
who, like his fellows, faces the dangers of Wood's coin ; as an unlearned shopkeeper who instructs those even less learned than he ;
as a modest commoner who can exhort the nobility and gentry ; as a
brave private citizen who is willing to fight Wood, and who looks
with contempt upon his adversary ; as a loyal subject of the King ; as a
humble typical Irishman who expresses all that he and his countrymen
have suffered at the hands of England. He is a plain man battling for
his freedom and that of other plain men. Either to present a modified
statement of one of Swift's sincere beliefs, or to make an ironical
utterance, every one of these forms of humility had its function in the
battle. One needs no more convincing proof of the success of this
persona than the fact that the English finally had to admit their inability
to force Wood's coin on Ireland.

NOTES TO CHAPTER IX

[1] This chapter analyzes Swift's method of argument rather than the economic validity of his case. Though Swift doubtless exaggerated, the Irish probably did have real objections to Wood's coin : that it would cause an outflow of foreign gold and silver coins, and that it would increase counterfeiting. For a summary, see A. Goodwin, 'Wood's Halfpence', *English Historical Review*, LI (October, 1936), 647–74.

[2] *Works*, VII, 346.   [3] *Ibid.*, IX, 323–4.   [4] *Ibid.*, VI, 8, note.

[5] Professor Landa says it is unclear whether Swift desired independence of action for all Irish or only for the English in Ireland. (' Swift's Economic Views and Mercantilism ', *ELH*, X [1943], 316–7, note.) It is generally agreed (though exact statistics are hard to obtain) that there was a great difference between the English Protestants in Ireland—who in 1672 reportedly owned two-thirds of the land and seven-eighths of the housing—and the far more numerous (8 : 3) native Irish, who lived in a nasty, brutish condition. (*Sir William Petty's Political Survey of Ireland*, 1672 [1719], p. 27). But Anglo-Irish writers other than Swift were thinking of the welfare of the country as a whole. Thomas Prior in 1729 deplores the extravagance of the men of fortune and the poverty of ' our ' natives. He opposes absentecism, as a drain on the Irish economy, and the restrictions on the Irish woollen manufacture. But (perhaps being realistic) he urges the English to encourage Irish manufacturing in order to increase ' our trade and riches ', which will be the surest way to increase the wealth of England. (*A List of the Absentees of Ireland* and *Observations on the Trade of Ireland*, in *A Collection of Tracts* [Dublin, 1861], II, 251, 292, 284–5). A more obviously devoted Englishman is Samuel Madden, who considers any attempt by Ireland to rival English trade as base ingratitude. Yet he speaks feelingly of the wretched poverty of ' our tenants ' and urges a programme similar to Swift's (including the encouragement of Irish manufacture) for the improvement of the whole country. (*Reflections and Resolutions Proper for the Gentlemen of Ireland*. [Dublin, 1738]). But see : *Correspondence*, III, 309.

[6] *Works*, VI, 18.   [7] *Ibid.*, 24–5.

[8] *Ibid.*, 18, 20. For another disjointed, trailing sentence, see the paragraph beginning : 'For suppose you go to an ale-house . . .' (*ibid.*, 17). In Harding's original text Wood's name was spelled ' Woods '; it was changed in the later editions. See : Herbert Davis, ed., *The Drapier's Letters* (Oxford, 1935), pp. lxviii–lxxix ; 4, note. Some of the Drapier's character is probably revealed in such punctuation and spelling in the original text. But curiously ' Woods ' is the spelling in the *Seasonable Advice*, which is not by the Drapier (*Ibid.*, 89, 91).

[9] *Works*, VI, 20.   [11] *Ibid.*, 34–5 .   [13] *Ibid.*, 190.
[10] *Ibid.*, 42.   [12] *Ibid.*, 88.

[14] *Ibid*. Few eighteenth century readers would have considered a draper to be among the really wretched Irish. Many drapers evidently bought brown linen for cash from weavers, contracted for its bleaching and finishing, and then sold it, usually to Dublin merchants. It was thus necessary for them to travel frequently from the northern provinces to Dublin. (Conrad Gill, *The Rise of the Irish Linen Industry* [Oxford, 1925], pp. 51, 57). Although many Catholics were engaged in the Ulster linen business (*ibid.*, p. 23), it is still more than likely that a draper would be, like most other middle class tradesmen, a Protestant, since no Catholics were admitted into the trade guilds. (Constantia Maxwell, *Dublin Under the Georges*, 1714–1830 [Harrap, 1936], p. 227). A woollen draper might carry English manufactures in his shop, though he ran the risk of having it raided by nationalist mobs. (*Dublin Evening Post*, May 14, 1734 ; quoted in Maxwell, *op. cit.*, p. 123) ; thus Swift is perhaps wise in choosing a draper, who could conceivably be an Anglo-Irishman and whose livelihood might depend upon English trade, as a spokesman for the Irish cause.

Finally, an eighteenth century reader would have been ready to accept the idea that the Drapier was reasonably prosperous : ' The merchants, citizens, and manufacturers in Dublin are very numerous, and many of them rich and in great credit, perfectly well understanding every branch of trade, of which their linen, woollen, silk, and hair-manufactured goods are specimens '. (Edward Lloyd, *A Description of the City of Dublin* [1732] ; quoted in Maxwell, *op. cit.*, p. 213). These background details are reinforced by what the Drapier says of himself.

[15] *Works*, VI, 13–15.   [16] *Ibid.*, IV, 185.

[17] Churton Collins, *Jonathan Swift, a Biographical and Critical Study* (1893), pp. 177, 178.

[18] *The Satire of Jonathan Swift*, p. 68.

[19] *Works*, IV, 183.	[24] *Ibid.*, 124.	[28] *Ibid.*, 25.
[20] *Ibid.*, 191.	[25] *Ibid.*, VI, 25.	[29] *Ibid.*, 198.
[21] *Ibid.*, 208.	[26] *Ibid.*, 21.	[30] *Ibid.*, 180.
[22] *Ibid.*, V, 111.	[27] *Ibid.*, 184.	[31] *Ibid.*, 192.
[23] *Ibid.*, XI, 116.		

[32] *Ibid.*, 190. The Drapier's reference in Letter V (*ibid.*, 174) to his ' learned works ' is probably equivalent to his comment in the same letter (*ibid.*, 163) that Letter IV was made out of ' the best Irish wool I could get ' and ' grave and rich enough to be worn by the best lord or judge of the land '.

[33] *Ibid.*, 21–4.	[38] *Ibid.*, 35–6.	[43] *Ibid.*, 65, 80.
[34] *Works*, VI, 102–3.	[39] *Ibid.*, 42–4.	[44] *Ibid.*, 78, 82.
[35] *Ibid.*, 41.	[40] *Ibid.*, 74–5.	[45] *Ibid.*, 68.
[36] *Ibid.*, 59.	[41] *Ibid.*, 69, 70.	[46] *Ibid.*, 90–1.
[37] *Ibid.*, 39.	[42] *Ibid.*, 78–9.	[47] *Ibid.*, 64.

[48] *Ibid.*, 90. Swift thus, in Letter III, is not ' hampered a little ' by his *persona*, as Dr. Davis says in his excellent ' Introduction ' to *The Drapier's Letters*, p. xxxv.

[49] *Works*, VI, 41.	[58] *Ibid.*, 38, 35.	[67] *Ibid.*, 60, 65.
[50] *Ibid.*, III, 206.	[59] *Ibid.*, 186.	[68] *Ibid.*, 120.
[51] *Works*, VI, 115.	[60] *Ibid.*, 34–9.	[69] *Ibid.*, 183–6.
[52] *Ibid.*, 39.	[61] *Ibid.*, 38.	[70] *Works*, VI, 119–21.
[53] *Ibid.*, 15, 19.	[62] *Ibid.*, 72–3.	[71] *Ibid.*, 141.
[54] *Ibid.*, 102, 103.	[63] *Ibid.*, 108.	[72] *Ibid.*, 116.
[55] *Ibid.*, 118.	[64] *Ibid.*, 86, 88.	[73] *Ibid.*, 141.
[56] *Ibid.*, 33–4.	[65] *Ibid.*, 170.	[74] *Ibid.*, 116.
[57] *Ibid.*, 102.	[66] *Ibid.*, 187.	[75] *Ibid.*, 20–1.

[76] *Ibid.*, 41. The Drapier (in Letter IV) writes with similar irony of Hugh Boulter, Archbishop of Armagh and one of Walpole's representatives in Ireland, who—the Drapier believes—' will be as good an Irishman, upon this article, as any of his brethren, or even of us who have had the misfortune to be born in this island ' ; for Boulter would not want to be paid in a debased coinage. The Drapier uses a like device, though without any bitterness, against Swift's friend Carteret, who as Lord Lieutenant of Ireland was supposed to persuade the Irish to take Wood's coin. The Drapier explains that Carteret can't be coming to help Wood, since the fight is between Wood and the Irish people, not the Irish and the King. He points out that there are few Irish public offices to be given to bribe people to support Wood's coin. And finally, he lists the methods—promises and threats— that would be used in corrupt times to force the coin on Ireland, adding that Carteret will not use these methods. Thus the Drapier gives both the Irish people and Carteret warning, while pretending merely to praise the new Lord Lieutenant. (*Ibid.*, 105–12).

[77] *Ibid.*, 103–4.   [78] *Works*, VI, 188.

[79] The Drapier's remarks on the Irish peerage in Letter VII are similar to his remarks on the English. He claims to be puzzled that many Irish peers prefer to live in London, where they have little or no prestige among so many others more illustrious than themselves, when they could shine in Ireland because of the scarcity

of competition. This ironical thrust at absentee ownership, which impoverished Irish farm land, he makes by way of a comment on the peers' desire to live in London where they can get the latest news earlier than they would in Dublin, add to the ring of coaches at Hyde Park, and appear at the chocolate-houses ; he cannot, however, see how these persons can be led to such a life by the usual motives of human actions—pleasure, profit, and ambition. Swift achieves the irony here by endowing the simple tradesman with false wonder. He intensifies the emotion behind the irony by using the accretive style of his attacks on Wood ; for in the Drapier's humble opinion ' to be wholly without power, figure, influence, honour, credit, or distinction is not . . . a very amiable situation of life '. (*Ibid.*, 190–1).

But Swift writes to his good friend Charles Ford, an absentee, that the Drapier, by opposing a debased coinage, is trying to help keep Ford and his kind in England. (D. Nichol Smith, ed. *The Letters of Jonathan Swift to Charles Ford* [Oxford, 1935], pp. 111–2).

80 *Works*, VI, 71. See also : *ibid.*, 84, where Swift apparently alludes to the facts that the Duchess of Kendal was receiving a yearly pension of £3,000 on the Irish Establishment, and that she was to share in Wood's profits. (Herbert Davis, ed., *Drapier's Letters*, p. 240, note).

81 *Works*, VI, 198.	85 *Ibid.*, 40–1.	89 *Ibid.*, 84.
82 *Ibid.*, 86.	86 *Ibid.*, 70–9.	90 *Ibid.*, 103–4.
83 *Ibid.*, 16.	87 *Ibid.*, 88.	91 *Ibid.*, 114.
84 *Ibid.*, 21, 24.	88 *Ibid.*, 67.	

92 In a clever addition to this statement, as Craik points out (*ibid.*, 114, note), the Drapier puts a suspicion of Jacobitism on his opponents by saying that if the Pretender were to become King of England, he, the Drapier, would fight to keep him from becoming King of Ireland.

93 *Ibid.*, 104.   94 *Ibid.*, 113, 115.

95 *Ibid.*, 132, note. This is the numbering of the Letters followed by Dr. Herbert Davis. In the Temple Scott edition the Letter to Midleton is numbered V and the Letter to Molesworth, VI.

96 *Ibid.*, 138–9.

97 Swift believes that even if the Drapier is guilty of indiscretion, his loyal ntention (to defend Ireland against the Pretender in spite of the statute binding England and Ireland under one king) should be ' at least some small extenuation of his crime '. In fact, on this point Swift must confess he agrees with the Drapier. (*Ibid.*, 143–5).

98 *Ibid.*, 151.   99 *Ibid.*, 136, 148.   100 *Ibid.*, 149.

101 See Davis, ed., *Drapier's Letters*, pp. 287–9, note. Swift, writing as a moderate Whig in 1723, had praised Molesworth's ' useful hints ' for improving Irish agriculture ; he respects Molesworth's opinions, ' excepting in what relates to the Church.' (*Some Arguments Against Enlarging the Power of Bishops*, in *Works*, III, 236).

102 *Works*, VI, 172. Actually the *Seasonable Advice* is written in forceful, straightforward, legalistic language similar to that of the petition at the end of Letter II. It contains no pretence of humility, and its ending is blunt : ' I will conclude all with a fable, ascribed to Demosthenes '—the fable of how, once the shepherds and mastiffs were taken away, ' the wolves without all fear made havoc of the sheep '. (*Ibid.*, 128).

103 *Ibid.*, 159, 162.   104 *Ibid.*, 174.   105 *Ibid.*, 162.

106 *Ibid.*, 164–7. This cringing passage must certainly have reminded readers of a forthright one from William Molyneux: 'If a villain with a pistol at my breast makes me convey my estate to him, no one will say this gives him any right. And yet just such a title as this has an unjust conqueror who with a sword at my throat forces me into submission.' (*The Case of Ireland's Being Bound by Acts of Parliament in England* [Dublin, 1698], p. 18).

107 *Works*, VI, 171.   108 *Ibid.*, 162–8.

109 *Ibid.*, 175–6. Letter VII (first published in 1735) merely continues the use of

the methods already discussed, though the character of the Drapier appears somewhat less vividly than in the other essays. The Drapier restates his intention to resist Wood's coin (*Works*, VI, 187). He continues to distinguish between the King, who intended the good of Ireland, and Wood, who intended Ireland's destruction (*ibid.*, 186). But this letter is different from the others in its enumerating to the English Parliament the general miseries of Ireland. Even in this description, however, the humility of the tradesman can be used : the Drapier says he wishes humbly that ' the reverend the clergy ' would set an example of wearing Irish manufactures (*ibid.*, 195), and he points out the bad practice of ' us tradesmen ' in selling these manufactures (*ibid.*, 196).

X

THE CHARACTER OF LEMUEL GULLIVER

Gulliver's Travels (1726), like the *Drapier's Letters*, appeared before the public with an air of mystery about its true authorship. As Alexander Pope wrote to Swift, even the publisher, Benjamin Motte, said that he got the manuscript ' he knew not from whence, nor from whom, dropped at his house in the dark, from a hackney coach '.[1] But although Gulliver, like the Drapier, enabled Swift—superficially at least—to keep his authorship a secret, the two masks are widely different.

For *Gulliver's Travels* goes far beyond immediate political and economic problems. The protagonist, Lemuel Gulliver, makes four voyages : the first to Lilliput, inhabited by tiny people who are sometimes ingenious, sometimes petty ; the second to Brobdingnag, the country of variously crude and magnanimous giants ; the third to Laputa, Balnibarbi, Glubbdubdrib, Luggnagg, and Japan—a trip on which he meets, among others, various sorts of mathematicians, scientists, and projectors ; and the fourth to the land of the Houyhnhnms, horse-like creatures of perfect reason who treat as inferiors a race of loathsome beasts—with human resemblances—called Yahoos. Swift uses these various fictitious peoples to comment on a wide range of virtues and abuses of morality and reason. In scope and execution this is the greatest of his works.

Gulliver himself, probably more clearly than any other of Swift's ' authors ', illustrates how extensively a lifelike and individualized *persona* can become a symbolic device for ironical satire. Both in his personal character and in his relation to the various peoples he visits, he is a *persona* who enables Swift to indulge in numerous forms of irony, which have a multiplicity of satiric purposes. This chapter will treat some of the aspects of Gulliver's character. The following will deal with his actions among his hosts and his relationships to them.

Although Gulliver has been called ' Everyman ',[2] or a typical human being who learns from his experiences,[3] his characteristics as an individual are of primary significance. In the first place, he is a seaman, a ship's surgeon.[4] We are reminded concretely of this as the Lilliputians make an inventory of the comb, pistols, razor, knife, and other things in his pockets ;[5] as he discovers that he has left aboard his ship the proper instrument for dissecting the huge Brobdingnagian

lice ;[6] and in his report that an hour before the attack of the pirates in
his third voyage, his observation showed the *Hopewell* to be in ' the
latitude of 46 N. and of longitude 183 '.[7] He takes a practical interest in
geography : map-makers, he says, should join the kingdom of the
Brobdingnagians to N. W. America,[8] and Hermann Moll should
follow Gulliver's advice and put New Holland three degrees farther
west.[9] The humour of these passages is obvious only in the light of the
fantastic nature of Gulliver's travels.

Gulliver writes like a seaman, at times using nautical language
which—he realizes—has been called old-fashioned.[10] He shows a
mastery of salt-water terms, for example, in his description of the
storm at the beginning of Voyage II (which Swift copied nearly
verbatim from a description by Samuel Sturmy in the *Mariner's Magazine*,
1679) :

> Finding it was likely to overblow, we took in our spritsail, and
> stood by to hand the fore-sail ; but making foul weather, we
> looked the guns were all fast, and handed the mizen. The ship
> lay very broad off, so we thought it better spooning before the
> sea, than trying or hulling. We reefed the foresail and set him, we
> hawled aft the fore-sheet ; the helm was hard a weather. The ship
> wore bravely. We belayed the fore-down-hall ; but the sail was
> split, and we hawled down the yard, and got the sail into the
> ship, and unbound all the things clear of it.[11]

Continuing at some length, this passage, as Professor Eddy says, adds
realism to the narrative.[12] In its exaggeration, as G. Ravenscroft
Dennis points out, it is a humorous parody on sea-language.[13]

Gulliver is further made concrete by his association with two well-
known nautical figures. The fictitious Richard Sympson, Gulliver's
' cousin ', attends to the publication of Gulliver's manuscript. The
name ' Sympson,' Professor Frantz has shown, would suggest to
contemporary readers that of Captain William Sympson, the well-
known—though fictitious—' author ' of *A New Voyage to the East
Indies* (1715).[14] Even more important, Gulliver tells Sympson he has
given his ' cousin Dampier ' advice on the latter's publication of *A
Voyage Round the World*.[15] This association between Gulliver and the
famous mariner, William Dampier, comes up again at the beginning of
Voyage IV, where Gulliver relates how he—captaining the *Adventure*
—met Captain Pocock at Teneriffe, going to the bay of Campechy to
cut logwood. Gulliver adds that Pocock lost his ship and his life in a
storm, because of his headstrong nature and his unwillingness to heed

Gulliver's advice.[16]   As Professor Bonner has shown, Pocock is modelled on Dampier. Like Pocock, Dampier made his last voyage from Bristol to Campechy and was known as an honest man and a good sailor, though his stubbornness in command gave him trouble with insubordinate crews. Dampier's ship also foundered, but unlike Pocock he escaped alive.[17] Of course even if a contemporary reader did not recognize the similarity between the two men, Pocock would add verisimilitude to Gulliver's narrative.

Gulliver himself in many ways resembles Dampier. Professor Bonner shows the similarity of Gulliver's and Dampier's progress from a minor office to the captaincy of several ships. Also, the dates and itineraries of Gulliver's first, second, and third voyages correspond roughly to Dampier's second, third and fourth voyages. Gulliver's fourth voyage corresponds to Dampier's first. Gulliver's course to Brobdingnag, and some details of the voyage—the ' very prosperous gale ' to the Cape of Good Hope, and the storms from a ' constant equal gale ' from the west for twenty consecutive days—come from Dampier. Like Dampier, Gulliver trades from Tonquin in Voyage III, and explores in the West Indies in Voyage IV.[18]

Moreover, Sympson says, in ' The Publisher to the Reader ', that partly by cutting out ' innumerable passages relating to the winds and tides ' he has reduced Gulliver's manuscript to half its length.[19] Dampier did the same thing, making of half his material a second volume in which one-third of the space contained technical details on winds, currents, and tides. Dampier removes some of his sea-language for the sake of clarity ;[20] Gulliver notes that some of the new-fangled mariners find his sea terms obscure and adds testily, ' I cannot help it '.[21] Dampier disagrees with Ringrose's map of Panama,[22] and, Professor Bonner says, Moll was able to correct certain maps by following the suggestions of Dampier (though not those of Gulliver!).[23] Finally, Gulliver resembles Dampier[24] in protesting that no one helped him write his book.[25]

Gulliver impresses the reader as being a real seaman in his genuine fondness for both his family and the sea.[26] He tells his Houyhnhnm master, for example, that he set sail in order to get riches to maintain himself and his family.[27] This was necessary because his early business attempts were unsuccessful.[28] He shows repeatedly understandable human emotions in his sad departure from his wife and family before Voyage II, [29] in his lamenting this voyage which resulted in encounters with the gigantic Brobdingnagians,[30] and in his dream of being safe at home with his family.[31] As his time in Brobdingnag drags on, he desires more and more to be no longer a prisoner of the giants, to be able to walk without fear of being stepped on, to converse with his own kind.[32] During the third voyage the King of Luggnagg makes Gulliver many attractive offers, but Gulliver decides it would be more consistent with prudence and justice to spend the rest of his life with his wife and family.[33]

Gulliver's overriding love of the sea makes him like a great many seamen. One feels, however, that his somewhat exaggerated passion for travel becomes an object of mild satire. It is not out of compelling necessity that Gulliver leaves on his second voyage, for his family is no longer in dire straits; in addition to the profit from his first voyage he has inherited an estate from his uncle John. But after two months at home, he says, ' My insatiable desire of seeing foreign countries would suffer me to continue no longer '. ' Condemned by nature and fortune to an active and restless life,' he sails for Surat[34] and finds Brobdingnag. When he returns, his wife says he shall never put to sea again.[35] But Captain William Robinson persuades Gulliver to go on Voyage III by making him lucrative offers and saying ' so many other obliging things '. Gulliver, after accepting the offer—since his *Wanderlust* continued ' as violent as ever '—induces his wife to consent ' by the prospect of advantage she proposed to her children '.[36] Returning from this trip after five and one-half years, he reports cryptically that he found his wife and family ' in good health '. He goes on to tell in less than two full sentences at the opening of Voyage IV how he stayed five months with his family, left his wife pregnant, and ' accepted an advantageous offer made me to be Captain of the *Adventure* '.[37] Gulliver's sea fever is extreme.

The *persona* is made lifelike, and sometimes amusing, by capabilities which he shares with such an admirable, well-respected, authentic mariner as Dampier. Gulliver shows a resourceful and practical ingenuity in, for example, his fashioning a boat in order to leave Blefuscu[38] and Houyhnhnmland,[39] or in his method of signalling for help from his box—with a handkerchief on a stick—after he left Brobdingnag.[40] Dampier also exhibits such ingenuity; in one instance he put his writings in a joint of bamboo plugged with wax in order to keep them dry when he crossed a river.[41]

Gulliver likewise is a competent leader of his men in adversity, which he is capable of facing matter-of-factly. Seeing, at the start of Voyage III, that his ship can offer no resistance to the pirates, Gulliver orders his crew to lie prostrate on their faces and submit.[42] He reports factually in Voyage IV how he was forced to surrender to the mutinous buccaneers he had taken aboard; they threatened to kill him if he tried to escape.[43]

But here Gulliver—perhaps humorously—is a less heroic leader than Dampier, whose bravery appears clearly through a modestly factual narrative.[44] Even more obviously courageous is Captain Siden, imaginary ' author ' of another source for *Gulliver*, the *Histoire des Sévarambes* of Denis Vairasse d'Alais. Siden relates, again modestly, how after the shipwreck the crew insisted by unanimous acclaim that he be their leader; this acclaim is preceded by a full public discussion of his many admirable qualities. An able administrator in his appointment of deputies,[45] he is cautiously just : after carefully questioning the owner of a sword found in the dead bodies of a woman and her lover, Siden decides that mere ownership of the sword constitutes no final proof of the seaman's guilt.[46]

Thus in some ways Gulliver resembles ' Dampier, or any other sturdy nautical wanderer of the period endowed with courage and common sense '.[47] Not all these resemblances are in virtuous qualities, however. When Gulliver is first invited into the Houyhnhnm house, he takes with him the sort of gifts which travellers usually give to savage Americans in the hopes of getting kind treatment—two knives, three bracelets of false pearl, a small looking-glass, and a bead necklace.[48] The inappropriateness of these cheap trinkets among creatures of perfected reason is soon apparent. Swift may have remembered Dampier's account of how he tried to bribe a native to conduct him and his men across a difficult and dangerous territory, by offering him beads, money, hatchets, and long knives. The native refuses to move, until finally his wife is presented with a sky-coloured petticoat. Then the hard journey begins.[49]

These concrete biographical details make Gulliver's narrative vivid. They also constitute a subtle burlesque on writers of travel literature. This combination of results continues in certain parallels between the intellectual and moral attributes of Gulliver and his predecessors. Though Dampier carried books and papers with him and spent his leisure hours making observations and writing his journals,[50] Gulliver appears more definitely as a scholar. For example, he is quick to learn languages, having a good memory. He acquires the knowledge of a number of them on his early voyages.[51] Thus he can address the Brobdingnagian farmer ' in several languages '[52] and amaze even the Houyhnhnms with his capacity for quickly imitating their speech.[53] In this ability he resembles the protagonists of two other sources of *Gulliver*. Cyrano de Bergerac, in the *Histoire Comique de la*

Lune, learns the language of the giants on the moon more quickly than does his fellow earth-dweller, Gonzales.[54] And Captain Siden learns the rudiments of the language of the Utopian Sevarambians in three or four months, expresses himself ' tolerably well ' in it in about a year, and after three years speaks it like a native ; his fellow voyagers learn more slowly.[55]

But Gulliver knows more than languages. He was a diligent student at Emmanuel College, Cambridge, from his fourteenth to his seventeenth year. Later he studied mathematics and navigation privately for four years, and medicine at the University of Leyden for two years and seven months. (Captain Siden studied and practiced law before going to sea.)[56] During his early travels Gulliver spent his spare time ' in reading the best authors, ancient and modern, being always provided with a good number of books '.[57]

Gulliver's knowledge of the ancients enables him to remark, when his noble Houyhnhnm master laughs at the futility of human systems of natural philosophy, that this is exactly the attitude of Socrates, as Plato reports it. Pointing out this identity of opinion is the greatest honour Gulliver can pay Socrates.[58] Gulliver's appreciation for both ancients and moderns enables him to say that at least the names of the principal virtues ' are to be met with in modern as well as ancient authors ; which I am able to assert from my own small reading.'[59]

Gulliver's tolerance of both groups of writers appears most clearly in Glubbdubdrib, where the sorcerers permit him to interview the illustrious dead. Though he desires mainly ' to see those ancients who were most renowned for wit and learning ', he also desires to see all their commentators. Gulliver introduces two commentators—Didymus and Eustathius—to Homer, and prevails ' on him to treat them better than perhaps they deserved '. Gulliver then has Descartes and Gassendi explain their systems to Aristotle, who says (recognizing their mistakes and his own) ' that new systems of nature were but new fashions, which would vary in any age '.[60] Gulliver can even resemble the modern commentator Bentley in etymologizing the name ' Laputa ' from ' *quasi lap outed*; *lap* signifying properly the dancing of the sunbeams in the sea, and *outed*, a wing '.[61] These characteristics of Gulliver remind us that Swift's aim is not merely to create a lifelike character, but to create one who can be used for satire.

Even more ironically satirical is Gulliver's misapplication of Latin quotations. For instance, in discussing the degeneracy of the European nobility he quotes what he believes to be a remark of Polydore Vergil about one noble house : ' *Nec vir fortis, nec femina casta.*'[62] As Professor

K

Case points out, this ' quotation ' has not been found in the writings of Polydore Vergil. It is, however, a reversal of the epitaph of Margaret Cavendish, Duchess of Newcastle : 'All the brothers were valiant, and all the sisters virtuous '.[63] Similarly, Gulliver praises the Houy-hnhnms by saying that if they should ever fight a European army, ' they would well deserve the character given to Augustus, *Recalcitrat undique tutus* '.[64] The phrase is from Horace's *Satires*.[65] Trebatius urges Horace to write in praise of Augustus Caesar. Horace, answering that one must be careful with such praise, and wait for an auspicious moment, adds, ' Stroke the steed clumsily and back he kicks, at every point on his guard '. Gulliver misapplies this figurative statement in what he considers a heroic compliment to the Houyhnhnms. The process reminds one of the author of *A Tale of a Tub*.

Gulliver's learning thus has faults which can be used satirically. The same is true of his moral character. It is not an innovation of Swift's that Gulliver is no embodiment of every moral virtue. Dampier and Siden, in their relative integrity, are unusual among Gulliver's predecessors in voyage literature. Among the travels which are openly fantastic, the protagonists are rather adventurous than admirable. Perrot d'Ablancourt, for example, has a sensual streak which leads him, on the Isle of Magicians, to chase a pack of howling cats into a cave, where the cats turn into a group of nude dancing women ; an orgy and feast follow, which suddenly end like a dream when d'Ablancourt remarks that his food lacks salt.[66] Elsewhere he watches raptly as the figures on a tapestry depicting Diana and her nymphs come to life ; these vanish, and another beautiful woman appears, but d'Ablancourt is restrained by an invisible hand as she disappears in flame.[67] He makes no apology for climbing a tree in order to watch in ease and safety the battle between the savages and the rebellious bears, ostriches, and crocodiles.[68]

Cyrano observes that a giantess on the moon is in love with him and wants to return to earth with him ; but beyond entertaining her with stories about the people on earth and their musical instruments, he takes no lasting interest in her.[69] Furthermore, in the Garden of Eden (located on the moon) Cyrano insults the prophet Elijah with blasphemy. Elijah drags Cyrano bodily out of the Garden, and on the way Cyrano steals an apple from the Tree of Knowledge, which he eats when he becomes hungry.[70]

One likewise looks in vain for much virtue among the crew of pilgrims whom Rabelais describes on their way to the Oracle of the Holy Bottle Bacbuc. When a storm arises at sea, Friar John, Epistemon

and Ponocrates help the seamen, but the hero Pantagruel prays and
holds onto the mast, and Panurge sits on the deck in a heap, half dead,
blubbering and calling on the saints to save him.[71]

Gulliver is by no means so frankly amoral as these predecessors.
His ethical character—as indicated in his resemblances to Dampier
and Siden—is a mixture of good and bad. At times he seems to voice,
or to represent, Swift's moral attitude. At other times Gulliver shows
definite limitations in his ethical views and in his behaviour. But the
most important unity of *Gulliver's Travels* is the unity of its satire ; both
Gulliver's idealism and his shortcomings are used to advantage by
Swift to satirize morals, whether of Europeans in particular or of
human beings in general.

Gulliver frequently points out his good qualities, though without
exaggeration. One admires him when he says that he went to sea
rather than make his living on land by bad business practices.[72] He
describes how the Lilliputians dispose of his excrement, in order ' to
justify my character in point of cleanliness to the world ', which his
' maligners ' have questioned.[73] As an example of his generosity he
tells how the Brobdingnagian dwarf who stuck him in a marrow bone
was given, at Gulliver's entreaty, only a sound whipping.[74] Gulliver
intercedes a second time for the dwarf, this time admitting it was his
own taunts which had provoked the dwarf to shake a giant apple onto
his head.[75] But when Gulliver pleads with the Brobdingnagian
farmer not to punish his son who has held Gulliver by his feet in the
air, he does so not out of generosity but because he fears the son's
later retaliation.[76]

Even more significant is Gulliver's plan, in Voyage III, for what he
would do if he were allowed to live forever as a *struldbrug*. The main
aim of his life would be, with other *struldbrugs*, to teach mankind by
precept and example, and thus to ' prevent that continual degeneracy
of human nature so justly complained of in all ages '.[77] But his plan for
achieving this aim is not an example of Swift's idealism. Gulliver, who
has thought long about this problem, says he ' would first resolve by
all arts and methods whatsoever to procure myself riches '. In two
hundred years, if he were clever, he could be the richest man in the
kingdom. Second, he would study ' arts and sciences ' in order to
' excel all others in learning '. Lastly he would record all public events
and ' set down the several changes in customs, language, fashions of
dress, diet and diversions '. He would become ' the oracle of the
nation '.[78] This individual's plan for saving the ' world ', with its
naiveté and personal ambition, is more typical than vicious.

One is furthermore uncertain of Gulliver's exact attitude toward tyranny. After conquering the whole navy of Blefuscu for the King of Lilliput, it is high-minded of Gulliver to refuse to reduce the enemy to complete subjection, as the King desires. In declining to ' be an instrument of bringing a free and brave people into slavery ', [79] Gulliver can remind readers of the ideals of Swift or of Swift's friends, Oxford and Bolingbroke, who opposed the Whig demand for complete subjugation of France in the War of the Spanish Succession. Yet Gulliver later offers the secret of gunpowder to the King of Brobdingnag, so that he could destroy any city in his kingdom that disputed ' his absolute commands '. When the King in horror refuses, Gulliver is surprised that ' a nice unnecessary scruple ' should keep him from being ' absolute master of the lives, the liberties, and the fortunes of his people '.[80]

Gulliver, like many men, holds beliefs which are contradictory to one another. His equivocal attitude toward absolute rulers is unmistakable as the Governor of Glubbdubdrib allows him to speak with the dead. It is significant that Gulliver's first desire is ' to be entertained with scenes of pomp and magnificence '. Accordingly he sees first Alexander the Great (mentioned in *A Tale of a Tub* as an ' enthusiastic ' conqueror), Hannibal, and Caesar and Pompey. But Brutus, as well as Caesar, talks with Gulliver, who is ' struck with profound veneration ' at Brutus's appearance. Here Gulliver is inspired to pay his famous compliment to six who heroically resisted tyranny : Brutus, Junius, Socrates, Epaminondas, Cato the Younger, and Sir Thomas More— a ' sextumvirate to which all the ages of the world cannot add a seventh '. For Gulliver is impressed most not by illustrious and powerful leaders but by ' the destroyers of tyrants and usurpers, and the restorers of liberty to oppressed and injured nations '.[81]

That Gulliver exhibits human imperfections and falls far short of representing an ethical ideal appears most clearly in the one quality in which he claims to be perfect. After his stay among the Houyhnhnms, he says, he cannot tell a lie. His Houyhnhnm master tells him that to say ' the thing which was not ' defeats the purpose of speech.[82] Gulliver learns from him ' an utter detestation of all falsehood or disguise ' and determines to ' sacrifice everything ' to truth.[83] After returning to Europe Gulliver tells his cousin Sympson that he has lost that ' infernal habit of lying, shuffling, deceiving, and equivocating '.[84] And Sympson informs the reader that Mr. Gulliver was known among his neighbours for his singular veracity.[85]

This ideal of perfect candour may be Swift's ideal. But for Gulliver to attain it a severe reform is certainly necessary. Deceit is one of his

primary weapons in his first two voyages. Twice he is tempted to break
his promise to the Lilliputians by trying to free himself and dash a
handful of them to death. The first time he remembers he is bound by
the laws of hospitality; the second time he is restrained by fear.[86]
Though he agrees to empty his pockets, he tries to keep his two fobs
and another pocket secret. The Lilliputian messengers discover and
search the two fobs but not the third pocket, which Gulliver does not
think himself ' bound in honour ' to reveal, since its contents are of no
value to anyone but himself.[87]

In Brobdingnag Gulliver walks into a giant mole-hill and makes up
' some lie not worth remembering, to excuse myself for spoiling my
clothes '.[88] He manages to escape from Brobdingnag by pretending
to be very ill so that he has to be taken to the seashore.[89] After his
visits to Laputa, Balnibarbi, Glubbdubdrib, and Luggnagg, leaving
Japan with Dutch sailors, he makes up a short and probable story
about his journey, concealing the greatest part. Understandably he
conceals his money and ' other little necessaries ' from the pirates who
leave him stranded in Voyage IV.[90] But among the Houyhnhnms
Gulliver conceals the appearance of his body by taking off his clothes
after the family is asleep and dressing before they awaken. He soon
realizes, however, that the truth will be known, because his clothing
will not last indefinitely. Yet Gulliver asks his master to keep the
secret from the other Houyhnhnms until Gulliver's clothing wears out,
and his master graciously agrees.[91]

Thus Gulliver is not perfectly frank, as he admits, before he is
educated by the Houyhnhnms. But it is difficult to believe his claim
that they have completely regenerated him. One admires him for
reporting fully the bad things the King of the Brobdingnagians said
about the English, since Gulliver's extreme love of truth wins out
over his patriotism.[92] Yet when the Houyhnhnms speak disparagingly
of human history, Gulliver refuses to record what they said.[93]

One is not surprised to find that Gulliver, talking with the King of
the Brobdingnagians, eludes artfully many of the King's embarrassing
questions about human nature and gives ' to every point a more
favourable turn by many degrees than the strictness of truth would
allow '.[94] Gulliver's extenuation of human faults makes the King's
subsequent indictment all the more crushing. But even in talking
with his Houyhnhnm master not only can Gulliver be ' silent out of
partiality to my own kind ' ;[95] but also, as the Houyhnhnm discovers,
he can conceal many details in order to favour the human race and
often says ' the thing which was not '. This deception occurs after

Gulliver announces his dedication to truth. 'It is some comfort to reflect,' he continues, that he extenuated the faults of his countrymen 'and upon every article gave as favourable a turn as the matter would bear '. He is not entirely apologetic when he says that anyone would 'be swayed by his bias and partiality to the place of his birth '.[96]

Furthermore, after Gulliver leaves the Houyhnhnms he does not hesitate to use old ruses in dealing with other people. He is picked up by the ship of the admirable Don Pedro de Mendez. Gulliver is angry that Don Pedro should consider his stay among the Houyhnhnms as merely a figment of his imagination, for Gulliver has completely forgotten how to lie. Yet when the ship arrives in Lisbon Gulliver asks Don Pedro to keep secret the tale about the Houyhnhnms, for he fears the Inquisition. When Gulliver leaves Lisbon on a merchant-ship bound for England, he avoids seeing the captain and crew by pretending to be sick and staying in his cabin.[97]

The dubiousness of Gulliver's veracity brings into question the truthfulness and consistency—within the framework of fantasy—of his whole narrative. Much has been written about certain of its technical details. Professor Case has noted inconsistent references to the time between Voyages I and II and between Voyages III and IV, and to the chronology of Voyage III.[98] But Gulliver himself blames the printer for such errors as these.[99] It could be, as Professor Case says, that the printer is responsible also for certain minor errors in the geography of the travels : the text gives an inland location for Lilliput and for the place where Gulliver was attacked by pirates.[100]

There are more significant details to be questioned within the frame of the narrative. The Houyhnhnms are presented as perfectly rational creatures, who are compelled to action by the dictates of reason,[101] which does not admit of a two-sided discussion, but which 'strikes you with immediate conviction '. Yet the Houyhnhnms can hold a grand assembly in order to carry on ' their old debate ' : whether the Yahoos should be exterminated from the earth.[102]

Furthermore, though Swift sticks carefully to his scale in Lilliput and Brobdingnag, one may note that Gulliver exhibits a definite tendency to exaggerate. In Lilliput the scale is one inch to one foot. Thus a Lilliputian man is six inches high. At first Gulliver mentions that forty Lilliputians mounted his chest.[103] Next ' above one hundred ' of them climb up bearing baskets of meat, though it is unclear whether they are all on his chest at once.[104] Later, despite his being guarded, he is sure ' there could not be fewer than ten thousand at several times, who mounted my body by the help of ladders '.[105]

Though perhaps these figures are credible, one wonders whether boys and girls roughly four and five inches tall could play hide-and-seek in Gulliver's hair,[106] whether he could hold twenty or thirty smaller Lilliputian fowl (a lark is slightly smaller than a fly) on the end of his knife, and whether he could pick up in one hand twenty six-inch waiters carrying food and drink.[107] The size of Gulliver's handkerchief is certainly exaggerated. Even if it were more than twelve inches (thus equivalent to twelve feet) square, it would still not be large enough to be a carpet for the Lilliputian King's ' chief room of state ',[108] or to be an area upon which twenty-four horsemen could exercise freely.[109]

Professor Augustus De Morgan was the first to demolish the likelihood that Gulliver could have captured the fleet of Blefuscu. Gulliver says that he dragged ' with great ease ' fifty of the enemy's ' largest men of war ' after him.[110] Since the mass of a Blefuscudian battleship would equal $\frac{1}{1728}$ of the mass of a battleship of Swift's day, De Morgan points out that Gulliver, up to his neck in water, could not possibly have dragged easily the equivalent of $\frac{50}{1728}$ of the latter mass.[111] Also, Gulliver says that after the Blefuscudians deserted their ships, there were at least thirty thousand of them at the water's edge (though it is unclear whether all these came from the ships).[112] De Morgan argues that thirty thousand Blefuscudians would equal in bulk and weight about seventeen Englishmen ; Gulliver could not easily have towed a boat which comfortably held seventeen of his countrymen.[113]

In Brobdingnag, where one inch is as large as an English foot, it is incredible that a doubled handkerchief should be nearly a foot thick.[114] Some of these details may be minor exceptions to the rule of consistency,[115] made deliberately for the sake of a temporary picturesque incident.[116] But such deviations from honesty are of only secondary importance in the satire on the credibility of voyagers and of men who say they tell the truth. The main incongruity lies in the strenuousness of Gulliver's claims to veracity and credibility in the light of the obviously fantastic nature of his adventures.

The claim that he is telling plain and simple facts in an unadorned style is one Gulliver shares with many of his sources. In the ' Preface ' to the *Voyage to New Holland* Dampier answers the objection that his style is dry by professing to tell only the truth, without ornament ;[117] in the ' Preface ' to the *New Voyage* he says that, except by omissions, he will not prejudice the sincere truth of his narrative.[118] Like *Gulliver*, the *History of the Sevarambians*, a Utopian voyage tale of Denis Vairasse d'Alais, pretends to be authentic. The ' manuscript ' of the ' author ',

Captain Siden, has been left (after the Captain's death) in the hands of an ' editor ', who carefully checks the authenticity of the story. In the ' Preface ' the ' editor ' argues that Siden's narrative is true, partially because it is written in so plain a manner that no one could doubt it.[119] His comment is similar to Sympson's about *Gulliver's Travels* : ' there is an air of truth apparent through the whole '.[120]

The simple narrative style of much of Gulliver's story certainly does seem appropriate to the seaman-author ; it appears at the very outset :

> My father had a small estate in Nottinghamshire ; I was the third of five sons. He sent me to Emanuel College in Cambridge at fourteen years old, where I resided three years, and applied myself close to my studies ; but the charge of maintaining me (although I had a very scanty allowance) being too great for a narrow fortune, I was bound apprentice to Mr. James Bates, an eminent surgeon in London, with whom I continued four years.[121]

Moreover, Gulliver himself periodically reminds the reader of the simplicity of his account. Describing Brobdingnag, he says, ' I have been chiefly studious of truth, without affecting any ornaments of learning or of style '. He has omitted certain details only because he does not want to be censured, like other travellers, for being trifling.[122] Later he reiterates that he tells no improbable tales.[123] In fact, he feels after his return from Brobdingnag that his experiences have been so commonplace by comparison with those found in other travel books that few readers will find them interesting.[124] And though severe critics might think his story exaggerated, he assures the reader that he has gone to the other extreme : the Brobdingnagians would think he had minimized his facts.[125]

With this sort of constant reminder to the reader, the incredible narrative proceeds. Like Dampier, who says ' without vanity ' that his travels will include many things new to the reader,[126] Gulliver carefully prepares his audience for the unusual. In Voyage III he tells how mathematics is taught by a method ' scarce imaginable to us in Europe ' : the student swallows a proposition written on a wafer.[127] Gulliver recognizes that the ghosts who serve the Governor of Glubb-dubdrib are domestics ' of a kind somewhat unusual.'[128] He realizes his account of the immortal *struldbrugs* ' seems to be a little out of the common way '.[129]

But Gulliver will allow no one to question the sincerity of his account. He tells Sympson he has never heard of any Yahoo Englishman so presumptuous as to dispute the existence of the Lilliputians or the Brobdingnagians, ' because the truth immediately strikes every reader with conviction '.[130] On the return voyage from Lilliput Gulliver convinces the ship captain of his honesty by showing him several Lilliputian black cattle and sheep—the same sheep which Gulliver hopes will aid the English woollen manufacture.[131] Returning from Brobdingnag he tells his adventures to another captain, who immediately believes in his veracity since ' truth always forceth its way into rational minds.'[132]

Among the sources of *Gulliver*, as Professor Eddy shows, Rabelais's satire contains exaggerated burlesque on the improbable fictions of travellers.[133] As Panurge, Pantagruel, and their companions travel in search of Truth, Epistemon, for example, buys a painting of the Ideas of Plato and the atoms of Epicurus.[134] At the end of an utterly fantastic trip, Bacbuc takes Panurge to hear the words of the oracle of the Goddess Bottle. She urges Panurge to drink, for truth is in wine.[135]

But the closest parallel to the method of Gulliver occurs in the book's most important source, Lucian's *True History*. Professor Eddy shows that both Lucian and Gulliver oppose falsified travels and want to be remembered for their singular veracity, that they record plain facts without bias, and that they omit long technical descriptions.[136] Lucian begins quite frankly by saying that he is going to tell ' all kinds of lies in a plausible and specious way ' and thus parody the ' poets, historians, and philosophers of old '. He names in particular Ctesias and Iambulus. Lucian claims to be truthful at least in saying that he is lying, that he is writing about things which do not and cannot exist, and which the reader should by no means believe in.[137]

Then the falsehood begins. Lucian can promise—as Gulliver, imitating Dampier, does[138]—future books of wonders for the reader.[139] Like Gulliver, Lucian can be deceitful : he opens and reads a letter from Odysseus to Calypso before delivering it.[140] Again like Gulliver, he warns his audience : ' Though I know that what I am going to recount savours of the incredible, I shall say it nevertheless.'[141] Lucian's adventures are as unbelievable as Gulliver's. Lucian is carried by a whirlwind to the moon, takes part in the war between Endymion and Phaethon (involving Vulture Dragoons, Grassplumes with wings like lettuce leaves, and Flea-Archers),[142] visits the city of animated lanterns, lives on an island twenty-seven miles long in the belly of a whale, and converses with the philosophers and heroes on the Island of the Blessed.[143]

Less rounded as a character than Gulliver, Lucian believes ironically in the reliability of Homer, who had only slight inaccuracies in his description of the city of the Isle of Dreams ;[144] and of Aristophanes, whose writings Lucian says are distrusted without reason.[145] But like Gulliver, Lucian is careful to convince his readers of his own veracity. He is reluctant to describe the removable and replaceable eyes of the moon-dwellers for fear the reader will think he is lying.[146] He tells how in a looking-glass on the moon he saw clearly his family and his whole native land. He adds that anyone who does not believe him will find, if he ever gets to the moon, that Lucian is telling the truth.[147]

Lucian makes his most extreme praise of his truthfulness when he comes to the Islands of the Wicked. Among all those tortured there, the severest punishments fell on ' those who told lies while in life and those who had written what was not true '; this group includes Ctesias and Herodotus. ' On seeing them,' Lucian says, ' I had good hopes for the future, for I have never told a lie that I know of '.[148]

This is a rather blunt parallel to the irony that appears with such magnificent adroitness when Gulliver, as Swift's most life-like *persona*, reassures the reader of his honesty. When all four voyages are over, Gulliver complains that travel books disgust him and abuse the credulity of mankind. For this reason he will adhere strictly to the truth, inspired by the teachings of his noble Houyhnhnm master. Gulliver reinforces his statement with a quotation from the *Aeneid* :

> . . . *Nec si miserum Fortuna Sinonem*
> *Finxit, vanum etiam, mendacemque improba finget.*[149]

As in his other misapplications of learning, Gulliver here believes he has shown that Fortune would not make him false as well as wretched. But his lines come from the speech in which Sinon convinces the Trojan leaders that the wooden horse, harmless, should be taken into the city.[150] As Gulliver, believing he is presenting a convincing case for his honesty, parallels himself with the greatest liar of antiquity, Swift subtly comments on the unsubstantiality of Gulliver's claim.

In thus making Gulliver considerably short of perfect, Swift is not merely satirizing the lack of truthfulness of voyage writers, or of human beings generally. Nor is he merely pointing out Gulliver's foibles and shortcomings as a seaman, an Englishman, or a man. Swift is creating a character who can serve his satiric ends. For Gulliver, though imperfect himself, is capable of having an idea of goodness or even perfection. He is not an impeccable hero ; yet he can sincerely express some of Swift's ideals. He can criticize as well as illustrate the faults of travel-writers, Englishmen, and human beings generally. This double function of Gulliver is clear not only in his personal character but also in his activities among his hosts.

NOTES TO CHAPTER X

[1] Pope to Swift, November (26), 1726. (*Correspondence*, III, 364). The citations from *Gulliver* have been checked against the variants in Faulkner's edition of 1735, which Sir Harold Williams and Dr. Herbert Davis have shown to be authoritative.

[2] H. O. White, ' The Art of Swift ', *Hermathena*, LXIX (1947), 5–6.

[3] W. A. Eddy, *Gulliver's Travels ; a Critical Study* (Princeton, 1923), p. 100.

[4] *Works*, VIII, 157.   [5] *Ibid.*, 33–4.   [6] *Ibid.*, 115.

[7] *Ibid.*, 159. The longitude is equivalent to 177° W. (*Ibid.*, note).

[8] *Ibid.*, 113.   [9] *Ibid.*, 295.   [10] *Ibid.*, 7–8.

[11] *Ibid.*, 86. Both Swift and Sturmy are quoted in full in Collins, *op. cit.*, pp. 206–7.

[12] *Gulliver's Travels*, pp. 65 6. This is the standard work on the sources of *Gulliver*. But for a *caveat* on the study of Swift's sources, see Sir Harold Williams' *Dean Swift's Library* (Cambridge, 1932), pp. 88–92.

[13] *Works*, VIII, 86, note.

[14] R. W. Frantz, ' Gulliver's " Cousin Sympson " ', *Huntington Library Quarterly*, I (April, 1938), 329–34. Professor Frantz cites other details Swift may have obtained from the *New Voyage*.

[15] *Works*, VIII, 5.   [16] *Works*, VIII, 229–30.

[17] Willard Hallam Bonner, *Captain William Dampier, Buccaneer-Author* (Stanford, 1934), pp. 165–6.

[18] *Ibid.*, pp. 167–72.   [19] *Works*, VIII, 3–4.   [20] Bonner, *op. cit.*, pp. 161–3

[21] *Works*, VIII, 7–8.   [22] *A New Voyage Round the World* (1927), p. 5.

[23] *Op. cit.*, pp. 175–6.

[24] *A Voyage to New Holland* (ed. James A. Williamson, 1939), pp. lxviii–lxix.

[25] *Works*, VIII, 7.

[26] See J. B. Moore, ' The Rôle of Gulliver ', *Modern Philology*, XXV (1928), 474–5.

[27] *Works*, VIII, 251.   [33] *Ibid.*, 215.   [39] *Ibid.*, 292–3.

[28] *Ibid.*, 18.   [34] *Works*, VIII, 82, 85.   [40] *Ibid.*, 148.

[29] *Ibid.*, 82.   [35] *Ibid.*, 154.   [41] *New Voyage*, p. 21.

[30] *Ibid.*, 89.   [36] *Ibid.*, 157–8.   [42] *Works*, VIII, 158.

[31] *Ibid.*, 95.   [37] *Ibid.*, 227–9.   [43] *Ibid.*, 230.

[32] *Ibid.*, 144.   [38] *Ibid.*, 79–80.

[44] See, for example, his handling of a mutinous crew, in *Voyage to New Holland*, p. 31.

[45] *The History of the Sevarambians* (anon. trans. from the French, 1738), pp. 13–16.

[46] *Ibid.*, pp. 30–1.

[47] Sir Walter Scott, ed., *The Works of Jonathan Swift* (1883), I, 317.

[48] *Works*, VIII, 236–7.

[49] *New Voyage*, p. 19. In another source for *Gulliver*, the sequel to Lucian's *True History* by N. Perrot d'Ablancourt, the author and his companions give the inhabitants of the Fire-Island perfume and receive fireproof shirts in return. (*Lucien de la Traduction de N. Perrot d'Ablancourt* [Paris, 1654], II, 651–2.)

[50] Bonner, *op. cit.*, pp. 164–5.

[51] *Works*, VIII, 18.   [52] *Ibid.*, 91.   [53] *Ibid.*, 235.

[54] Cyrano de Bergerac, *A Voyage to the Moon* (tr. A. Lovell, 1899), p. 121.
[55] *The History of the Sevarambians*, pp. 117–8.
[56] *Ibid.*, pp. 2–3.　[57] *Works*, VIII, 17–18.　[58] *Ibid.*, 279.　[59] *Ibid.*, 305.
[60] *Ibid.*, 206–7. The satire in this section on the commentators is derived from Lucian's *True History*. (Eddy, *Gulliver's Travels*, p. 55).
[61] *Works*, VIII, 166, and note.　[62] *Ibid.*, 208.
[63] Arthur E. Case, *Four Essays on Gulliver's Travels* (Princeton, 1945), p. 92.
[64] *Works*, VIII, 305.　[67] *Lucien*, II, 677.　[69] *Voyage to the Moon*, p.128.
[65] II, i, 20.　[68] *Ibid.*, 645.　[70] *Ibid.*, pp. 67–9.
[66] *Lucien*, II, 671–3.
[71] Rabelais, *Works*, II, 668–70. The protagonists are similarly amoral in some less certain sources for *Gulliver*. In the *Voyages et Avantures de Jacques Massé*, of Simon Tyssot de Patot (1710), Massé connives at the seduction by his companion La Forêt of the Queen of the country they are visiting. (John Robert Moore, 'A New Source for *Gulliver's Travels*', *Studies in Philology*, XXXVIII [Jan., 1941], 78). In Gildon's 'Fortune Shipwreck', Morris deserts to the enemies of the people he visits. (Philip Babcock Gove, 'Gildon's "Fortune Shipwreck" as Background for *Gulliver's Travels*', *Review of English Studies*, XVIII (Oct., 1942), 476–7).
[72] *Works*, VIII, 18.　[75] *Ibid.*, 118.　[78] *Ibid.*, 218.
[73] *Ibid.*, 29.　[76] *Ibid.*, 92.　[79] *Ibid.*, 54.
[74] *Ibid.*, 111.　[77] *Ibid.*, 219.
[80] *Ibid.*, 138–9. Similarly, Gulliver observes that the King of Laputa 'would be the most absolute prince in the universe' if he could get a ministry to join with him. (*Ibid.*, 176).
[81] *Ibid.*, 204–5.　[91] *Ibid.*, 242–5.　[101] *Works*, VIII, 291.
[82] *Ibid.*, 248.　[92] *Ibid.*, 137.　[102] *Ibid.*, 278, 282.
[83] *Ibid.*, 269.　[93] *Ibid.*, 289.　[103] *Ibid.*, 20, and note.
[84] *Ibid.*, 9.　[94] *Ibid.*, 137.　[104] *Ibid.*, 22.
[85] *Ibid.*, 3.　[95] *Ibid.*, 275.　[105] *Ibid.*, 26–7.
[86] *Ibid.*, 23–4.　[96] *Ibid.*, 270–1.　[106] *Ibid.*, 38.
[87] *Ibid.*, 33, 37.　[97] *Ibid.*, 298–300.　[107] *Ibid.*, 65.
[88] *Ibid.*, 120.　[98] *Four Essays*, pp. 61–7.　[108] *Ibid.*, 33.
[89] *Ibid.*, 145.　[99] *Works*, VIII, 7.　[109] *Ibid.*, 41.
[90] *Ibid.*, 226, 231.　[100] Case, *Four Essays*, pp. 55–61.　[110] *Ibid.*, 52.
[111] In *Notes and Queries*, ser. II, vol. VI (Aug. 14, 1858), p. 124.
[112] *Works*, VIII, 52.
[113] *Op. cit.*, p. 124. Professor De Morgan also criticizes Swift for assuming that the gravity in Lilliput is the same as anywhere else; for if it were, the Lilliputians would be unable to support their own weight. Also he believes that Swift should not have said the Laputans cut their meat, which is three-dimensional, into triangles and rhomboids, which are two-dimensional.
[114] *Works*, VIII, 91. Professor Eddy says that the relative lack of figures on the Brobdingnagians is due to Gulliver's inability to measure them. (*Gulliver's Travels*, p. 137).
[115] Eddy, *Gulliver's Travels*, p. 95.　[116] Case, *Four Essays*, pp. 57–8.
[117] P. lxviii.　[118] P. 3.
[119] P. vi. See Geoffroy Atkinson, *The Extraordinary Voyage in French Literature before* 1700 (1920), pp. 92–3.　[120] *Works*, VIII, 3.
[121] *Ibid.*, 17.　[125] *Ibid.*, 117.　[129] *Ibid.*, 224.
[122] *Ibid.*, 96.　[126] *New Voyage*, p. 3.　[130] *Ibid.*, 8.
[123] *Ibid.*, 302.　[127] *Works*, VIII, 194.　[131] *Works*, VIII, 81–2.
[124] *Ibid.*, 152.　[128] *Ibid.*, 203.　[132] *Ibid.*, 151.
[133] *Gulliver's Travels*, pp. 18–19.
[134] Rabelais, *Works*, II, 635.　[135] *Ibid.*, 868–9.
[136] 'A Source for *Gulliver's Travels*', *Modern Language Notes*, XXXVI (Nov., 1921), 419–20. See also Eddy, *Gulliver's Travels*, p. 18.

[137] *The Works of Lucian* (tr. A. M. Harmon, 1913), I, 249–53.
[138] Bonner, *op. cit.*, p. 180.   [139] Lucian, *Works*, I, 357.
[140] *Ibid.*, 341.   [144] *Ibid.*, 337.   [147] *Ibid.*, 281.
[141] *Ibid.*, 299.   [145] *Ibid.*, 285.   [148] *Ibid.*, 335, 337.
[142] *Ibid.*, 263.   [146] *Ibid.*, 279.   [149] *Works*, VIII, 303.
[143] *Ibid.*, 283–331.
[150] Virgil, *Aeneid* (tr. H. R. Fairclough, 1925), bk. II. ll. 79–80.

XI

GULLIVER AND HIS HOSTS

As Gulliver moves through his adventures, his character is made plain through his relationships with various hosts. The *persona* of an English seaman is interesting in itself : Swift has much to say about this representative man's habits, ethics, and thoughts. But the narrator becomes far more interesting, and the satire far more complex, as he describes his adventures among men no bigger than his hand, among giants who could carelessly crush him underfoot, among wild and visionary projectors, and among creatures of perfect rationality.

It has often been said that Gulliver is a naive individual whose experiences turn him into a wise and sceptical misanthrope.[1] Gulliver's being a sailor, unfamiliar with the ways of rulers,[2] enables him at times to express Swift's views with simple understatement. When Gulliver learns to his surprise that the King of Lilliput, desiring complete conquest of Blefuscu, is ungrateful for the mere capture of the enemy fleet, he first begins ' to conceive some imperfect idea of courts and ministers '.[3] Knowing nothing of ' the gratitude of courtiers ', he respects his obligations to the King despite the latter's severe treatment of him. Ingenuously he at first believes the Lilliputian Council's decision to blind him is cruel, though (and here the process of his ' enlightenment ' leads him to exaggerate) later encounters with courts and ministers show him that they are capable of so many worse things that to him blinding seems mild by comparison. But his revealing experience in Lilliput makes him unwilling later to trust the generous offers of the King in Blefuscu, or the word of any other ministers or princes.[4]

In Brobdingnag Gulliver still can believe naively that he is complimenting the giant Queen and his nurse, Glumdalclitch, by saying that their persons, in contrast to the odiousness of the huge maids of honour, are ' as sweet as those of any lady in England '.[5] But in Laputa he can understand that his story of the *liaison* between a great lady of court and an old deformed footman may remind readers of similar occurrences at home in England and Europe.[6] Though he still venerates crowned heads, he sees clearly the corruptions of the nobility,[7] so much so that when his Houyhnhnm master compliments him by saying he must be of noble birth, he shows his master how the English nobility is characterized by idleness, luxury, weak and diseased bodies, and sallow complexions.[8] When the ghosts of Glubbdubdrib show Gulliver the corruptions among the famous dead, he loses more of ' that profound veneration which I am naturally apt to pay to persons of high rank.'[9] And Gulliver, at first ecstatically happy over the possibility of immortality, is so sobered by the sight of the helpless and wretched old *struldbrugs* that his ' keen appetite for the perpetuity of life was much abated '.[10]

Gulliver is not only a naive individual. He is also a patriotic Englishman. As an individual he at times represents inexperienced idealism in the midst of corruption. As an Englishman he usually exhibits the common sense of values of his countrymen (and Europeans generally) among more or less idealized people. The inappropriateness of Gulliver's attitude appears concretely in Voyage I, as he believes he ' defends ' a criminal by saying the crime was only a breach of trust— which the Lilliputians believe is the most serious of offenses.[11] In Brobdingnag Gulliver shows the contents of his purse to a giant farmer, who has no interest in English money.[12]

But Gulliver, provincial like all men, believes so strongly in the values of the English that his praise for them becomes, from Swift's point of view, nearly mock-heroic. In conversation with the King of Brobdingnag he hears with indignation

> our noble country, the mistress of arts and arms, the scourge of France, the arbitress of Europe, the seat of virtue, piety, honour, and truth, the pride and envy of the world, so contemptuously treated.[13]

When asked about his country he wishes ' for the tongue of Demosthenes or Cicero ' in order to honour it fittingly. He praises extravagantly England's illustrious Parliament, holy and wise bishops, venerable justices, and brilliant victories by sea and land.[14] When the King nonetheless concludes that Gulliver's descriptions prove the English an utterly contemptible people, Gulliver, who has admittedly magnified England's virtues and minimized her vices, is resentful.[15] But his confidence is unshaken : are not the King's prejudice and narrow thinking due to his limited experience with the manners and customs of the world ?[16] Similarly, though in Voyage III Gulliver clearly sees the faults of the nobility in general, he says that his remarks about them do not apply to the English.[17]

It is true that Gulliver's faith in humanity has undergone extensive changes by the end of Voyage IV. Yet it is a mistake to see *Gulliver's Travels* as the simple history of a steadily increasing wise misanthropy.[18] Admittedly, by contrast to the conversations between Gulliver and the

King of the Brobdingnagians, Gulliver is less aggressive in his patriotism and more sparing with his praise as he describes human customs to his Houyhnhnm master. In Brobdingnag his aim was to convince the King that these customs were good. In Houyhnhnm-land his problem is simply to describe clearly these customs, which are scarcely credible to a creature of perfect reason. Thus in the later voyage the facts primarily speak for themselves when Gulliver outlines such things as the practices of 'ignorant and stupid' lawyers, who prove that white is black; the injustices of judges; the value of money; the necessity of extensive trade to provide a lady her breakfast; the vices brought in from foreign countries; the necessity of wine to make people merry; illnesses which come from an excess of eating and drinking; the ability of surgery to remedy these illnesses; and the violent desire of prime ministers for 'wealth, power, and titles'.[19]

But even here Gulliver can show thoroughly English qualities in his standard of values. Early in Voyage IV, after the experiences of the first three journeys, Gulliver still claims that 'there were few greater lovers of mankind, at that time, than myself'.[20] He regards it as a compliment that his Houyhnhnm master is bright enough to arrive at 'a competent knowledge of what human nature in our part of the world is capable to perform'. (This is of course a double-edged statement through which Swift as well as Gulliver speaks, and with a different meaning.)

Even Gulliver's exposition to his master contains evidences of the same patriotism, though less aggressive, that appeared in Voyage II. He says it is 'very justifiable' to invade a country weakened by famine and a 'very kingly, honourable' practice for a ruler to turn against his allies. Also honourable is the trade of a soldier, who kills in cold blood as many as possible. 'To set forth the valour of my own dear countrymen', Gulliver describes how they had blown up one hundred of their enemies during a siege.[21] A surgeon himself, he praises the 'great excellency' of his colleagues in predicting death and administering a 'seasonable dose' if recovery should begin.[22]

When the Houyhnhnm master speaks slightingly of human beings, Gulliver registers less violent anger and scorn at his host's narrow education than he had in Brobdingnag, but he always attempts to come to the aid of his fellows. The Houyhnhnm, for example, thinks that since men are less able fighters than Yahoos, human wars could not be dangerous. Gulliver says, 'I could not forbear shaking my head, and smiling a little at his ignorance'. Then he describes cannon and other implements of war.[23] The Houyhnhnm master implies that court favourites among men must be like the Yahoo leader's favourite, who is hated by all the other Yahoos and is discarded when a worse favourite can be found. Gulliver reports that he ' durst make no return to this malicious insinuation, which debased human understanding below the sagacity of a common hound ', for even a dog has sense enough to follow the ablest leader. When his master says that human beings, like Yahoos, must be singular among animals for filthy habits, Gulliver resolutely offers the defence that pigs are certainly dirtier.[24]

Gulliver, even in Voyage IV, considers the participants in the War of the Spanish Succession ' the greatest powers of Christendom '.[25] First among these is undoubtedly England, ' the dear place of my nativity ', with its ' excellent constitution, deservedly the wonder and envy of the whole world '.[26] Even after his return to England from Houyhnhnm-land, in refusing to disclose the exact location of the four kingdoms because he fears the attempt of vicious Europeans to colonize them, Gulliver says he does not refer to English colonists, ' who may be an example to the whole world for their wisdom, care, and justice '.[27] While Gulliver's admiration for human institutions has been modified, his patriotism has been by no means completely shattered.

Along with Gulliver's exaggerated ingenuousness and his extreme patriotism goes his powerful admiration for the work of mathematicians, scientists, and projectors. Gulliver's admiration for mechanical schemes undergoes scarcely any change during the entire course of his travels. His book itself has a utilitarian purpose. Dampier, his friend, deferentially presents his works to the Royal Society in order to advance knowledge ;[28] similarly Gulliver can present three Brobdingnagian wasp-stings to Gresham College,[29] as well as describe seemingly insignificant bathroom details in Brobdingnag in order to help philosophers enlarge their thoughts and ' apply them to the benefit of public as well as private life, which was my sole design in presenting this and other accounts of my travels to the world.'[30]

Gulliver respects the practical mathematical ingenuity of the Lilliputians who skilfully construct a stage from which to observe him, build an engine to carry him,[31] compute that his body is 1,728 times as large as theirs,[32] and find the circumference of his wrist by measuring his thumb and doubling the answer.[33] Under the circumstances the Lilliputian cleverness is commendable, and Swift doubtless shares Gulliver's admiration for the useful application of their knowledge. But in Brobdingnag Gulliver expresses merely his own opinion as he praises the three learned scholars who examine him and determine he is *lusus naturae*. This conclusion, he says, is comparable to those of

L

modern European philosophy; where the followers of Aristotle merely disguised their ignorance, the modern professors, in Gulliver's opinion, ' have invented this wonderful solution of all difficulties, to the unspeakable advancement of human knowledge '.[34]

Although Gulliver admired concrete demonstrations of the Lilliputians' mathematical skills, he finds the learning of the Brobdingnagians—with such an exception as the one above—generally defective from a modern European's point of view. Their King is educated in philosophy, particularly mathematics.[35] But mathematics is applied only to the useful arts, and thus would be little esteemed in Europe. In addition, the Brobdingnagians know only morality, history, and poetry. Gulliver tries in vain to make them understand ' ideas, entities, abstractions, and transcendentals '. Furthermore, they have not ' reduced politics into a science, as the more acute wits of Europe have done '.[36]

It is in Voyage III that one becomes most conscious that Gulliver prefers speculative to practical learning. Occasionally, as a hard-headed Englishman, he can condemn as impractical the political projectors of Lagado who desire to have monarchs reward wisdom, virtue, and merit. [37] In Laputa he observes that using a quadrant to measure a man for a suit of clothes is different from the European method,[38] but he nonetheless has a number of things in common with the Laputans. They are interested only in mathematics and music; Gulliver knows something about both.[39] Like a mathematician, he draws a diagram and provides a verbal explanation to show the way the flying island of Laputa was manoeuvred. He understands the mathematical proof that the satellites of Mars are governed by the same law of gravitation that influences other heavenly bodies. The Laputan astronomers, he believes, should publish their discoveries of ninety-three different comets, since the theory of comets is very backward.[40] But despite the excellence of the Laputans in two sciences which Gulliver esteems, he still finds them rather too abstracted to be good companions.[41]

Accordingly Gulliver leaves the flying island for the real island, Balnibarbi, below. There he finds the metropolis, Lagado, with its Academy. The activities here, as well as in Laputa, may symbolize the experiments of the Royal Academy[42] and thus contain a satire on the new science.[43] They may symbolize the newfangled schemes of political projectors.[44] Or they may symbolize certain elements of both. At any rate, many of the details of the Academy are taken from Rabelais's account of the court of Queen Whims.[45] There Panurge and the other pilgrims see such wonderful things as experiments to putrefy beetles, to make figs from thistles, and to make churches jump over steeples.[46] Furthermore, the reaction of the pilgrims to these sights is one of unqualified praise and wonder. Repeatedly the Queen (who can cure incurable diseases) is given adulation for her excellence : ' We saw there such new, strange, and wonderful things, that I am still ravished in admiration every time I think on't.'[47]

This is exactly the reaction of Gulliver to much of what he sees on his third voyage, particularly in Lagado. Gulliver can, of course, appreciate the ' wise observations ' of the ' great lord ' at the court of Laputa, who was considered stupid because he never learned mathematics and music. He also notes objectively the prosperity of the lands of Lord Munodi and the nobility of his house ' built according to the best rules of ancient architecture ', in contrast to the wretched appearance of the lands awaiting the fulfilment of the projectors' schemes.[48] Although Munodi is entirely content with the ways of his ancestors, he does not hate the innovators. It is because they dislike him that he declines to accompany Gulliver through the Academy. Therefore he introduces Gulliver to a friend who will be his guide. In doing so Munodi refers to Gulliver as ' a great admirer of projects, and a person of much curiosity and easy belief '. This, Gulliver adds, ' was not without truth ; for I had myself been a sort of projector in my younger days '.[49]

Except for briefly registering disgust at the filth of the man turning excrement into food, Gulliver reacts to the projects with spontaneous admiration. It is a ' most ingenious ' architect who builds houses from the roof down.[50] Gulliver is ' highly pleased ' with a scheme for using hogs to plow the earth, and ' fully convinced ' that silk can be coloured by the colour of flies eaten by spiders. He promises that on his return to England he will obtain recognition for the inventor of the wonderful word-machine, which enables the most ignorant person to write books on any subject by a mechanical method. He scorns the women, the vulgar, and the illiterate who oppose the unique scheme of abolishing all words and replacing them with objects to be carried about.[51] Writing in the manner of the medical projector himself, he reports the plan of ' a most ingenious doctor ' for curing the diseases of the body politic, which corresponds strictly to the natural body and must therefore ' be cured by the same prescriptions ', with ' lenitives, aperitives, abstersives, corrosives, restringents, palliatives . . .'[52] When one professor reveals his project for discovering plots against the government by examining the diet of suspected persons, Gulliver goes even further and outlines for him the method of the Tribnians, who are supremely skilful at reading hidden anagrammatic meanings in letters of suspects.[53] Later, in Glubbdubdrib, he admires the ' great strength of reason ' with which three dead kings prove that corruption is necessary to government. And one reason he is thrilled at the prospect of being a *struldbrug* is that he will be able to witness the discovery of the longitude, the perpetual motion, and the universal medicine.[54]

These are a number of the ways in which Gulliver's attitude differs radically from Swift's, and enables Swift to point up ironically the events Gulliver witnesses. As Professor Robert C. Elliott has shown, many of the naive, patriotic, foolish, or otherwise questionable attitudes which Gulliver shows in the early voyages are reported not as the ideas solely of the still unwise Gulliver who makes Voyages I–III, but as the ideas of the disillusioned, clear-eyed Gulliver who has been through Voyage IV and who then writes about his travels. Professor Elliott concludes that the misanthropic Gulliver-author, portraying his earlier character, speaks naively or foolishly with conscious irony ; thus in the ironical accounts of the early voyages there is little difference between Gulliver-author and Swift himself (Professor Elliott does point out a difference which develops in Voyage IV).[55] To see Gulliver as an ironist is one possible way of solving this problem ; it tends to make him a consistent character and gives the book a well-defined point of view, in Henry James's sense. But since Swift often uses his *personae* quite freely for his main purposes of irony and satire, without a novelist's primary regard for the absolute integrity of the fictitious character itself, and since he seldom shares his ironical omniscience with an ' author ', it seems more likely that Swift saw Gulliver could be useful in two primary capacities : as a naive voyager and as a disillusioned misanthrope. There is a technical problem involved in presenting these two sides of his character. Before the Houyhnhnms enlighten him, he appears as frequently foolish, both as voyager and as author, in the manner of other travel writers. To a person who had not read Book IV the inconsistency in the character of Gulliver-author would not, practically speaking, be a glaring one, for the character of the reformed Gulliver is suggested with real force only in the ' Letter to Sympson '. It receives no thoroughgoing treatment until Voyage IV, where it becomes very important to the satire. Yet even here in several passages, as we have seen, Gulliver can resemble his former naive self, in a manner which looks less like conscious irony on his part than like a free use of the mask on Swift's. It is these passages which would bother readers more, yet the satire in them is effective, and that, as always, seems to have been Swift's main concern in creating his mask.

— Swift does not overwork the irony in *Gulliver's Travels*. In many instances, Gulliver is merely an objective reporter ; here Swift lets the events speak for themselves. In Lilliput, for example, Gulliver describes straightforwardly many of the good qualities of the inhabitants.[56] His report resembles Dampier's factual account of people, animals, and vegetation, and Captain Siden's objective description of the ways of the Sevarambians, though it is clear that Siden considers his hosts practically perfect by contrast with Europeans.[57] Gulliver observes the picturesqueness of Lilliput.[58] He also notes that the laws and customs of the country have good points, though they are ' directly contrary ' to those of England. If a man is found innocent, his accuser is put to death. Fraud is a greater crime than theft, public officials are chosen more for their morals than their abilities, and parents do not raise their own children. The women, like the men, are afraid of being cowards and fools. Begging is unknown in the country.[59] The Emperor is an impressive leader of his people, taller than any of his court, with an Austrian lip and arched nose, graceful gestures, and a clear and articulate voice.[60] He stands bravely as Gulliver flourishes his scimitar and fires his gun.[61]

But the Emperor also is ambitious in desiring to subjugate Blefuscu ;[62] and before any cruel execution he makes a speech on his great lenity and tenderness.[63] These qualities reflect the fact that the Lilliputians can exhibit, in addition to some non-English merits, some very English faults.[64] Showing that the pure original institutions of Lilliput have fallen into corruption,[65] Gulliver describes how political offices are given to rope-dancers (Flimnap, the Prime Minister, is the best) and how candidates jump over a stick in order to win blue, red, and green ribbons.[66] There is factionalism in the kingdom between the High-Heels and the Low-Heels and between those who break their eggs on the big end and those who break them on the small end.[67] Purely out of hatred Skyresh Bolgolam and others of the Council impeach Gulliver and demand his death.[68] The Lilliputians are amusingly proud of their mighty Emperor, the ' delight and terror of the universe '.[69] And they are sure there are no regions beyond Lilliput and Blefuscu.[70]

Similarly, Gulliver reports both good and bad qualities in Brobdingnag. The King has a real interest in new discoveries in art and nature.[71] Hating mystery, intrigue, and secrets of state, he believes government should be confined to common sense and reason. The laws in the

country are limited to twenty-two words, the people have few books
in their libraries,[72] and they write a clear, masculine, smooth style.[73]
Furthermore, after questioning Gulliver, the King reflects in an extreme
form some of Swift's most pessimistic feelings in his conclusions about
England. Gulliver himself can only in helpless anger record the King's
judgment—and it is the King's—that 'ignorance, idleness, and vice
are the proper ingredients for qualifying a legislator', that English
institutions have become hopelessly corrupt, and that 'the bulk of
your natives' are 'the most pernicious race of little odious vermin
that nature ever suffered to crawl upon the surface of the earth'.[74]

Although the Brobdingnagians are the least corrupted of the
'Yahoo nations',[75] they have faults.[76] A struggle for power goes on
among their king, nobility, and people.[77] Their moralists, like those
in Europe, write books on the present weakness of men and on how
there must once have been giants in the world.[78] An avaricious master
exploits Gulliver as an oddity.[79] One can feel only disgust at the
nakedness of the huge nurse[80] and maids of honour,[81] and the quantity
eaten by the Queen.[82]

Although Gulliver expresses frequent admiration throughout
Voyage III, much of the satire is in his objective descriptions. For
example, he reports the appearance of the Laputans, whose clothes
are decorated with figures of the sun, moon, stars, and musical instruments ; their need for flappers in order to communicate ; the mathematicians' puzzling interest in politics ; the lack of right angles in
Laputan buildings; their concern over the health of the sun ;[83] and
the King's lowering the flying island gently, supposedly out of tenderness to his people, but really because he is afraid the adamantine
bottom of the island will crack.[84]

In Voyage IV Gulliver describes the good qualities of the Houyhnhnms and the vices of the Yahoos. He is still objective, though it
becomes increasingly clear that he admires the one and detests the other.
Going far beyond the Brobdingnagians, the Houyhnhnms have no
idea of books and literature.[85] Since they use no alphabet, their
knowledge is all traditional.[86] Having few wants and passions, they
require few words,[87] and their conversations consist only of useful
information. They enjoy perfect health[88] and have no comprehension
of law,[89] being completely virtuous and rational. Friendship and
benevolence are their principal virtues,[90] the frequent subjects of their
conversations, and the exalted theme of their poetry.[91] They propagate
and educate their offspring rationally for the good of the race, not
because of strong marital and paternal attachments.[92] When a Houy-

hnhnm dies, his friends and relatives express neither joy nor grief.[93] Like the King of Brobdingnag, the Houyhnhnm master speaks for Swift in his condemnation of human war,[94] natural philosophy,[95] and the human corruptions of reason that are worse than brutality.[96]

On the other hand, Gulliver depicts the Yahoos as completely loathsome. Five of them fight over enough food for fifty. They dig coloured stones and heap them in their kennels and devour herbs, roots, and flesh with undistinguishing appetites. Pregnant females continue to admit males, and males and females fight.[97] The Yahoos are unteachable, cowardly, cruel,[98] filthy, deformed, malicious animals.[99]

One must not conclude, however, that Swift is merely contrasting, in the abstract, qualities which he admired with those he disliked. As a satire, the main purpose of *Gulliver's Travels* is to show certain shortcomings in eighteenth century European society, not to depict ideal and base societies which should be imitated or avoided. If we return to the first paragraph on the good qualities of Lilliput, for example, we must ask in what sense Swift meant they were unlike those of England. In the statement that, if a man is found innocent, his accuser is put to death, Swift is probably merely pointing out ironically that England lacks punishment for false accusers, not that they should invariably be executed. In saying that fraud is a greater crime than theft, he is probably indicating that fraud should be recognized as a serious crime, that it can be a form of theft. In remarking that in Lilliput public officials are chosen more for their morals than their abilities, Swift is not saying that men with ability should not have public office; he is leading the reader to surmise that in England officials with bad morals get into office. That Lilliputian parents are not allowed to raise their own children suggests more the reality that parents do not treat their own children rationally than that not having them rear their own children will solve the problem. That the Emperor of Lilliput has a clear voice and graceful gestures is less a statement with a moral than a concrete detail which gives colour to the narrative, though it contains the devastating hint that the ungainly George I lacks some of the good qualities of the ruler who is only six inches high.

Much of the satire in *Gulliver's Travels* consists in the details of what Gulliver sees. The book could doubtless have enjoyed a certain amount of success if Swift had contented himself merely with describing the four imaginary kingdoms. The effectiveness of this facet of the work is reflected in Dr. Johnson's superficial comment that when Swift had thought of little men and big men, his principal job was done. But

Gulliver's Travels, probably even more than any of Swift's other great works, owes its excellence to the fact that its satire is in purpose not single but multiple. Swift achieves part of this multiplicity by making Gulliver not merely an observer but also an active participant in the events he describes. Here the most important thing is the extent to which Gulliver identifies himself with his hosts. The main object of this part of the satire is human pride.

The reader easily sees the difference between Gulliver and the Lilliputians as first they bind him and then agree to release him if he will consent to the terms they set. In the picture of the human being towering above the diminutive society there is a convincing comment on how petty various social institutions could appear if one could see them as Gulliver sees those of the Lilliputians. This form of the satire, clearly illustrated (for example) as Gulliver effortlessly picks up members of the court or gives the horsemen his handkerchief to exercise upon, is one of the results of differentiating Gulliver (who seems to be a colossus) from his tiny hosts.

But as the story goes on, one is aware that Gulliver has adapted himself to the Lilliputian scale. He worries that Bolgolam is his ' mortal enemy '[100] and defends himself against the gossip that the Treasurer's wife came privately to his lodging.[101] Towards the diminutive monarchs he behaves like any other subject : he lies on his side to kiss the hand of the Queen, prostrates himself at the feet of the King of Lilliput[102] and the King of Blefuscu.[103] To avoid the charge of vanity, he does not repeat the compliments given him by the Lilliputian King.[104] The Lilliputian palace[105] and the Blefuscudian ambassadors seem to him magnificent.[106]

The device of ridiculing Gulliver and raising his hosts to a mock-heroic level continues as Gulliver performs his valorous deeds. When Blefuscu threatens Lilliput, Gulliver says he is ready ' with the hazard of my life ' to defend the King and state against all invaders.[107] After conquering the enemy fleet, he cries out, ' Long live the most puissant Emperor of Lilliput ', and is created a Nardac on the spot.[108] Later he prides himself on being a Nardac, while the Treasurer is only a Glum-glum. At dinner at the court he eats more than usual ' in honour to my dear country, as well as to fill the court with admiration '.[109] Such actions, he proudly recalls later, ' will be recorded forever in the chronicles of that empire '.[110] The satire on human pride is doubly intense : the Lilliputians act proud of their tiny systems, and the human Gulliver acts proud of the part he has in them.

The various relationships between Gulliver and the Brobding-

nagians serve still more satiric ends. Gulliver is distinguished from
them by his obvious inferiority in size. This makes him ridiculous and
even contemptible, for he is beneath even animals and children. A
Brobdingnagian farmer watches him carefully, as Gulliver would watch
a weasel in England.[111]. A dog carries him in his mouth, and Gulliver
tries to conceal the story for the sake of his reputation.[112] He breaks
his shin on a snail's shell and is forcibly fed by a monkey who carries
him to the top of a high roof.[113] Glumdalclitch, nine years old, dresses
and undresses him and regards him as a replacement for her pet lamb,
butchered a year before.[114] A schoolboy throws a hazel nut at his
head and nearly knocks out his brains.[115]

Despite his diminutive size, Gulliver continues to show pride in
his accomplishments as he had in Lilliput. For an audience he gallantly
flourishes his hanger ; a piece of straw is his pike.[116] He bravely kills a
' nimble and fierce ' rat,[117] dexterously cuts flies to pieces with his
knife, courageously fights off four wasps which try to steal his piece
of cake,[118] resolutely draws his hanger when a kite swoops at
him, triumphantly knocks down a linnet, and forces a frog out of
his boat.

Yet the Brobdingnagians merely laugh at his pretensions to courage
when he claims he would have fiercely wounded a monkey had his
fears not prevented him.[119] Gulliver's claims for the grandeur of
England and the English are likewise crushed. After he has been ' a
little too copious in talking of my own beloved country ', the King
takes him up in his hand and, laughing, asks him whether he is Whig
or Tory. Then the King remarks on how human grandeur can be
' mimicked by such contemptible creatures '.[120] The satire on pride
acquires a new kind of force here. The smallness of the Lilliputians is
seen through Gulliver's objective report. Even when he criticizes
their bad customs he treats them as corruptions due to ' the degenerate
nature of man '. He is not a giant scorning his hosts. When he
becomes involved in the war, moreover, he cannot condemn its pettiness, since he looks upon it as being of glorious importance. But the
King of Brobdingnag can speak with crushing contempt of human
smallness, since (unlike Gulliver) he never is led to consider it great.
In the one instance Swift's message must be implied from the way
Gulliver behaves among people one-twelfth his size. In the second the
message is reflected in the words of the King.

Yet the satire in Voyage II is not simple, with giants looking down
contemptuously upon a man. Since the Brobdingnagians are large,
their size can be used to point out in a magnified way certain forms of

human crudeness. The farmer who finds Gulliver, sits with his friends in a circle observing Gulliver without understanding his speech. The farmer's wife, upon seeing Gulliver, screams and runs, as though he were a toad or spider.[121] The giant Queen is commonly referred to as ' the Ornament of Nature, the Darling of the World, the Delight of her Subjects, the Phoenix of the Creation '.[122]

As in Voyage I the satire takes on a new dimension when Gulliver manages to accept the giant scale of the Brobdingnagians.[123] He refers to a dwarf thirty feet high[124] as a ' malicious little cub '[125] and makes jokes on his deformity.[126] He can share the Brobdingnagians' humorous contempt for the idea of English lords and ladies dressed in their finery.[127] And when he is rescued by English sailors he regards them as ' the most little contemptible creatures I had ever beheld.'[128] What Gulliver says, like what the King says, reflects Swift's message. Human beings *are* contemptible. Yet Gulliver has forgotten—as his creator has not—that he is a human being, capable as anyone of the folly of pride in human accomplishments.

In Voyage III the attack on pride does not come primarily through identification between Gulliver and his hosts. It comes rather in the portrayal of the satisfaction the hosts feel over their mechanical schemes. There are minor exceptions, of course. Gulliver is allowed to lick the dust before the footstool of the King of Luggnagg and to address the decidedly imperfect monarch with ' May your Celestial Majesty outlive the sun, eleven moons and a half '. During this voyage, however, Gulliver mostly looks upon his hosts as would an observant and frequently admiring outsider. As a reporter, in addition to praising the various inventions he sees, he can note (forgetting his own failings) that the Luggnaggians are not without ' that pride, which is peculiar to all Eastern countries '.[129]

Voyage IV contains Swift's clearest attack on human pride. This attack depends upon the identification between Gulliver and the Yahoos, Gulliver and the Houyhnhnms. Gulliver actually is neither Yahoo nor Houyhnhnm. As his dwelling is six yards from the Houyhnhnm house and separate from the Yahoo stable,[130] so he is in reason as inferior to the Houyhnhnms as the Yahoos are to him.[131] He is a Yahoo with ' some glimmerings of reason '[132] and is therefore regarded as a prodigy.[133] Yet perverted human reason, the Houyhnhnms realize, can be a means of discovering vices unknown to the Yahoos.[134]

In many details Gulliver is identified with the Yahoos. They sense that he is one of them, and hate him for the favouritism the Houyhnhnms show him. As he bathes, a female Yahoo attempts to embrace him.[135]

Although he regards the Yahoos at first with loathing,[136] he later sees that they have a ' perfect human figure ', distorted only as it is among savage peoples.[137] Gulliver's body differs from theirs only to his disadvantage in strength, speed, and activity.[138] He observes the similarity between the Yahoos' sucking a juicy root and human beings' drinking wine. Hearing about coquetry among the Yahoos, Gulliver understands that this vice has ' place by instinct in womankind '.[139] He forms the habit of referring to his fellow men as ' Yahoos,'[140] who use reason only to multiply their vices ; he is horrified at his own reflection.[141]

On the other hand, Gulliver's rationality, however small, and his ability to recognize the loathsomeness of his Yahoo characteristics enable him at times to be partially identified with the Houyhnhnms. He is allowed to listen to their discourses,[142] from which he obtains all the knowledge of any value he possesses. Regarding all men as Yahoos, he has love and gratitude for the Houyhnhnms' condescending to distinguish him from the rest of his kind.[143] So great is his love for his hosts that he resolves never to return to mankind again.[144] As he makes such a resolution, briefly his patriotism disappears. Even when the Houyhnhnm assembly forces Gulliver, whom they consider a Yahoo, to leave, his master, ' partly out of kindness ', sees him in his canoe and gives him his hoof to kiss. Gulliver says his detractors will hardly believe he has received such an honour.[145] For this noble creature, unlike the monarchs in the first three voyages, truly deserves Gulliver's respect.

Part of the difficulty in Voyage IV comes from the temptation to see Gulliver as either Yahoo or Houyhnhnm, not as both. From the beginning, of course, the Houyhnhnms see him as a Yahoo and finally drive him away for being one ; his master kindly makes the exception that Gulliver is an unusual Yahoo in possessing some reason. The Yahoos, too, recognize Gulliver as one of their own kind, though they are jealous of his relations with the Houyhnhnms. Gulliver himself, however, begins by hating the Yahoos, whom he considers far inferior to him. As the Houyhnhnms compare him with a Yahoo and constantly refer to him as one, he realizes the resemblance with a shock. Then he attempts to dissever himself from his kind. Like the Houyhnhnms, he regards his fellow men as Yahoos (distinguished primarily by their different shape and their perversion of reason) and loathes them. But he is always aware of his similarity to them.

One must remember that Gulliver's identification with the idealized Houyhnhnms (like his identification with the Lilliputians and Brob-

dingnagians) is not complete when he looks down upon the human
race generally as unregenerate Yahoos. His scorn for

> gibers, censurers, backbiters, pickpockets, highwaymen, house-
> breakers, attorneys, bawds, gamesters, politicians, wits, splenetics,
> tedious talkers, controvertists, ravishers, murderers, robbers,
> virtuosos

is more like the angry condemnation of the King of Brobdingnag than
the calm disapproval of the Houyhnhnm master. Though in part
voicing Swift's message, Gulliver is still himself. As he writes, he
cannot even approximate the Houyhnhnms' expressions in ' our
barbarous English '.[146] After leaving Houyhnhnm-land, when first he
sees a European ship, he tries to escape to the barbarians rather than
return home. The smell of Captain Pedro de Mendez and his men
nearly makes him faint,[147] as his wife's kissing him actually does.[148]
Moreover, some of the habits Gulliver has acquired from the Houyhnhnms seem humorous—his neighing speech,[149] his trotting like a
horse,[150] and his daily conversations with his own horses.[151] As on his
arrival home from Brobdingnag, when (still thinking of himself as a
giant) he was afraid of trampling on the apparently tiny Englishmen,
Gulliver at the end of Voyage IV is somewhat ridiculous in his failure
—being among men—to return at once to imperfect human ways and
to accept with resignation the inescapable and humbling fact that he is
like the other human beings whom he so violently rejects. Yet at the
same time it is improbable that Swift regards him here as merely an
object of comedy and thus condemns completely his misanthropy
and his worship of the Houyhnhnms.[152] In censuring men in general,
as in censuring human pettiness or lying in particular, Gulliver is
both explainer and object of Swift's satiric message. Gulliver is doubtless wiser now than when he first greeted the Houyhnhnms by whistling
at them like a jockey, while they received his ' civilities with disdain '.[153]
He has seen (and so has the reader) the shocking difference between an
ideal and actuality. Regarding his fellows—because of this difference
—with contempt, he can have no more benevolence and friendship
for them than the Houyhnhnms have for the Yahoos. His preferring
the company of horses to that of men is not only an amusing reflection
on his unwillingness to be identified with those of his own kind, and
an indication that—unlike Swift, who could ' heartily love John, Peter,
Thomas '—he has become a misanthrope ' in Timon's manner '.[154]
It is also a bitter commentary on the imperfections of human life.

After living among the Houyhnhnms Gulliver cannot give his
highest praises even to Queen Anne, whom he formerly reverenced.

He tells Sympson that he despairs completely of reforming the English Yahoos, and that it was only a recurrence of some of his own former Yahoo corruptions that made him attempt such a reform.[155] If such recurrences indicate a moral readjustment to normality comparable to Gulliver's physical readjustment after Brobdingnag (not Lilliput),[156] it is decidedly an unfortunately necessary readjustment to imperfection. Furthermore, it is not a total change. For though Gulliver has managed to stand the sight of ' a lawyer, a pickpocket, a colonel, a fool, a lord ', he heartily detests the vice of pride : ' but when I behold a lump of deformity, and diseases both in body and mind, smitten with pride, it immediately breaks all the measures of my patience.'[157]

We may hear the voice of Swift in this harsh judgment, but we should also distinguish the voice of Gulliver. Ready to denounce his fellow men for pride, he must set himself apart from them in order to do so. He writes for the noblest end, ' to inform and instruct mankind, over whom I may, without breach of modesty, pretend to some superiority, from the advantages I received by conversing so long among the most accomplished Houyhnhnms '. Pride in one's moral superiority may be consistent with *true* humility. But Gulliver's pharisaical self-evaluation makes his perfection of humility suspect. One feels this shortcoming as he warns any ' English Yahoo ' who has ' any tincture ' of pride not to ' presume to come in my sight '. Moreover, Gulliver's hatred of pride is conspicuously coupled in the final chapter of his book with his hatred of falsehood. Having seen his veracity as questionable, one is apt to doubt his humility. Yet as he seems to speak for Swift, his own shortcomings intensify the moral satire. One thinks of the nominal Christian and (later) of the ' defender ' of Carteret, who support Swift's cause but not for Swift's reasons.

Falsehood, perversion of reason, and pride—these faults seem to be the most definite objects of the satire in *Gulliver's Travels*. As Swift attacks them Gulliver can be said to symbolize man, in his traditionally imperfect state as a ' proud and yet a wretched thing ' or

> Sole judge of truth, in endless error hurled ;
> The glory, jest, and riddle of the world!

Yet Gulliver also displays, and comments upon, the shortcomings specifically of writers of travel literature ; of contemporary scientists, commentators, nobles, courts, and kings ; of the accepted human scheme of values ; and of the values of patriotic Englishmen. All these elements are interwoven in a narrative which, apart from its symbolic significance, contains details which have given imaginative delight to generations of readers.

NOTES TO CHAPTER XI

[1] J. B. Moore, *op. cit.*, 469–80 ; and Case, *Four Essays*, pp. 115–21. Professor Moore emphasizes Gulliver's admirable qualities in order to show that when he becomes a misanthrope, it must be for a genuinely good reason. See also Ruby V. Redinger, ' Jonathan Swift, the Disenchanter ', *The American Scholar*, XV (1946), 221–6.

[2] *Works*, VIII, 68.   [7] *Ibid.*, 208.   [12] *Ibid.*, 91.
[3] *Ibid.*, 54–5.   [8] *Ibid.*, 268.   [13] *Ibid.*, 109.
[4] *Ibid.*, 74–9.   [9] *Ibid.*, 210.   [14] *Ibid.*, 130–2.
[5] *Ibid.*, 121.   [10] *Ibid.*, 217, 223.   [15] *Ibid.*, 136–7.
[6] *Ibid.*, 171.   [11] *Ibid.*, 60.

[16] *Works*, VIII, 138. Cyrano makes a similarly patriotic defence to the rational giant moon-dwellers. He refuses to argue against those who deny Aristotle's philosophy (*Voyage to the Moon*, p. 127), defends the customs of treacherous war (*ibid.*, p. 132) and burial (*ibid.*, p. 198). The giants laugh at him for saying the earth is a world and the moon is merely a moon ; he is forced to reverse his opinion (*ibid.*, pp. 138–43).

[17] *Works*, VIII, 209.   [21] *Ibid.*, 252–6.   [25] *Ibid.*, 253.
[18] J. B. Moore, *op. cit.*, 475–80.   [22] *Ibid.*, 265.   [26] *Ibid.*, 263–6.
[19] *Works*, VIII, 259–66.   [23] *Ibid.*, 255.   [27] *Ibid.*, 305.
[20] *Ibid.*, 239.   [24] *Ibid.*, 273–4.

[28] *New Voyage*, p. 1. Professor Eddy shows that Cyrano goes to distant worlds in order to get scientific information from the inhabitants, and adds that this element of scientific speculation is not in *Gulliver*. (*Gulliver's Travels*, p. 40).

[29] *Works*, VIII, 112.   [31] *Ibid.*, 21, 25.   [33] *Ibid.*, 64.
[30] *Ibid.*, VIII, 96.   [32] *Ibid.*, 45.

[34] *Ibid.*, 106. The source of the puzzled examination of a human being by giants is Cyrano's *Histoire de la Lune*. (Eddy, *Gulliver's Travels*, p. 126).
[35] *Works*, VIII, 105.   [36] *Ibid.*, 140, 139.   [37] *Ibid.*, 195.
[38] *Ibid.*, 166–7. This detail is from the writings of Tom Brown. (E. N. S. Thompson, ' Tom Brown and the Scientists ', *Modern Language Notes*, XXXII [1917], 92–3). Professor De Morgan points out that a quadrant measures an angle, not distance. (*Op. cit.*, 125).
[39] *Works*, VIII, 167–8.   [40] *Ibid.*, 175–6.   [41] *Ibid.*, 180.

[42] A correspondence has been shown between some of the experiments described in the *Philosophical Transactions of the Royal Society* and such details in the Laputa episode as the use of quadrants to determine altitude, the analogy between musical and mathematical theory, and astronomers' knowledge of comets. In Lagado, the description of the Grand Academy may reflect the plans of the Royal Society for expanded quarters. Such experiments in the Academy as the attempt to strike sunbeams from cucumbers and to put a sun-dial on a weather cock, as well as the Balnibarbian method of managing land, are exaggerated parallels of actual Royal Society experiments. (Marjorie Nicolson and Nora M. Mohler, ' The Scientific Background of Swift's Voyage to Laputa ', *Annals of Science*, II [1937], 299–334.) See also George R. Potter, ' Swift and Natural Science ', *Philological Quarterly*, XX (April, 1941), 97–118 ; this article shows Swift's familiarity with science, scientists, and the satire on them.

[43] Dr. Potter says that Swift did not see how natural science could affect religion and morals ; thus he did not take science so seriously as political vices as an object for condemnation. (*Ibid.*, 117). Professor Landa, on the contrary, says that while Swift satirizes the corruptions of science, not science itself, he probably was aware of many of the philosophical implications of science. (Review of Potter's ' Swift and Natural Science,' *Philological Quarterly*, XXI, 220.)

[44] Professor Case argues that Balnibarbi represents the British Isles under George I and the Whigs, with their political innovations and schemes. (*Four*

Essays, p. 87). The Grand Academy, he says, resembles Whitehall more than the Royal Academy. The projectors of Lagado are interested in get-rich-quick schemes, while the Royal Academy carried on primarily experiments in pure science. (*Ibid.*, p. 89.)

⁴⁵ Eddy, *Gulliver's Travels*, pp. 19, 60. Professor Eddy shows that details come also from Lucian's *True History* (*ibid.*, p. 16); Joseph Hall's *Mundus Alter et Idem* (*ibid.*, pp. 44–5); Tom Brown's *Amusements Serious and Comical* (*ibid.*, pp. 36–7); and possibly Baron Holberg's *Voyage of Nicholas Klimius to the World Underground* (*ibid.*, pp. 160–1).

⁴⁶ Rabelais, *Works*, II, 815–18. Swift also owes to Rabelais the idea of the distillation of human excrement, of making air tangible, of the anal pump, and of the malleability of fire. (Eddy, *Gulliver's Travels*, p. 162.)

⁴⁷ Rabelais, *Works*, II, 815.

⁴⁸ *Works*, VIII, 180–3. Professor Case says that Lord Munodi represents Oxford : Munodi had formerly been Governor of Lagado ; he was discharged for inefficiency and subsequently lived in retirement. Munodi's estate symbolizes the good old Tory way, as against Whig innovations which were ruining the country. (*Four Essays*, p. 87.) His being persuaded by the projectors to change his old mill for a new one refers to Oxford's sponsoring the South Sea scheme, urged by such projectors as Defoe. (*Ibid.*, pp. 88–9.)

⁴⁹ *Works*, VIII, 185.

⁵⁰ *Ibid.*, 187. This detail comes from Tom Brown. (Eddy, *Gulliver's Travels*, p. 163.)

⁵¹ *Works*, VIII, 187–93.

⁵² *Ibid.*, 195–6. The analogical proof reminds one of the *Tale of a Tub*.

⁵³ *Ibid.*, 200–1. ⁵⁴ *Ibid.*, 209, 219.

⁵⁵ ' Gulliver as Literary Artist ', *English Literary History*, XIX (1952), 49–63.

⁵⁶ Professor Eddy shows that Perrot d'Ablancourt's sequel to Lucian's *True History* is similar to *Gulliver* in making the human viewpoint the abnormality and that of the pygmies normal. (*Gulliver's Travels*, p. 87). D'Ablancourt's pygmies are ruled by a benevolent king and are ingenious in domestic affairs (*ibid.*, pp. 55–6); they make glasses out of pits of cherries and drink dewdrops (*ibid.*, p. 86). They valorously oppose their larger enemies, the cranes (*ibid.*, p. 85). Professor Eddy (*ibid.*, pp. 88–9) mentions the *Gerania* of Joshua Barnes (1675) as the longest account of pygmies before *Gulliver* ; Barnes's pygmies are skilled in sciences, and have neither desire of riches nor deceit.

Other possible sources of *Gulliver* give accounts of pygmies and small people who have good, though not heroic, qualities : Ned Ward's *The Humors of a Coffee-House* (F. S. Rockwell, 'A Probable Source for *Gulliver's Travels*,' *Notes and Queries*, 169 (Aug. 24, 1935), 132–3); *The Weekly Comedy* of May 10, 1699 (G. S. McCue, 'A Seventeenth Century Gulliver ', *Modern Language Notes*, L[Jan., 1935], 32–3); and *The Wanderings of the Tuath Luchra* (Margaret R. Grennan, ' Lilliput and Leprecan : Gulliver and the Irish Tradition,' *English Literary History*, XII [Sept., 1945], 194).

For the concept of the Lilliputians' symbolizing European faults, Swift perhaps combined the point of view of Menippus, who flies above the earth and sees how petty it is (Lucian, *Icaromenippus*) with the experience of Rabelais's pilgrims, whose hosts—in the Land of Pettifogging and Pope-figgland—are satirical representatives of European vices. (Eddy, *Gulliver's Travels*, pp. 109–10, 18–19). Professor Pons shows a connection between the Lilliputian language and Rabelais's experiments in coining words. (' Rabelais et Swift à propos du Lilliputien ', *Mélanges Offerts à M. Abel Lefranc* [Paris, 1936], pp. 225 ff.

⁵⁷ *History of the Sevarambians*, bks. III and IV. Gulliver's attributes make him a good observer of various civilizations. (Case, *Four Essays*, p. 115). He is not a symbol for the ' egotistic ' Swift, seeing himself as the only sane and normal person in an abnormal world. (M. M. Rossi and J. M. Hone, *Swift, or the Egotist* (1934), pp. 320–1).

58 *Works*, VIII, 28.   59 *Ibid.*, 59–64.

60 The Emperor is evidently the antithesis of the ungainly George I, who dressed badly and spoke guttural English (Case, *Four Essays*, p. 71).

61 *Works*, VIII, 36.

62 *Ibid.*, 53–4.

63 *Ibid.*, 74.

64 This ' inconsistency ' in the symbolism of Lilliput has been often pointed out : Eddy, *Gulliver's Travels*, p. 112 ; Quintana, *Mind and Art of Jonathan Swift*, p. 309 ; G. Wilson Knight, *The Burning Oracle* (1939), p. 121. The good qualities of the Lilliputians, however, do not contradict the bad ones. And neither Lilliput nor Brobdingnag is supposed to be a complete Utopia, although each country can in certain respects be a salutary example for the English to follow. Throughout the book the Houyhnhnms and Yahoos are the only whole groups represented as consistently good and bad.

65 *Works*, VIII, 61.   67 *Ibid.*, 48–50.   69 *Ibid.*, 43.

66 *Ibid.*, 38–9.   68 *Works*, VIII, 69–73.

70 *Ibid.*, 49. The allegorical significance of this voyage has been studied in great detail. Sir Charles Firth believes that the low and high heels refer to low and high church sentiments ; that Blefuscu is France ; and that the Emperor—a Low-Heel— is George I. The 'inconsistencies' in the descriptions of Lilliput and the Emperor are due to Swift's revising his book, begun before 1714, after 1720. Thus also, in the first version Gulliver, who extinguished the palace fire by urinating, represents Swift the satirist, whose *Tale of a Tub* Queen Anne disliked ; Bolgolam is Swift's enemy Nottingham. But in the revision Gulliver becomes Bolingbroke, Flimnap the Prime Minister is Walpole, and the moderate Reldresal—who opposes executing Gulliver—is Lord Carteret. (' The Political Significance of *Gulliver's Travels*,' *Proceedings of the British Academy*, IX [1919], 240–6.)

Professor Case argues that Gulliver's career in Lilliput represents the joint political fortunes of Oxford and Bolingbroke (*Four Essays*, p. 70). Thus, among other differences from Firth's analysis, Gulliver's method of extinguishing the fire in the Queen's apartment refers to the negotiation of the Peace of Utrecht, which was illegal and conducted by Harley, who was frequently drunk and contemptuous of the dignity of Queen Anne (*ibid.*, p. 76). Bolgolam is Nottingham, but as an enemy of Harley's, not Swift's (*ibid.*, pp. 72–3). Reldresal is Charles, Viscount Townshend, the insincere friend of the Tories after their fall. The proposal to blind Gulliver refers to the barring of Oxford and Bolingbroke from political activities for the rest of their lives. (*Ibid.*, p. 78.)

But as Swift wrote to the Abbé des Fontaines, *Gulliver* was not written ' for one city, one province, one kingdom, or even one age.' (Quoted in Case, *Four Essays*, p. 123). The political allegory contains only a part of the significance of the book.

71 *Works*, VIII, 139. The giants in Cyrano's *Voyage to the Moon* (p. 183) have an atomic theory like that of Epicurus.

72 *Works*, VIII, 140. Professor Eddy believes the giants' small libraries indicate lack of intelligence. He parallels the pacifism of their King with that of Grangousier (*Gulliver's Travels*, p. 135). But the Utopian Sevarambians also have fewer books than Europeans do (Vairasse d'Alais, *op. cit.*, p. 118). Swift here, in his usual method, is arguing not for small libraries but against the plethoric production of worthless reading matter.

73 *Works*, VIII, 141.

74 *Ibid.*, 135–6. Swift can write strong invective in works which do not involve a mask. See, for example, the *Letter to a Young Lady*, where he says of the ' bold, swaggering, rattling Ladies, whose talents pass among coxcombs for wit and humour. . . . I have often thought that no man is obliged to suppose such creatures to be women ; but to treat them like indolent rascals disguised in female habits, who ought to be stripped and kicked down stairs.' (*Ibid.*, XI, 123). In the same essay Swift can put an extreme statement into imaginatively concrete terms, in a manner which

looks forward somewhat to the condemnations of the Brobdingnagian King and, later, of Gulliver himself :

> . . . so your sex employs more thought, memory, and application to be fools, than would serve to make them wise and useful. When I reflect on this, I cannot conceive you to be human creatures, but a sort of species hardly a degree above a monkey ; who has more diverting tricks than any of you ; is an animal less mischievous and expensive, might in time be a tolerable critic in velvet and brocade, and for ought I know would equally become them. *Works*, XI, 120).

[75] *Works*, VIII, 303. Dr. Samuel Kliger concludes that Brobdingnag is an ' attainable ' Utopia. (' The Unity of *Gulliver's Travels* ', *Modern Language Quarterly*, VI [1945], 405–7).

[76] Professor H. M. Dargan shows that the allegory in Voyages I and II is based on the assumption that smallness is equivalent to pettiness and largeness to nobility, though these equivalents may be reversed. ('The Nature of Allegory as Used by Swift ', *Studies in Philology*, XIII [1916], 172–4).

[77] *Works*, VIII, 143.

[78] *Ibid.*, 141–2. For possible sources of such a book, see Eddy, *Gulliver's Travels*, p. 123 ; and Potter, *op. cit.*, p. 103. It seems clear, however, that such a complaint from a Brobdingnagian can be only humorous satire on European moralists.

[79] *Works*, VIII, 101, 103.   [81] *Ibid.*, 120.   [83] *Ibid.*, 163, 168–70.
[80] *Ibid.*, 94.   [82] *Ibid.*, 108.

[84] *Works.*, VIII, 177. Sir Charles H. Firth (*op. cit.*, 252–8), says Laputa represents England, and its adamantine bottom English interest in Ireland. Professor Case, however, says that Laputa is the Court, and that the allegory is of the tyranny of a would-be absolute monarch. (*Four Essays*, pp. 82–4)

[85] *Works*, VIII, 243.   [88] *Ibid.*, 287–8.   [91] *Ibid.*, 285, 288–9.
[86] *Ibid.*, 284.   [89] *Ibid.*, 256–7.   [92] *Ibid.*, 279–80.
[87] *Ibid.*, 250.   [90] *Ibid.*, 278–9.

[93] *Ibid.*, 285. Despite Swift's depicting the Houyhnhnms as ' the perfection of nature ' (*ibid.*, 243) their excellence has not always been appreciated. Coleridge disliked them for their lack of progressiveness and affection. (' Coleridge on *Gulliver's Travels*,' pub. G. A. Aitken, *Athenaeum*, II, 224). Professor Eddy says they are stupid, ignorant, and incapable of seeing that Gulliver's body is better than theirs for the ' common needs of life '. (*Gulliver's Travels*, pp. 50, 188). These statements could be possibly valid only if one were testing the Houyhnhnms by the standards of imperfect human life, which Swift is not doing. Also, writers have insisted upon calling the Houyhnhnms ' horses, nothing else ' (Eddy, *Gulliver's Travels*, pp. 174–5) and ' the wise and kindly horses ', guided by animal nature and instinctive behaviour, who are better than men. (Kliger, *op. cit.*, 413–4.) See also : Kathleen M. Williams, ' Gulliver's Voyage to the Houyhnhnms ', *English Literary History*, XVIII (Dec., 1951), 275–86. Swift does not condemn the Houyhnhnms for being completely rational, without either numerous or non-rational (i.e., non-social) emotions, though he evidently realizes that men, being men, will never become so. He implies that men could do well to become more like the Houyhnhnms than like the Yahoos, in having reason govern emotion. Before singling out the Houyhnhnms for their cold and inhuman rationality, one should compare Houyhnhnm-land with Plato's Republic and Lycurgus's Sparta.

[94] *Works*, VIII, 255.   [96] *Ibid.*, 256.   [98] *Ibid.*, 277.
[95] *Ibid.*, 279.   [97] *Ibid.*, 271–4.

[99] *Ibid.*, 282. Swift's sources for the Yahoos were probably the descriptions of Hottentots in voyage literature. These are ' men who are degraded to the lowest conceivable brutish condition '. They are not far from the apes. (R. W. Frantz, ' Swift's Yahoos and the Voyagers ', *Modern Philology*, XXIX [1931], 51–6)

[100] *Works*, VIII, 43.   [101] *Ibid.*, 66.   [102] *Ibid.*, 47, 45.
[103] *Ibid.*, 80.   [104] *Ibid.*, 45.   [105] *Ibid.*, 47.

M

[106] *Works*, VIII, 54.   [107] *Ibid.*, 50.   [108] *Ibid.*, 53.
[109] *Ibid.*, 67, 66.
[110] *Ibid.*, 89. There is mock-heroism in Addison's *Machinae Gesticulantes* and *Battle of the Pygmies and the Cranes*. (Eddy, *Gulliver's Travels*, pp. 108–9, 79.) Lucian also speaks with pride of being among the bravest of the troops of the King of the Moon. (*True History*, in *Works*, I, 265.)
[111] *Works*, VIII, 89.   [113] *Ibid.*, 125.   [115] *Ibid.*, 100.
[112] *Ibid.*, 119.   [114] *Ibid.*, 97, 99.
[116] *Ibid.* For a parallel to these episodes, see Cyrano's *Histoire de la Lune* (*Voyage to the Moon*, pp. 121–5). Cyrano proudly displays his great wit to the giants.
[117] *Works*, VIII, 95.   [122] *Ibid.*, 104.   [127] *Ibid.*, 110.
[118] *Ibid.*, 112.   [123] *Ibid.*, 153.   [128] *Ibid.*, 153.
[119] *Works*, VIII, 119–26.   [124] *Ibid.*, 106.   [129] *Ibid.*, 214–6.
[120] *Ibid.*, 109.   [125] *Ibid.*, 110.   [130] *Ibid.*, 241.
[121] *Ibid.*, 90–1.   [126] *Ibid.*, 118.
[131] *Ibid.*, 284. See T. O. Wedel, ' On the Philosophical Background of *Gulliver's Travels*,' *Studies in Philology*, XXIII (Oct., 1926), 442–4.
[132] *Works*, VIII, 244.   [134] *Ibid.*, 270, 289.   [136] *Ibid.*, 231–2.
[133] *Ibid.*, 242.   [135] *Ibid.*, 276, 278.   [137] *Works*, VIII, 238.
[138] *Ibid.*, 250, 270, 271. The giants in Cyrano's *Histoire de la Lune* find four-legged animals more noble than men. (*Voyage to the Moon*, pp. 123–4).
[139] *Works*, VIII, 273, 275. [140] *Ibid.*, 251.
[141] *Ibid.*, 289. W. B. C. Watkins overstates Swift's aim in concluding that Gulliver is completely identified with the Yahoos, and that Swift's laceration of himself and all mankind is not detached satire, but tragedy. (*Op. cit.*, pp. 20, 23.)
[142] *Works*, VIII, 288.   [143] *Ibid.*, 289.
[144] *Ibid.*, 269. Lucian weeps when he is forced to leave the Island of the Blest to resume his travels. (*True History*, in *Works*, I, 331). Cyrano admires the people on the moon, but returns to earth because of his love of country. (*Voyage to the Moon*, pp. 212–13). Captain Siden has a violent desire to leave the Utopian Sevarambians and return home, in spite of all his reason. (Vairasse, *op. cit.*, pp. 407–9).
[145] *Works*, VIII, 293.   [150] *Works*, VIII, 290.   [154] *Correspondence*, III, 277.
[146] *Ibid.*, 288, 253.   [151] *Ibid.*, 301.   [155] *Works*, VIII, 5–9.
[147] *Ibid.*, 296, 298.   [152] Ross, *op. cit.*, pp. 188–96 [156] Cf. Kliger, *op. cit.*, 403–4
[148] *Ibid.*, 301.   [153] *Works*, VIII, 233.   [157] *Works*, VIII, 307.
[149] *Ibid.*, 297.

XII

THE ECONOMIC PROJECTOR

In the years following *Gulliver's Travels* Swift energetically continued his fight for an improvement in the condition of Ireland. His efforts came to a climax in 1729 in the supreme piece of bitter ironical satire, *A Modest Proposal*. But the superb *persona* which accounts for the irony of the *Proposal* did not come about through spontaneous generation. Swift wrote a number of other pamphlets on the state of Ireland, protesting against, among other things, English restrictions on Irish trade and against the absenteeism of many Irish landowners. Frequently he used fragmentary ironical poses—poses which remind us how close irony is to the creation of character and yet how crucial is the final turn of imagination which brings an ' author ' to life.

In *Maxims Controlled in Ireland* (1724?) Swift undertakes to show that in Ireland the economic maxim is not true, ' that people are the riches of a nation '. He will grant, however, he says ironically, that if

> we had the African custom, or privilege, of selling our useless bodies for slaves to foreigners, it would be the most useful branch of our trade, by ridding us of a most unsupportable burthen, and bringing us money in the stead.

But now ' at least five children in six who are born ' cannot be employed

> And a very skilful computer assured me, that above one half of the souls in this kingdom supported themselves by begging and thievery.

Because the poor cannot find work, Swift concludes, he has often wished that all the ' unnecessary mortals ' could be transported to America ;

> as drawbacks are sometimes allowed for exporting commodities, where a nation is overstocked. I confess myself to be touched with a very sensible pleasure, when I hear of a mortality in any country parish or village, where the wretches are forced to pay for a filthy cabin, and two ridges of potatoes, treble the worth ; brought up to steal or beg, for want of work ; to whom death would be the best thing to be wished for on account both of themselves and the public.[1]

Here, in an ironical pose in a largely straightforward pamphlet, are some of the ingredients which later would go into the *Proposal* : the treatment of people as commodities, the interest in statistical computation, the inhuman ' pleasure ' which the news of a death can bring.

Swift felt that Ireland's improvement depended ultimately upon liberty of trade, ' a share of preferments in all kinds, to the British natives ', and a return of the absentees, who by living abroad drained off much of the nation's wealth. Immediately the Irish should ' encourage agriculture and home consumption' and stop importing foreign luxuries.[2] Again and again he urges such measures in his pamphlets of the 1720's. But Ireland's condition is not reformed, and in time he comes to express a pessimistic view of his efforts :

> What will it import, that half a score people in a coffeehouse may happen to read this paper, and even the majority of those few differ in every sentiment from me ?[3]

After suggesting several practical measures in *A Letter to the Archbishop of Dublin, Concerning the Weavers* (1729), he can add with weary ironical acceptance of Ireland's plight :

> And if at the same time they [Irish parliamentarians] could banish tea and coffee, and chinaware, out of their families . . . we might possibly be able to subsist, and pay our absentees, pensioners, generals, civil officers, appeals, colliers, temporary travelers . . . with all other smaller drains, by sending our crude unwrought goods to England, and receiving from thence and all other countries nothing but what is fully manufactured, and keep a few potatoes and oatmeal for our own subsistence.[4]

It becomes understandable how Swift could take the imaginative step which produced *A Modest Proposal* (1729), ' written ' not by the Dean of St. Patrick's[5] but by an economic projector who after long thought has found a practical way to solve Ireland's problems : a scheme for the methodical butchering of the Irish children.

But although there are suggestions of all these ideas, feelings, and ironical attitudes[6] in *A Modest Proposal*, even more important to the *persona* is Swift's active dislike of the views and methods of certain economists who were working out what he considered impractical plans to help Ireland. He can accuse such men of ignorance or even selfishness :

> Were you ever out of Ireland ? Or were you ever in it till of late ? You may probably have a good employment, and are saving all you can to purchase a good estate in England. But . . . it is plain you are either naturally or affectedly ignorant of our present condition.[7]

The *Answer to 'The Craftsman'* (1730)[8] shows clearly how Swift's dislike for certain systematic, unsound economists could lead to the creation of an imaginative mask ; in this respect it points up one of the main lines of satire in the earlier *Modest Proposal*. In both tracts Swift writes as a projector and thus ridicules the author. At the same time part of the author's message directly reflects Swift's sincere attitudes. The purpose of any project is to propose a remedy for certain present bad conditions. In the criticism of these conditions the author frequently speaks for Swift ; in his proposed remedy he speaks for himself.

Although the 'author' of the *Answer to 'The Craftsman'* is the same projector who wrote *A Modest Proposal*, the method of the *Answer* is somewhat different from that of the *Proposal*. The author, as he writes in the *Answer*, is no uneducated person ; but, as an Englishman living in Ireland, he shows throughout the essay a lack of intelligent understanding of the Irish economy. He can quote Virgil's account of the sheep-raising Scythians ('*et lac concretum cum sanguine bibit equino*') in order to describe the diet—the blood of cattle mixed with buttermilk—of the Irish, who likewise raise sheep, despite English restrictions on exporting wool. But he believes the Irish are fond of their diet (though by using the blood of cattle rather than, like the Scythians, of horses they have lost some of their 'ancestors'' warlike quality). In his opinion England should rightfully dominate Ireland, especially since Henry II conquered Ireland 'amicably' and 'without bloodshed'. (William Molyneux, whose writing Swift admired, had used the same fact to show that Ireland had never been really 'conquered' and so should not be considered a dependent state.) Swift begins satirizing the author's intelligence in the first sentence of the essay : 'I detest reading your papers, because I am not of your principles, and because I cannot endure to be convinced.'

Sir John Browne was typical of the sort of Anglo-Irish economist who (as in his *Essay on Trade*, 1728) could propose 'remedies' to improve the Irish economy and at the same time talk optimistically of the advances Ireland had made since Sir William Petty's survey of 1676. For this he had been attacked by the anonymous author (Swift, Arthur Dobbs, or someone else) of *Considerations on Two Papers* (Dublin, 1728) and *A Letter in Answer to a Paper Entitled 'An Appeal to the Rev. Dean Swift'* (1729).[9] In *An Answer to a Paper Called 'A Memorial'* (1728), Swift had criticized the author of the *Memorial* (Browne, according to Sir Walter Scott and Temple Scott) for calling Ireland a 'rich country' (while urging a ruinous scheme for importing wheat into Ireland and taxing the Irish to pay the importers) because he was 'either naturally or affectedly ignorant of our present condition '. In the *Answer to ' The Craftsman '* Swift has the ridiculed ' author ' say that he loves Ireland and cannot express ' how much I desire to see it flourish in trade and opulence, even beyond its present happy condition '. Whether this ironical reversal of facts shows the author's insincerity, his genuine ignorance of the state of Ireland, or both, it contrasts flatly with the passages in which the author speaks not as an unwise person, but as Swift himself—the passages describing the present difficulties of Ireland. Quite simply the author summarizes Swift's view by saying that no kingdom is so unhappy as Ireland, in both exports and imports ; Ireland imports goods of no intrinsic value, and exports goods for which the Irish receive nothing in return.

With the poverty of Ireland established, it remains only to discover a remedy. The author rejoices to find that the English government wants the French army (and, he hopes, that of Spain) to get recruits from Ireland. Like such economists as Browne and Dobbs,[10] he is adept at methodical computation, figuring statistically the amount which can be saved the country by exporting six thousand young Irishmen to France and Spain. With mad certainty he works out all the details: the maintenance of a tall, hungry Irishman costs (ironically!) five pounds a year. With the above number of soldiers exported, the saving to the country would thus be thirty thousand pounds a year. Excited by the prospect, the author imagines the great saving ' if thirty, forty, or fifty thousand (which we could gladly spare) were sent on the same errand '. As a good English Protestant economist, he has inhuman visions of a war between France and Spain which will kill off masses of these Irishmen whom (as in *A Modest Proposal*) he calls Papists and Jacobites.

The first project in *The Answer to ' The Craftsman '* is this idiotic scheme which reflects Swift's view (as in *Maxims Controlled in Ireland*) that in Ireland, because of English policy, people seem to be a liability rather than an asset to the national economy. It also shows how the English plan for exporting Irish soldiers would further impoverish the country, if people were (as they should normally be) really the riches of a nation. The second project, equally mad, consists of a list of current English abuses, carried to an extreme conclusion. All the farm land should be turned into pasture ; there should be a standing army of twenty thousand Englishmen to keep out the Pretender ; all landowners should be required to live in England ; all Irish commodities should be sent only to England, and Ireland should import commodities only from England ; tithes should be reduced ; the only money used in Ireland should be made from leather, and that should be coined in England.

Thus Swift manages to point out the impoverishment of Ireland for which English policy is responsible, both by his sincere statement of it and by the ironical implications in the project. There is irony in the fact that the Anglo-Irish author claims that his plan would serve ' the true interests of both kingdoms ', for both of which he professes a fondness. Whether as a result of his stupidity or his insincerity, his scheme would obviously serve only the English interest, for he accepts without criticism the bad English policies. His alleged ' remedy ' merely carries them to an extreme. Both Browne and Dobbs (and, significantly, the ' author ' of *A Modest Proposal*) try to remedy the Irish economy by accepting many of the English restrictions and encouraging the Irish to develop industries which don't interfere with those of England. Therefore they tend to minimize Irish grievances and to speak optimistically of Ireland's potentialities. Although Dobbs (if he was the anonymous author of *Considerations* and *A Letter*) may have censured Browne for going too far in this direction (the *Letter* says Ireland's ' consumption ' requires not unrealistic optimism but ' the skill of the most cautious physician '), he himself could write :

> instead of being splenetic or grumbling at any restrictions put upon us by our ancestors, let us endeavour to promote the enjoyment of what we have with pleasure and satisfaction, that we may all in our several spheres cheerfully contribute to support the power, wealth, fame, and commerce of the British Empire, of which Ireland is no inconsiderable member.[11]

In Browne's memorable figure, Ireland is a sponge which sucks up treasures from the ocean ' in order to squeeze them out again into the grand receptacle of all the riches of her dependencies, Great Britain.'[12]

Though Browne in particular speaks of Irish miseries, and Dobbs urges—for the good of both countries—the removal of certain restrictions, and though both deplore absenteeism,[13] these men are far more hopeful than Swift about Ireland's chances for prosperity under English restrictions. In his optimism (he sees Ireland becoming a new Arcadia) and his lack of a genuine understanding of Ireland, the *persona*-author of the *Answer* is to Swift a person like the author of the *Memorial* (Browne ?), who—Swift said—thinks of schemes for importing grain instead of urging his tenants to plough, who seems to write as a foreigner from a free country, and who saves his money in order to eventually to buy a good estate in England.[14] Unlike Browne, Dobbs, the author of the *Memorial*, or the ' author ' of the *Answer*, Swift does not accept the restrictive English policies. The implication of the *Answer to ' The Craftsman '* is that these policies must be changed.

In *A Modest Proposal* Swift exploits his mask far more extensively, in a way that has made the tract a landmark among all the ironical works of literature. Mr. Leavis argues that the intensity of the irony in this essay is essentially negative and destructive ; any positive idea appears only as ' a kind of skeletal presence, rigid enough, but without life or body '. He comments on Swift's habit of surprising the reader after betraying him ' into an incipient acquiescence ', and on the energy ' generated ' by the tension between the matter-of-fact tone, which ' induces a feeling and a motion of assent ', and the burden of the message, which ' compels the feelings appropriate to rejection '.[15] Professor Landa points out that the essay is a protest against the unqualified maxim that people are the riches of a nation. The irony of the essay, he says, is increased by the fact that Swift's audience consisted of readers who were strongly conscious of this maxim ; Swift attacks the unqualified maxim in this essay by saying ironically that people are the riches of Ireland only if the Irish are allowed to eat their babies.[16] Dr. Herbert Davis notes the very different sort of irony contained in Swift's parody of himself and in his attitude that he no longer has any political power.[17].

By reading the essay from the point of view of the author one can see how these and other forms of irony are introduced. Though the main qualities of the author appear through his ideas, Swift supplies just enough of his other attributes so that we can visualize him as a real person who lives and acts during the course of the tract. The author has turned his thoughts for many years on the important subject he considers, and has maturely weighed the schemes of other projectors. He has a ' worthy ' friend who proposed that children between twelve and fourteen should be used for venison. He has another friend from America who got the idea of killing youths from the famous Psalmanazar, who told him how much money youthful carcasses brought in Formosa ; this friend assured the author that the flesh of males between twelve and fourteen is tough and lean. A gentleman of the County of Cavan has informed the author that there are few instances of stealing before the age of six, even in that area of thieves. Finally, the author says that his youngest child is nine years old and his wife is past child-bearing.

These details are enough to give the author considerable concreteness and verisimilitude. Yet his character as revealed by his ideas is far more important. The purpose of this essay is not only to ridicule the speaker, but also to present trenchant social criticism. The author (though one of Swift's most peculiar characters) must be made as credible as possible, in order to give the real problems he discusses aching intensity : his mad world must merge imperceptibly with the real world of Irish misery. No modern reader ever put down this essay with a feeling that the problems in it were not tragically serious.

One of the author's most noticeable habits of mind, one which does much to establish his credibility, is his calm reasonableness. The manner of the essay is simple and factual, with none of the invective, none of the accumulations of names characteristic of much of Swift's angry writing. The aim of the projector is certainly stated in a fashion that anyone would agree with : to ' find out a fair, cheap, and easy method of making these children sound useful members of the commonwealth '.

But though the author is carefully kept in periodic contact with reality, it soon becomes clear that he has an unemotional standard of values all his own. For he is, as Professor Wittkowsky has shown, a political arithmetician ; like Petty, Browne, Dobbs, and others, the ' author ' analyzes economic problems primarily by means of cold statistical computations. He regards people as animals and labour as a commodity.[18] His manner of working out the project to the last detail is nearly diabolical in its calculation. Of one hundred and twenty thousand children, he says, one hundred thousand are to be sold for meat. One child will make two dishes for entertaining friends, while a fore or hind quarter is adequate for a family dining alone : in addition the meat can be boiled on the fourth day, with salt and pepper. He has computed the weight of a child at birth to be twelve pounds, and at one year twenty-eight pounds. He has figured that a year after Lent the market will always be glutted, that a mother can make eight shillings a year profit, that the skin of the children will make good gloves and boots, and that the best way to serve them is to buy them alive and dress them hot from the knife. These details, satirizing the inhuman methods of some economists, are so carefully interwoven with details from everyday life that we hardly realize the import of the *persona's* message ; it is hard to believe that we are in a world where normal human values no longer hold true, and where the murder of infants can be accepted as a matter of course.

On the surface the author seems to make the quiet presentation of his incredible scheme in a manner which is admirably modest, as the title indicates.[19] His attitude is even deferential as he says of the project,

' I . . . humbly offer it to public consideration ' only after having spent many years thinking about it. But though he restrains himself, it is clear that he is proud of his accomplishment, which has advantages ' of the highest importance ', and which (as far as he can see) is not liable to any objection. He is indeed sure of his own modesty, which he reminds us of periodically. When he says that he is interested not in himself but in finding a solution to the problem, that he would support another proposal if it should prove to be as good as his, one remembers how varied are Swift's uses of modesty. The gloriously self-confident Isaac Bickerstaff was also fond of ' modestly ' expressing his devotion not to himself but to the nobly philosophical true art of astrology. Like Bickerstaff, the author of the *Modest Proposal* has spent many years on his calculations, ' maturely ' weighing and contemptuously rejecting the invariably ' grossly mistaken ' schemes of other men. Anyone who can successfully solve Ireland's problem, he says, ' would deserve so well of the public, as to have his statue set up for a preserver of the nation ' ; one will later detect a distant similarity in Simon Wagstaff's ' modest ' belief that in return for his work in perfecting English conversation, he should be worshipped as a god. But the humour, such as it is, in the unassuming author of the *Proposal* intensifies by contrast Swift's mordant indignation.

In attacking the cold-hearted methods of political arithmeticians and economic projectors, Swift could not afford to make the author just a monster or a fool. He expresses certain moral values, though in doing so he speaks for himself rather than for Swift. There is a suggestion of generosity in his admiration for the ' very worthy person, true lover of his country, and whose virtues I highly esteem ', the man who is ' so excellent a friend and so deserving a patriot ', the man who suggests using young adolescents for venison. It is human feeling which causes the author to reject this suggestion, on the grounds that other people would criticize him for cruelty. For surprisingly, the author, whose emotions can seem ice-cold, insists that ' cruelty . . . hath always been with me the strongest objection against any project, however so well intended '. His feeling is unmistakably intense as he says that the horrid picture of women murdering their bastard children ' would move tears and pity in the most savage and inhuman breast '. The author's understanding of cruelty and pity is not, however, Swift's. For the reader sees, as the *persona* does not, the incongruity between his sympathy and his proposal.

Because the author is not simply an inhuman monster, he can describe convincingly the wretched state of Ireland. The essay begins with so pathetic a picture of the many children for whom their parents cannot adequately provide that a reader is soon ready to listen to the remedy of any projector. Most frequently the author unfeelingly uses such facts as mere details in support of his theory. Some of these details are not well fused with his character. When he says, for example, that infants' flesh can't be kept long in salt, ' though perhaps I could name a country, which would be glad to eat up our whole nation without it ', the reader feels that the author has stepped somewhat out of his pose to express—in extreme terms— Swift's feelings. For the most part, however, the two points of view— Swift's and the author's—are well integrated. The author feels that the food of the children will be expensive, and ' therefore very proper for landlords, who, as they have already devoured most of the parents, seem to have the best title to the children '. In a lighter vein, but still in trenchant satire, the author says that the country could do worse than to sell for meat several plump young girls in Dublin who ' without a single groat to their fortunes, cannot stir abroad without a chair, and appear at the playhouse and assemblies in foreign fineries, which they will never pay for '. No project is necessary for the old, diseased, and maimed people who are daily dying from cold, famine, filth, and vermin ; or for the young who pine away in idleness for want of nourishment.

These passages balance the remedy on the one hand against the evil on the other. Elsewhere Swift weaves his hard facts into the proposal itself. For instance, the author's programme is economically sound because an Irish mother can nurse her child for a year on two shillings, acquired by begging. As a result of the sale,

> the squire will learn to be a good landlord, and grow popular among his tenants, the mother will have eight shillings net profit, and be fit to work until she produces another child.

In his statistical computations also, the author interweaves facts with his proposal. He enumerates that there are a million and a half people in Ireland. Of these, two hundred thousand are breeding couples. So far Swift has provided empty statistics. But then comes the point : thirty thousand women can maintain their own children ; fifty thousand women have miscarriages or have their children die by disease or accident ; one hundred and twenty thousand can't provide for their children at all, having neither jobs nor homes.

This device of working essential facts into a system which also includes non-essential facts is characteristic of the essay. The reader is

kept shifting between the world of basic factual satire and the world of
the mad project. A good example is the six-point list of advantages that
would result, the author says, from his proposal. First, the project
would lessen the danger from the Papists, ' in the absence of so many
good Protestants, who have chosen rather to leave their country, than
stay at home, and pay tithes against their conscience, to an Episcopal
curate '. This point—as in the *Answer to ' The Craftsman '*—makes the
author something of a fool, in his fear of popery (in the *Modest Proposal*,
too, there is no danger of ' disobliging England ') ; it also suggests
the fact of emigration, and hits at the dissenters' arguments. Second,
the proposal would give the poorer tenants some wealth, ' their corn
and cattle being already seized, and money a thing unknown '. Third,
the nation's stock would be increased by fifty thousand pounds a year;
also, a new dish would be introduced ; and the product would
circulate only among the Irish, being only of Irish growth and manufacture. The first two parts of point three, diabolical jokes, suggest
Irish poverty ; the third contains one of Swift's major ideas—that
the Irish should use only their own products. Fourth, Irish
mothers will gain not only eight shillings a year but will also be
rid of the trouble of bringing up their children. The reader
reflects : Is it not hard to raise Irish children ? And where
are the feelings of the economic planners ? The fifth point—
that the new food would bring business to taverns, which could
specialize in dressing it to perfection, and thus attract fine gentlemen
and epicures—is again a terrible and heartless idea, designed to increase
the reader's horror. Sixth, the proposal would be a great inducement to
marriage ; it would increase the tenderness of mothers to their children,
and of husbands to their wives, since the better the child, the more
money it would bring. This point is most despairing of all. For the
author suggests (with perhaps some justification)[20] that Ireland is a
nation of people so oppressed and so dehumanized that the two most
fundamental human emotions can be encouraged only by the prospect
of gain. Yet the power of this statement owes much to the fact that it
occurs in a context of seemingly inconsequential trivialities. After this
climactic point the author goes straight on, seemingly unaware that
he has expressed anything horrible, to enumerate ' many other advantages '—the addition of children's carcasses to the Irish exports of
beef, and the possibility of serving a child at a Lord Mayor's feast.

Thus the reader is continually surprised and shocked by the powerful message concealed under the seemingly matter-of-fact tone in
which the author speaks. This mask is nearly flawless ; the satire

progresses relentlessly. Yet the effect of the essay is not merely destructive. Swift does have a positive plan. Professor Landa says that this positive idea is that people can be the riches of a country if they are given an opportunity to work, and that the *Modest Proposal* is an argument for the opportunity.[21] This attempt to answer the economists who said that people were *always* the riches of a country is certainly one purpose of the essay. But Swift himself has supplied a fuller positive message in detail, and it shows that his interest was humanitarian and moral as well as economic. Beginning with the statement that almost seems out of character in its intensity—that he has proposed his remedy only for the kingdom of Ireland ' and for no other that ever was, is, or, I think, ever can be upon earth '—the author lists ' other expedients ' which he objects to not because they are bad, but because they will not work. These expedients are to tax absentees ; to use clothes only of Irish manufacture ; to reject imports of foreign luxuries ; to cure women of pride, vanity, idleness, and gaming ; to introduce parsimony, prudence, and temperance ; to introduce love of country ; to end animosities and factions ; to be cautious ' not to sell our country and our consciences for nothing ' ; to teach landlords to have some mercy towards their tenants ; to put a spirit of honesty, industry, and skill into the Irish shopkeepers.

Though Swift probably felt a certain genuine weariness from his efforts to help Ireland, there is still irony in the author's statement that he has no confidence these reforms will succeed, that men will adopt only a mad ' proposal '. The despair of Swift himself is no more absolute in this late work than in the early *Project for the Advancement of Religion* or *Argument Against Abolishing Christianity*. In each of these early essays an ideal is set up which the author believes cannot be reached. In the *Argument*, the author does not want to reach it ; he is interested not in true Christianity but in the practical things—business and gambling—of the polite everyday world. In the *Project*, the author says that the ideal (a nation of genuinely moral people) is desirable, but difficult to attain ; probably the best that can be hoped for is a nation of hypocritical people who pretend to be moral. In the *Modest Proposal*, Swift's ideal is incorporated in the measures which the author rejects as impossible.

The mere fact that Swift can formulate an ideal should indicate that his satire is not completely negative. Idealism, of course, in accordance with the literary form Swift has chosen to use, can be introduced only to have the *persona* reject it. But a positive satiric and ethical message, heightened and intensified, not obscured by the irony,

is present in the *Modest Proposal*. The details, largely a result of Swift's
handling of his mask, remain indelibly fixed in the reader's mind. At
the same time the impact of these details is not merely depressing. For
while we can be shocked by the inhumanity of the author's terrible
picture of Ireland, at the same time we can find a form of comic relief in
the fact that the author, with his serious confidence, cannot see the
slightest objection to his scheme. The real force of the essay is moral; it
defines for us once again how great is the difference between the world
as Swift wanted it and the world as he saw it. In his project to butcher
the Irish children, the *persona*, weary of ' vain, idle, visionary thoughts ',
has at last found something ' solid and real '.

NOTES TO CHAPTER XII

[1] *Works*, VII, 70–1. Cf. George Wittkowsky, ' Swift's *Modest Proposal*, the
Biography of an Early Georgian Pamphlet ', *Journal of the History of Ideas*, IV (1943),
90–1. Swift also briefly adopts a pose of humility. Although his friend Charles
Ford was an absentee landlord, Swift claims to ' have not the honour of the least
acquaintance with anyone among ' the absentee lords and squires, ' (my ambition
not soaring so high) '. (*Works*, VII, 71). See : Nichol Smith, ed., *The Letters of
Jonathan Swift to Charles Ford*, pp. xxi, 111–2. Swift customarily addresses Ford as
' Charles Ford Esquire ' ; he refers to him in a note as ' The Squire ' (*ibid.*, p. 65).
[2] *Answer to Several Letters from Unknown Persons* (1729), in *Works*, VII, 121–2, 124.
[3] *Ibid.*, 125.   [4] *Ibid.*, 143.
[5] ' By Dr. Swift' appeared on the title page of the Dublin edition. This fact is
further evidence that Swift's aim was not trickery but the creation of a symbolic
persona.
[6] There are other ironical poses—fragmentary or extended—in several of these
tracts of the late 1720's : *A Short View of the State of Ireland*, 1728 (*Works*, VII,
88–91) ; *An Essay on the Fates of Clergymen*, 1728, with its ' realistic' adoption of a
worldly set of values, its ironical praise of mediocrity and implied censure of ability
(*ibid.*, III, 291–8) ; *An Answer to a Paper Called 'A Memorial '*, 1728, ending with its
inverted praise of the evil character of Justice Whitshed (*ibid.*, VII, 111–6) ; *A
Letter to the Archbishop of Dublin Concerning the Weavers*, 1729, in which Swift expresses
his solemn belief in exaggerations (*ibid.*, 138–9).
[7] *Ibid.*, 113. See also : *ibid.*, 123–4, 138.
[8] *Works*, VII, 217–24.
[9] Although these tracts have been attributed to both Swift and Dobbs, the
authorship is by no means certain.
[10] See, for example, Browne's *Seasonable Remarks on Trade* (Dublin, 1728), pp.
40–1 ; and Dobbs' *An Essay on the Trade and Improvement of Ireland*, in *A Collection of
Tracts and Treatises* (Dublin, 1861), II, 410–12. Swift knew well the sort of economic
methods and ideas represented in these works. The second part of Dobbs' essay,
however, did not appear until 1731 ; it is dedicated to Lionel, Duke of Dorset, who
became Lord-Lieutenant in 1730. For a summary see Wittkowsky (*Op. cit.*, 75–104).
[11] *Op. cit.*, 419. See also the ' Dedication '. Dobbs wrote these parts of the *Essay*
after Swift's *Answer*. But his view is representative, and it shows clearly where
Swift stood.
[12] *Seasonable Remarks*, pp. 33, 37–9.

¹³ See Browne's *An Essay on Trade in General* (Dublin, 1728), pp. 34–5, 38–9, 88–9 ; his *Appeal to the Reverend Dean Swift*, in *A Collection of Tracts* (London, 1729), pp. 113, 127–8 ; and his *Reflections Little to the Purpose on a Paper Less to the Purpose* (Dublin, 1729). On the sincerity of his concern for Ireland see the ' Dedications ' to his *Seasonable Remarks* and *Essay*; his letter to Swift of April 4, 1728, asking for mercy after Swift had attacked him for testifying in England for the introduction of Wood's halfpence (*Correspondence*, IV, 24–7) ; his letter to Faulkner of February 14, 1750, describing the monument Browne erected on the lawn of his estate to the memory of Swift (*ibid.*, 463–4) ; and Dr. Davis's summary, in *The Drapier's Letters*, pp. 226–8, note. Dobbs, like Swift, urges Irish women to wear Irish silks (*op. cit.*, 366), opposes extravagance and the importation of luxury items (*ibid.*, 365–6, 440–1), proposes a law to force beggars to remain in their own parishes (*ibid.*, 452) ; and argues against high duties on exports and imports (*ibid.*, 430–8) ; he goes further than Swift in cautiously urging a greater toleration for the Catholics (*ibid.*, 482). On the mercantilist ideas which Swift shared with Browne and Dobbs, see L. A. Landa, ' Swift's Economic Views and Mercantilism ', 310–35. Professor Landa concludes that Swift rejects not mercantilism but a dependent status for Ireland.

¹⁴ *An Answer to a Paper Called 'A Memorial'*, in *Works*, VII, 113–5. The ' author ', one should add, says he was born in England. Both Browne and Dobbs were members of Anglo-Irish families which went back several generations. The ' author ' represents neither Browne nor Dobbs personally, but some of the ideas they held.

¹⁵ F. R. Leavis, *op. cit.*, 365–8.

¹⁶ '*A Modest Proposal* and Populousness,' *Modern Philology*, XL (November, 1942), 161–70.

¹⁷ *The Satire of Jonathan Swift*, p. 108.

¹⁸ *Op. cit.*, 96–8. See also Professor Landa's review of this article in *Philological Quarterly*, XXIII (1944), 178–9.

¹⁹ Wittkowsky also points out that the modest title, as well as the project itself, is a burlesque on the methods of current economic tracts. (*Op. cit.*, 88–9).

²⁰ On the way the poorer Irish disfigured their children in hopes of financial gain, see Dobbs, *op. cit.*, pp. 443–4. Dobbs here shows more dislike for the laziness of the poor than sympathy for their children.

²¹ '*A Modest Proposal* and Populousness,' 170.

XIII

SIMON WAGSTAFF AND OTHERS

Because of the greatness of Swift's writings in the 1720's, it has been unfortunately easy for readers to consider the last fifteen years of his life as ' closing years ', notable mainly for the illness which made him finally ' a driv'ler and a show '. But such a view overlooks the fact that in the decade following *A Modest Proposal*, Swift—then in his sixties—yet showed a remarkable energy and humour. He administered the affairs of St. Patrick's Cathedral (as late as 1741 he was not to be conquered by a ' rebellious choir '). He had by no means lost his interest in questions of public welfare and the good of the Church. He could write with wit to his friends and indulge in the playful humour of questionable verses. And he continued actively to create *personae* for his varied satirical purposes.

(a) AGAINST THE WHIGS AND DISSENTERS

When Swift's friend, the Lord-Lieutenant of Ireland, was charged with ' favouring none but Tories, high-churchmen, and Jacobites ', Swift came to his defence in a characteristically inventive manner. Through the ' author ' of *A Vindication of His Excellency, John Lord Carteret* (1730) he supports his Lordship and attacks the Whigs. The ' Whig ' author shows a clear lack of wisdom. A mis-educated person, he repeatedly makes obvious errors in classical references. He does not know exactly who Augustus Caesar is, for example, nor does he particularly care to. In ' old English story books ' he remembers reading about 'Agesilaus ', adding that it doesn't much matter whether he has spelled the named correctly, since most of his readers won't care. A Greek tragedy to him is just a play ' written by some heathen author ', which may have contained (he isn't sure) Tory or High-Church principles.

Moreover, the author cannot always reason clearly and independently. Facts are likely to be true, he thinks, because the book where he found them is in print. His opinion he submits to ' that happy majority, which I am confident is always in the right '.[1] But the greatest evidence of his folly—and the one which carries the most satiric force—is his inverted sense of values. It would be a misfortune, in his opinion, for ' an original or proselyte favourer of the times ' to be ' born to those useless talents which in former ages qualified a man to be a poet or a philosopher '.[2] Carteret's ancestors were ' too much distinguished ' for their bravery in defending Charles I. And Carteret himself could never eradicate the 'tincture of his University acquirements and dispositions'.[3] Just as the author censures Carteret for his good qualities, he praises Swift's enemies for their vices.[4]

These various evidences of folly make the *persona* concrete. When joined to the fact that the author is a Whig, who dislikes the Royalists during the time of Charles I and who has little interest in the traditional classical education, they result in satire. But Swift's main purpose in the essay is not to satirize the Whigs but to vindicate Carteret. Swift does this, first of all, by making the author tolerant of the ' weaknesses ' of Carteret. Though he ' freely acknowledges ' that the studies of Greek, Latin, and philosophy are ' his Excellency's failings ', he says that ' philosophers and divines ' agree ' that some allowance ought to be given to human infirmity, and the prejudices of a wrong education '.[5] Carrying the case further, he urges that Carteret's ' failings ' be tolerated because they are harmless. It is an ' unfortunate ' weakness that he has about him ' one or two gentlemen ' distinguished for their wit, taste, and learning ; yet because these men may be stigmatized as Tories, Carteret may be forced to banish them. 'What harm can one or two men do ? ' the author asks. Why not let Carteret indulge in ' an infirmity which is not morally evil ' ? He should be allowed to talk over ' old exploded readings ' with friends.[6]

Up to this point it is obvious that Swift's method in part is to fabricate a character who reveals many obvious shortcomings, introduce him as a defender of Carteret against his enemies, and thereby weaken the seriousness of the charges against Carteret. The style of the author for the most part reflects the ironical superficiality of his attitudes. There is a tense, balanced control when the author says that Carteret was educated at Oxford, ' from whence, with a singularity scarce to be justified, he carried away more Greek, Latin, and philosophy than properly became a person of his rank '. But this control does not last throughout the essay. There is savage directness in his statement, ' This was the utter ruin of that poor, angry, bustling, well-meaning mortal Pistorides ' (Richard Tighe, enemy to Carteret) and ' How hath he been pelted, pestered, and pounded by one single wag, who promiseth never to forsake him living or dead! ' Such an angry outburst, which causes the author to pile up terms of abuse, is not characteristic of him. Neither is the vivid picture of the surgeon who hoped to stuff the carcass of the Earl of Galway in retaliation for injuries,[7] or the disgustingly trenchant picture of the body of Traulus

N

(Lord Allen)—'so open, so foul, and so full of sores'—and of the surgeon who will 'flay, and dissect him alive, and to the view of mankind lay open all the disordered cells of his brain'. These two different styles cannot be the work of a single *persona*. When control of language gives way to fury, the character of the simple, mild-mannered Whig, who above all represents a world of falsely superficial opinions, disappears. The reader faces the hard surfaces and sharp outlines of reality as Swift himself speaks.

In the main satiric pattern in this essay, the author presents a fact, on which he is in agreement with Swift, and by which alone he vindicates Carteret. Then the *persona* stands apart from Swift stupidly to add that the fact is no credit to a Lord : this device reduces the charges against him to an absurd level. Finally the author concludes 'impartially' that in spite of this fact, Carteret should not suffer by being accused of some enormous offence. This step does not justify Carteret ; it renders the issues of the controversy ridiculous. As in the ' defences ' made by the nominal Christian and the adviser of the young poet, the multiple effect of the satire is clear.

In 1732 Swift again creates a Whig *persona*, in *An Examination of Certain Abuses in the City of Dublin*. The author is ridiculed for his far-fetched suspicions. On a sign advertising punch, he sees a Jacobite symbol ; he is sure Oxford was a Papist ; when he hears women hawking plaice in the streets, he thinks they are selling places at court.[8] Swift also writes, in 1732, as an impossible projector (a recent arrival in Ireland) who makes *A Proposal for an Act of Parliament, to Pay Off the Debt of the Nation, Without Taxing the Subject*.[9]

In *The Advantages Proposed by Repealing the Sacramental Test*, adopting a method which recalls the much more skilful *Argument Against Abolishing Christianity*, he writes on the serious subject—another attempt to repeal the Test in Ireland—'impartially . . . , not only as a mere secular man, but as one who is altogether indifferent to any particular system of Christianity '.[10] But, as in the pamphlets against Burnet and Steele (1713), the ironical pose of deferential, non-religious objectivity (it can be satirically overthrown)[11] never becomes a full *persona*. In 1733 he handles the same problem by writing as a Catholic in *Reasons Humbly Offered to the Parliament of Ireland for Repealing the Sacramental Test in Favour of the Catholics*. The ' author' is relatively indistinct. He argues that Catholics are ' brethren of the dissenters ' ; both want to see the Test abolished. Moreover, he can't see why the dissenters, whose predecessors murdered their King and abolished ' the whole system of government . . . should pretend to a better share

of civil or military trust, profit, and power than the Catholics ', who
were persecuted for their loyalty to kingly power. He concludes with
a petition that the Catholics' 'incapacity for civil and military employments may be wholly taken off, for the very same reasons (besides
others more cogent) that are now offered by their brethren the dissenters '.[12] The author speaks for Swift (somewhat inconsistently
with his professions of brotherhood) in his strong condemnations
of the dissenters. And in arguing for his own rights, he puts the
dissenters' plea for repeal in a bad light.

(b) FOR WITTY AND SPARKLING TALK

In the same year (?) Swift becomes a spokesman for the footmen of
Dublin, humbly and urgently presenting a mock-petition to the House
of Commons.[13] His poems of the early 1730's also contain fictitious
characters, though these for the most part are not technically *personae*.[14]
But the clearest and most significant of his late masks is Simon Wagstaff, the ' author' of the 'Introduction' to *Polite Conversation* (published
in 1738, though parts of it probably date from much earlier in Swift's
career).[15]

Simon is a degenerated type of the character that was at its best in
the Isaac Bickerstaff of the *Predictions* and the *Vindication*. Presenting a
manual which claims to contain everything choice in polite conversation, Simon says he can enable anyone in society to make witty and
sparkling talk. The contents of this unusual book are drawn from the
current talk of the more fashionable classes, for although at times
conversation ' even in the most select companies . . . falls, and drops
to nothing, like a fire without a supply of fuel ' (and thus demands
Wagstaff's remedies), still ' my dear country hath outdone all the
nations of Europe in advancing the whole art of conversation to the
greatest height it is capable of reaching '. The way to wit and humour
is plain ; one must ' by hard labour ' commit to memory every
sentence in the book. Then, having a ready supply of correct questions
and answers, one must develop the proper bodily movements to go
with them. For just as there is a ' business ' of poetry—at least to the
young poet's adviser—so there is a ' Science ' (and it is a serious and
methodical affair) of amusing repartee.

Like Bickerstaff, Wagstaff is no one to hide his distinction. When
he was about thirty-six, in 1695, he began his important work, dining
with the best families and recording the best expressions in their
conversations. He judges that he has passed more time than any other

man of his age and country in visits and assemblies. And he can name distinguished (fictitious) friends of his who have also invented sets of words and phrases—the Hon. Col. James Graham, the D—— of R——, the E—— of E——, and Right Hon. the Lord and Lady H——. Like Bickerstaff, the author is meticulous, exceeding the advice of Horace to keep his piece nine years, and requesting anyone who finds anything of the least importance omitted from his work to write to him ' (they paying the postage).'

But Bickerstaff, writing against Partridge, could never have included such a ridiculous detail as this last one. Wagstaff lacks the superb and subtle gravity of the great astrologer. His knowledge of Horace comes from ' Mr. Creech's admirable translation '.[16] As with other fashionable people, his learning is superficial; except for a smattering of French, he is what ' pedants and scholars call, a man wholly illiterate ', although he is well read in English, at least in ' most of the plays and all the miscellany poems of twenty years past '. In addition, he knows the entire works of the prolific Tom Brown and has ' had the honour to be his intimate friend, who was universally allowed to be the greatest genius of his age.'[17]

Wagstaff's admired friends—this is sheer mockery from Swift— include many of Pope's dunces : Gildon, Ward, and Dennis, each of whom has carefully read Wagstaff's work five times ;[18] Colley Cibber, ' our most illustrious laureate ' ; Theobald, which he spells ' Tibbalds '; and the translators Ozell and Stevens. With the help of such great men Wagstaff can scornfully tell the Popes, Gays, Arbuthnots, and Youngs to burst with envy at the praises he and his friends receive from court and kingdom. For Pope's dunces, this is guilt by association with Wagstaff.

As one might expect, intelligence is not Wagstaff's *forte*. He is guilty of the old mistaken opinion that Tories are ' all Jacobites, and consequently Papists in their hearts '.[19] Like the author of *A Tale of a Tub*, he trusts the perfection of a mechanical scheme ; he can ' boldly affirm, that the whole genius, humour, politeness, and eloquence of England are summed up ' in his own system. In a curiously technical and humourless fashion he analyzes the cause of laughter : anatomically, it is ' a natural, involuntary distortion of muscles ' ; it is also ' the undoubted mark of a good taste ', acquired after much observation, long practice, and sound judgment.[20]

With Wagstaff's intellectual shortcoming—which is unlike Bickerstaff's rationality—goes the author's uncontrolled pride, which is less humourous than Bickerstaff's grave and noble self-confidence. Wagstaff, envisioning his book established by the House of Lords as a standard grammar in all the principal parts of the kingdom, sees himself with the responsibility of approving all the schoolmasters to teach his method ; after all, he says, Lilly got as much reward for teaching words in useless Latin.[21] ' Without the least violation of modesty ', he believes that he, more than any other man, deserves encouragement from the Crown, parliament, and the ministry toward perfecting his great work. Were not several heroes of antiquity worshipped as gods for having civilized a barbarous people ? [22]

Wagstaff claims that every witty statement in his book has the approbation of at least one hundred years, that all are ' genuine, sterling, and authentic '.[23] No one would disagree who had read such a sample as this[24] of good talk at tea time :

Colonel rising up

Lady Smart. Colonel, where are you going so soon ? I hope you did not come to fetch fire.

Colonel. Madam, I must needs go home for half an hour.

Miss Notable. Why, Colonel, they say, the devil's at home.

Lady Answerall. Well, but sit while you stay ; 'tis as cheap sitting as standing.

Colonel. No, madam ; while I'm standing I'm going.

Miss Notable. Nay, let him go ; I promise him we won't tear his clothes to hold him.

Lady Smart. I suppose, Colonel, we keep you from better company ; I mean only as to myself.

Colonel. Madam, I am all obedience.

Colonel sits down

Lady Smart. Lord, miss, how can you drink your tea so hot ? Sure your mouth's paved. . . .

Wagstaff's pretensions are foolish and exaggerated. To compare him with Bickerstaff is to show the superb artistry which made Bickerstaff a fully rounded, credible character, partially a butt of subtle and deft humour. In contrast, Wagstaff's ridiculous qualities are carried to an extreme. He is a not very successful object of relatively crude satire (indifferent to religion, he had considered including a catalogue of oaths in his system)[25] which lacks playful detachment. Remembering that even in the *Tatler* papers Bickerstaff had lost some of the excellence of his first appearances, one concludes that Wagstaff's apparent defi-

ciencies are due less to Swift's failing powers at the age of seventy
than to the unique brilliance of his elaborate joke on Partridge years
before.

(c) On the Death of Dr. Swift

Although Swift was interested in these characters, by 1731 he had
created his greatest satiric masks. In the ' Verses on the Death of
Dr. Swift ' he could with irony and humour look back on himself and
his career and look forward to the day when Dublin and London
would hear the news, ' the Dean is dead '. The ' Dr. Swift ' of the
poem is, like all men, selfish and envious : he ' resents ' (in ironical
and friendly compliment) the excellences of Pope, Gay, and Arbuthnot:

> To all my Foes, dear Fortune, send
> Thy Gifts, but never to my Friend :
> I tamely can endure the first,
> But, this with Envy makes me burst.

Like the Dean in the Imitation of Horace (1713), and like Cadenus, this
' Dr. Swift ' should not be taken too seriously.

With keen and imaginative humour he hears the voices of those—
friends and non-friends—who survive him ; among them

> My female Friends, whose tender Hearts
> Have better learn'd to act their Parts.
> Receive the News in doleful Dumps,
> ' The Dean is dead (and what is Trumps ?) '.

The poem is not pure gaiety, however, even in these ironically comic
passages. And in the latter section, an ' impartial ' account of Swift's
character by a speaker at the Rose Tavern, we have a summary which
(if one does not read it with absolute literal seriousness, and if one
recognizes Horatian overtones) describes with a certain justice much
of the career and nature of its exceedingly complex subject.

> ' Perhaps I may allow, the Dean
> Had too much Satyr in his Vein ;
> And seem'd determin'd not to starve it,
> Because no Age could more deserve it. . . .
> His Satyr points at no Defect,
> But what all mortals may correct ;
> For he abhorr'd that senseless Tribe,
> Who call it Humour when they jibe :
> He spar'd a Hump or crooked Nose,
> Whose Owners set not up for Beaux.'

And then, a frequently overlooked side of his nature :

> ' He knew an hundred pleasant Stories,
> With all the Turns of Whigs and Tories :
> Was chearful to his dying Day,
> And Friends would let him have his way.'

His humour and satire had always been close to ' his vein ironically grave '. It was irony

> Which I was born to introduce,
> Refin'd it first and shew'd its Use.

And irony, for Swift, was generally the function of a mask.

(d) BEHIND THE MASK

In considering Swift's masks as a whole, we can distinguish certain satiric themes common to many of his works. Perversion of reason, inversion of values, pride : we encounter them again and again. It is curious that a writer frequently labelled as proud and egoistic should have lashed the vice of pride as he saw it in others. Or is this apparent anomaly due to our willingness to use the utterances of Swift's *personae* as proof of their author's self-centredness ? Whether or not Swift himself was proud—and our judgment must certainly become less frenetic than it has been in the past—he undoubtedly had no sympathy for such various kinds of conceit as characterize Bickerstaff, the author of the *Tale*, and Gulliver. In this respect Swift, though with very different weapons, fights the same battle Milton fought, for a humble, just, and ordered view of oneself in relation to the world, and against the kind of distortion of values which deludes a man into over-estimating his own importance : ' But when a man's fancy gets astride of his reason . . . the first proselyte he makes is himself '. Swift satirized not the hunchback, but the hunchback who saw himself as a beau.

In pointing out this recurrent theme in Swift's work, one should not lose sight of the diversity of his satire and his *personae*. It is difficult to find a single characteristic common to all Swift's masks. As in the *Sentiments of a Church of England Man* and the *Letter to a Young Clergyman*, the mask can be simply a means of establishing an objective point of view from which Swift can present his message better than he could writing as an Anglican clergyman. More frequently, however, the mask is an ironical device. The *Examiner* sets up a falsely objective point of view which is periodically overthrown in order to attack an enemy. The Drapier and the Member of the Irish Parliament are humble characters, whose humility can be used freely in a variety of ways to attack England's policy toward Ireland. Bickerstaff, in his self-assurance, expresses himself so that both he and his fellow-astrologer Partridge are ridiculed.

Much of Swift's irony, Mr. Leavis has noted, lies in the contrast between his restrained, matter-of-fact tone and the intensity of his actual message.[26] Professor Sutherland has called this ' perhaps Swift's unique contribution to English literature '.[27] But even this characteristic is frequently a direct result of the use of a *persona*. Such characters as the authors of the *Argument Against Abolishing Christianity*, *A Modest Proposal*, and *A Tale of a Tub* are so different from Swift that a great deal of the ironical power of Swift's message lies simply in the contrast between what they are saying and what we must infer Swift means. The authors calmly assume that the reader of course agrees that Irish children should be butchered or that madness is the most admirable human condition. It is quite so.

Though some *personae* are primarily the embodiment of an ironical point of view, Swift's greatest masterpieces are written by ' authors ' who are clearly conceived and, for the most part, consistently maintained individuals. Their biographical details add a narrative interest to the satire and enable Swift to present many of his arguments through concrete illustrations. Most important, by making the ' author ' seem as real as possible, Swift intensifies the force of the incredible ironical things the ' author ' says.

Swift's ability to put himself, like a dramatist, into the place of a created character thus produced a gallery of masks which can only be called heterogeneous. In a period in which, according to Professor Sutherland, *personae*, though widely used, closely resembled in personality the authors who created them,[28] Swift's accomplishment is a remarkable one. Not one of Swift's *personae* can be considered (as the Drapier has been) as a mere name over a program,[29] which Swift could neglect, and which has no connection with his irony. In fact, the influence of the *personae* is so marked that it modifies even Swift's style : for evidence one need only notice the sweeping allusions and daring images of *A Tale of a Tub*, the impersonal calculations of *A Modest Proposal*, the blunt counselling of the author of the *Letter to a Young Clergyman*, and the plain narrative of Gulliver. Some of these stylistic characteristics are, of course, parodies. But Swift's parodies are always in a style appropriate to the general attitude of a supposed author. They are not mere spasmodically brilliant satirical fragments. Nowhere is this fact clearer than in *A Tale of a Tub*, where Swift gives one definite and steadily consistent author the stylistic traits of several groups of moderns. At the same time the literary medium of the mask necessitates that most of Swift's *personae* share one quality : as they speak—even (as in the *Tale* and *Drapier*) at the expense of absolute stylistic uniformity in a work—they must be able somehow to use language so powerfully that they communicate Swift's own ironic or humorous point.

Just as Swift's *personae*, like the creations of any careful dramatist, appear as a heterogeneous group, so each of the *personae* is able to accomplish a multiplicity of satiric ends. This accomplishment would hardly have been possible without the mask device. When one considers the great variety of the satire in *Gulliver's Travels* as well as that in the *Project for the Advancement of Religion*, the *Argument Against Abolishing Christianity*, and *A Tale of a Tub*, it is hard to see how all these ends can be accomplished without affecting the power and coherence of the individual work. It is in fact Swift's use of a fictitious author that enables him to create a point of view from which such multiple satire becomes possible.

The success of the device which provides this richness becomes at once apparent when one contrasts the many cross currents of ironical satire in the *Tale* or *Gulliver* with the irony (also excellent in its way) of Gibbon. The author of the *Decline and Fall* is Gibbon, though with a pose. Restraining his true feelings about early Christianity, he writes :

> The great law of impartiality too often obliges us to reveal the imperfections of the uninspired teachers and believers of the Gospel ; and, to a careless observer, *their* faults may seem to cast a shade on the faith which they professed. . . . The theologian may indulge the pleasing task of describing Religion as she descended from heaven arrayed in her native purity. A more melancholy duty is imposed on the historian. He must discover the inevitable mixture of error and corruption which she contracted in a long residence upon earth, among a weak and degenerate race of beings.

Here the false attitude of impartiality heightens our interest in the devastating facts which Gibbon carefully sets down. It is one of the successes of the *Decline and Fall* that he maintains this pose so impeccably. Certainly it is the main source of the humour in the history, as it is in his ' fair ' observation in the *Autobiography* that Pope's Homer had every excellence except similarity to the original. But the irony in itself is fairly simple to see through and fairly simple in its purpose. Once the reader has rejected the surface affectation, he discovers usually a single clear meaning. Gibbon's satire does not, like Swift's, strike at once in many directions. Because Gibbon's irony depends completely upon a single pose of detachment which cannot for a moment be broken, it lacks the capacity for emotional power which Swift's—depending upon fully rounded character—has.

But the mask device has a still greater effectiveness. If one thinks of a *persona* as a sort of dramatic character with a life and ideas of his own, apart from Swift's, one can make a rough distinction between Swift's satires which depend mainly upon allegory (in which the character of a supposed author is of only secondary importance) and those which depend mainly upon the establishment of a mask and consequently a semi-dramatic situation. *Gulliver's Travels*, of course, contains many allegorical elements, though its general framework—the adventurous voyages of a seaman—depends upon the creation of the character of Gulliver. In allegory the main problem of the writer is to find a set of symbols which consistently throughout a narrative stand for certain general concepts. Thus in the morality play *Everyman*, in sections of *The Faerie Queene*, and in *The Pilgrim's Progress*, the characters stand for certain virtues—such as faith, hope, charity—or for certain vices—idleness, intemperance, greed. In the narrative sections of *A Tale of a Tub*, Peter, Martin, and Jack consistently represent Catholicism, Lutheranism, and Presbyterianism. The action goes on simultaneously on two levels, that of the characters themselves and that of their allegorical significance. Once the reader has discovered the key to the allegory, he can usually throughout the work simply substitute the real meaning for the symbol. The excellence of this type of literature (as in *The Battle of the Books*) depends not so much upon the demand made on the reader to discover the true meaning as upon the interest of the action and the ingenuity with which the symbols themselves are conceived.

In Swift's satire which depends upon a *persona*, however, the reader must be much more active. The words of the ' author ' do not correspond automatically to a real meaning behind them. There is no key. There are only clues. The reader must be constantly alert to see these clues and to use each of them to infer the real message. This demand is not an easy one, for Swift's *personae* have a number of ways of distorting this message. One must see through the exaggerated self-importance of Bickerstaff, the humility of the Drapier, and the inverted values of the author of *A Tale of a Tub* in order to understand what Swift is saying. Even the satiric point should not be taken too literally : it is not Swift's final, considered opinion, for example, that modern critics should commit suicide, that real Christianity would turn English courts into deserts, that Whigs are savage animals, and that men are odious vermin. One must be ready to see that an ' author ' can in some ways agree with Swift and in others disagree with him. Most important, no ' author ' distorts the message in one way alone. The reader must examine carefully every step of the argument.

In *Gulliver's Travels*, in addition to an author and his ideas, there are characters, and their ideas. As a result the reader must judge the meaning of these symbolic characters as well as of the words of the author. The minuteness of the Lilliputians should remind him of the littleness of man, just as the hugeness of the Brobdingnagians should remind him of human grossness. The excellence of certain Lilliputian and Brobdingnagian customs, and the extreme mechanism of the *virtuosi* in Laputa and Lagado should recall the inadequacies of certain English customs and the excesses of which English experimenters are capable. The exalted reason and benevolence of the Houyhnhnms make painfully clear the fact that human beings frequently pervert reason for ignoble purposes. The baseness of the Yahoos is a sobering reminder that men are often like beasts and, in their perversion of reason, even worse than beasts.

These pictures are distortions of what really exists. The distortion, as in irony and exaggerating invective, can be made in a great number of ways : Swift can make men smaller and better, smaller and more petty, larger and nobler, larger and cruder, more mechanistic, more bestial, or more rational than they really are. This fact should imply that Swift is not simply saying that the English should pick out all the good qualities in Lilliput, Brobdingnag, and Houyhnhnm-land and imitate them. Swift presents not so much models of what should be or what should not be, as criticisms of what is ; his positive message must be inferred from each individual criticism. When Gulliver, for example, says that begging is unknown in Lilliput, Swift probably means that, in this one respect, the English would do well to imitate the Lilliputians. But when Gulliver says that the Brobdingnagians have not many books and the Houyhnhnms none at all, Swift probably means the Europeans would be wise to have fewer and better books. The demand made upon the reader to do part of the work in getting Swift's meanings doubtless accounts for much of the intellectual and emotional force his writings have.

There is of course difficulty in the fact that when Swift uses irony and symbolism he appeals to a norm,[30] a system of values and ideas which the reader must bring to the work. Obviously the irony in an

' author's ' inverted sense of values will fail unless the reader's sense of values is not inverted. One cannot, as in *A Tale of a Tub*, ironically condemn Homer for (unlike the moderns) his failure to understand the Church of England and the circulation of the blood unless one's readers are aware that Homer has excellences which cannot be touched by such criticism. Mistakes have been made when critics have tried to interpret Swift in the light of their own idea of a norm rather than his. Thus the Brobdingnagians have been called stupid because of their small libraries. The Houyhnhnms have been condemned as unsympathetic, inhuman, cold creatures, who are unintelligent because they read nothing and have no comprehension of the intricacies of human warfare. But one must clearly recognize that Swift's appeal to a norm is in most instances a source of strength, not confusion. For the values he appeals to most frequently are permanent ones—the belief, for example, that fraud, war, and madness are bad and that truthfulness, reason, and humility are good. That he can make such appeals should suggest that he does not regard all men as totally depraved. It is, among other things, the powerful and surprising way in which he reminds readers of these values that gives his works significance in any period.

As a satirist, Swift had phenomenal success, typified in the results of his efforts against prolongation of the War of the Spanish Succession and against Wood's halfpence, to say nothing of his ridicule of Partridge. Part of this success is due to the power of his irony. But part is also due to the brilliant and amusing playfulness of his writing. This quality, though it appears excellently in the narrative of *A Tale of a Tub* and in the *Battle of the Books*, is also in large part reflected in his use of *personae*. It means that readers have always found *A Modest Proposal* an extremely interesting, as well as extremely sobering, essay. Much has been written about Swift's cynicism and misanthropy. But one needs to remember what is suggested in Dr. Johnson's remarking that Swift's favourite maxim was ' *Vive la bagatelle* '.[31] It is partly this play of intellect, this attention to minute and ingenious dramatic detail, that keeps Swift's serious works from being enervating.[32]

In part it is Swift's playfulness of intellect which enables him to see his *personae* as individuals and so not to identify himself with them. When a writer gives a *persona* too many of his own ideas and attitudes about a depressing subject (as is true in certain of Housman's poems) the result can be likewise depressing. But when an author keeps his *persona* individualized, even on a serious subject the result can be powerful and yet at the same time humorous. Part of the strength of

Swift's works (as in great tragedy) comes from our realization that the author is apart from the drama, presenting a problem, not being overcome by it. In tragedy we feel not merely pity and fear but the catharsis of these emotions. In Swift's satire we often feel not only agony over the failings of human beings ; we also admire the power of mind in the author who can portray these failings with intellectual control. In addition, humour frequently results from our recognition that the *persona* is not omniscient, that we can see through his words (and frequently his pretence) to the true meaning behind them. This sort of humour characterizes not only the Bickerstaff papers and du Baudrier's *New Journey* but also *A Tale of a Tub* and *Gulliver's Travels*.

To say that Swift's *personae* are ' individuals ' is not to say that they are ' real people '. The Church of England Man and the friend of the young clergyman, of course, are relatively true to life. But the greater part of Swift's *personae* are plainly fictitious characters whose attributes are exploited freely for ironical satiric ends. They are masks. And in Swift, in Greek drama, in the Noh plays of Japan, as for children on Halloween, the character of the message is dependent upon the character of the mask. The perceptive spectator sees the play within the play. Upon the contrast between the apparent and the real meaning rests part of the power of the closing, ' *La commedia è finita* '.

If one considers *Gulliver's Travels* Swift's masterpiece, it is probably because it contains more playfulness of mind, more ingenuity, more multiplicity of satire, and more concrete realization of character than any other of Swift's works. Yet even more praiseworthy than his creation of a single great character is his creation of a whole host of them, each with a particular task to do in the harsh and humorous world of satire. They are responsible for much of the drama, irony, intensity, and humour that cause Swift's work to be continually popular. They symbolize much of what he found contemptible in humanity ; and they express some of his immediate, as well as distant, ideas of how to improve mankind. They reflect, without losing their dramatic integrity, facets of the character of the complex man who was ' Presto ' to the Duchess, Dean of St. Patrick's, a moralist, a political pamphleteer, a Christian, a savage critic, and a humourist. They remind us that even in a great pessimist, the spirit of *saeva indignatio* can join triumphantly with that of *la bagatelle*.

NOTES TO CHAPTER XIII

[1] *Works*, VII, 239–41.

[2] *Ibid.*, 239.

[3] *Ibid.*, 231–2.

[4] *Ibid.*, 237.

[5] *Ibid.*, 231, 233.

[6] *Ibid.*, 238–41.

[7] *Ibid.*, 235.

[8] *Ibid.*, 272–7.

[9] *Ibid.*, 253–8.

[10] *Ibid.*, IV, 77.

[11] *Ibid.*, 80–2.

[12] *Ibid.*, IV, 87–101. See also *The Presbyterians' Plea of Merit* (1733), in which Swift adopts, at the beginning of his relatively straightforward argument against repeal, an attitude of impartiality. (*Ibid.*, 31).

[13] *Ibid.*, VII, 307–8. In *Considerations Upon Two Bills* (1732) Swift, writing on two bills concerning the Church, pretends, for rhetorical purposes, to have no acquaintance with ' one single prelate of the kingdom '. He creates no mask. (*Ibid.*, III, 261).

[14] See, for example : 'A Beautiful Young Nymph Going to Bed ' (*Poems* II, 580–3) ; ' Strephon and Chloe ' (*ibid.*, 584–93) ; ' Cassinus and Peter ' (*ibid.*, 593–7) ; ' The Beasts Confession ' (*ibid.*, 601–8) ; 'An Answer ', spoken by a cloud (*ibid.*, 616–22 [manuscript version] ; 623–8 [printed version]) ; ' Traulus ' (*ibid.*, III, 795).

[15] *Works*, XI, 197, note ; see also : *Correspondence*, IV, 258, 309. Swift has been called the primary author of *The Miscellaneous Works of Dr William Wagstaff* (1726), which contains a satirical character of Steele. The name 'Walter Wagstaff' was used by William Oldisworth in his annotations on the *Tatler*, published in 1711. (Sir Henry Craik, *Life of Swift*, 1882, pp. 295–7, note).

[16] *Works*, XI, 201–9.

[17] *Ibid.*, 221. Professor Eddy calls this ' Swift's tribute to Brown '. (' The Wits vs. John Partridge, Astrologer ', 35).

[18] *Works*, XI, 221–2. Dr. Gove concludes from this passage that Swift knew Gildon. (*Op. cit.*, 471).

[19] *Works*, XI, 222–8.

[20] *Ibid.*, 203–4.

[21] *Ibid.*, 216.

[22] *Ibid.*, 223–4.

[23] *Ibid.*, 204–5.

[24] *Ibid.*, 233–4.

[25] *Ibid.*, 210–12.

[26] *Op. cit.*, 368.

[27] ' Some Aspects of Eighteenth Century Prose,' in *Essays on the Eighteenth Century Presented to David Nichol Smith*, p. 97.

[28] *Ibid.*, p. 99.

[29] Rossi and Hone, *op. cit.*, pp. 309–10.

[30] Cf. the full discussion of Swift's rhetorical method in Kelling, *op. cit.*, ch. 3–5.

[31] ' Swift ', in *Lives of the Poets* (ed. G. Birkbeck Hill, Oxford, 1905), III, 45–6.

[32] See the excellent essay of Professor Bredvold, ' The Gloom of the Tory Satirists ', in *Pope and his Contemporaries* : *Essays Presented to George Sherburn*, pp. 1–19.

BIBLIOGRAPHY

Aitken, G. A. 'Coleridge on *Gulliver's Travels*,' *Athenaeum*, II (Aug. 15, 1896), 224.

—— ed. *The Tatler*, London, 1898, 4 vols.

Atkinson, Geoffroy. *The Extraordinary Voyage in French Literature before 1700*. New York : Columbia University Press, 1920.

Ault, Norman, ed. *The Prose Works of Alexander Pope*. Oxford : Blackwell, 1936.

Ball, F. Elrington, ed. *The Correspondence of Jonathan Swift, D.D.* London : G. Bell, 1910–14, 6 vols.

Baugh, Albert C., ed. *A Literary History of England*. New York : Appleton-Century-Crofts, 1948.

Bonner, Willard Hallam. *Captain William Dampier, Buccaneer-Author*. Stanford : University Press, and London : Oxford University Press, 1934.

Brown, Huntington. *Rabelais in English Literature*. Cambridge : Harvard University Press, 1933.

Browne, Sir John. *An Essay on Trade in General*. Dublin, 1728.
—— *Reflections Little to the Purpose on a Paper Less to the Purpose*. Dublin, 1729.

—— *Seasonable Remarks on Trade*. Dublin, 1728.

Case, Arthur E. *Four Essays on Gulliver's Travels*. Princeton : University Press, 1945.

Churchill, Winston S. *Marlborough, his Life and Times*. New York : Scribner's, 1933–8, 6 vols.

Clifford, James L., and Louis A. Landa, edd. *Pope and his Contemporaries : Essays Presented to George Sherburn*. Oxford : Clarendon Press, 1949.

A Collection of Tracts and Treatises. Dublin, 1861, 2 vols.

A Collection of Tracts Concerning the Present State of Ireland. London, 1729.

Collins, John Churton. *Jonathan Swift, a Biographical and Critical Study*. London : Chatto and Windus, 1893.

Considerations on Two Papers Lately Published. Dublin, 1728.

Craik, Sir Henry. *The Life of Jonathan Swift*. London, 1882.

Cyrano de Bergerac, Savinien. *A Voyage to the Moon*, tr. A. Lovell, ed. Curtis Hidden Page. New York : Doubleday and McClure, 1899.

Dampier, William. *A New Voyage Round the World*, introd. Sir Albert Gray. London : Argonaut Press, 1927.

—— *A Voyage to New Holland*, ed. James A. Williamson. London : Argonaut Press, 1939.

Dargan, H. M. 'The Nature of Allegory as Used by Swift,' *Studies in Philology*, XIII (1916), 159–79.

Davis, Herbert, ed. *The Drapier's Letters to the Whole People of Ireland*. Oxford : Clarendon Press, 1935.

—— ed. *The Prose Works of Jonathan Swift*. Oxford : Blackwell, 1939–.

—— *The Satire of Jonathan Swift*. New York : Macmillan, 1947.

—— ' Swift and the Pedants,' *Oriel Review*, I (1943), 129–44.

Delany, Patrick. *Observations Upon Lord Orrery's Remarks*. London, 1754.

De Morgan, Augustus. ' Swift : *Gulliver's Travels*,' *Notes and Queries*, series II, vol. VI (Aug. 14, 1858), 123–6.

Directions Concerning the Matter and Stile of Sermons, . . . by J. A., D.D. London : 1671.

Eddy, William A. *Gulliver's Travels* ; *a Critical Study*. Princeton : University Press, and London : Oxford University Press, 1923.

—— 'A Source for Gulliver's First Voyage,' *Modern Language Notes*, XXXVII (June, 1922), 353–5.

—— 'A Source for Gulliver's Travels,' *Modern Language Notes*, XXXVI (Nov., 1921), 419–22.

—— ' Tom Brown and Partridge the Astrologer,' *Modern Philology*, XXVIII (Nov., 1930), 163–8.

—— ' The Wits vs. John Partridge, Astrologer,' *Studies in Philology*, XXIX (Jan., 1932), 29–40.

Ehrenpreis, Irvin. ' The Date of Swift's " Sentiments ", '*Review of English Studies*, III (1952), 272–4.

Elliott, Robert C. ' Gulliver as Literary Artist,' *English Literary History*, XIX (1952), 49–63.

—— ' Swift's *Tale of a Tub* : an Essay in Problems of Structure,' *Publications of the Modern Language Association*, LXVI (June, 1951), 441–55.

Ellmann, Richard. *Yeats, the Man and the Masks*. New York : Macmillan, 1948.

Essays on the Eighteenth Century Presented to David Nichol Smith. Oxford : Clarendon Press, 1945.

Fairclough, H. R., tr. Horace, *Satires, Epistles, and Ars Poetica.* Cambridge : Harvard University Press, and London : W. Heinemann, 1942.

—— tr. *Virgil.* London : W. Heinemann, and New York : Putnam, 1925–7, 2 vols.

Firth, Sir Charles H. ' The Political Significance of *Gulliver's Travels* ', *Proceedings of the British Academy,* IX (1919–20), 237–59.

Frantz, R. W. ' Gulliver's " Cousin Sympson ",' *Huntington Library Quarterly,* I (April, 1938), 329–34.

—— ' Swift's Yahoos and the Voyagers,' *Modern Philology,* XXIX (1931), 49–57.

Freud, Sigmund. *New Introductory Lectures on Psycho-Analysis.* New York : Norton, 1933.

Gill, Conrad. *The Rise of the Irish Linen Industry.* Oxford : Clarendon Press, 1925.

Godley, A. D., tr. *Herodotus.* Cambridge : Harvard University Press, and London : W. Heinemann, 1930–8, 4 vols.

Goodwin, A. ' Wood's Halfpence,' *English Historical Review,* LI (October, 1936), 647–74.

Gove, Philip Babcock. ' Gildon's " Fortune Shipwreck " as Background for *Gulliver's Travels,*' *Review of English Studies,* XVIII (Oct., 1942), 470–8.

Grennan, Margaret R. ' Lilliput and Leprecan : Gulliver and the Irish Tradition,' *English Literary History,* XII (Sept., 1945), 188–202.

Guthkelch, A. C., and D. Nichol Smith, edd. *A Tale of a Tub to which is added The Battle of the Books and the Mechanical Operation of the Spirit. By Jonathan Swift.* Oxford : Clarendon Press, 1920.

Harmon, A. M., ed. and tr. *Lucian.* London : W. Heinemann, and New York : Putnam, 1925–47, 5 vols.

Jaeger, Werner. *Paideia : the Ideals of Greek Culture.* New York : Oxford, 1945, 3 vols.

Johnson, Samuel. *Lives of the Poets,* ed. G. Birkbeck Hill. Oxford : Clarendon Press, 1905, 3 vols.

Jones, W. H. S., and H. A. Ormerod, tr. Pausanias, *Description of Greece.* London : W. Heinemann, and New York : Putnam, 1918–35, 5 vols.

o

Kelling, Harold D. *The Appeal to Reason*: *a Study of Jonathan Swift's Critical Theory and Its Relation to his Writings*. Unpublished doctoral dissertation, Yale University, 1948.

Kliger, Samuel. 'The Unity of *Gulliver's Travels*,' *Modern Language Quarterly*, VI (1945), 401–15.

Knight, G. Wilson. *The Burning Oracle*. London and New York: Oxford University Press, 1939.

Krappe, Edith S. 'A *Lapsus Calami* of Jonathan Swift,' *Modern Language Notes*, LIII (1938), 116–7.

Landa, Louis A. '*A Modest Proposal* and Populousness,' *Modern Philology*, XL (Nov., 1942), 161–70.

—— Review of Potter's 'Swift and Natural Science,' *Philological Quarterly*, XXI (April, 1942), 219–21.

—— Review of Quintana's *Mind and Art of Jonathan Swift*, *Modern Philology*, XXXV (Nov., 1937), 202–4.

—— Review of Wittkowsky's 'Swift's *Modest Proposal*,' *Philological Quarterly*, XXIII (April, 1944), 178–9.

—— 'Swift's Economic Views and Mercantilism,' *English Literary History*, X (1943), 310–35.

Leavis, F. R. 'The Irony of Swift,' *Scrutiny*, II (1934), 363–78.

Lecky, W. E. H. *History of England in the Eighteenth Century*, new ed. New York: D. Appleton, 1892–3, 7 vols.

Levin, Harry. *Toward Stendhal*. Murray, Utah, 1945. (*Pharos*, No. 3).

Madden, Thomas. *Reflections and Resolutions Proper for the Gentlemen of Ireland*. Dublin, 1738.

Mann, Thomas. *Essays of Three Decades*. New York: Knopf, 1947.

Maxwell, Constantia. *Dublin Under the Georges*, 1714–1830. London: Harrap, 1936.

McCue, G. S. 'A Seventeenth Century Gulliver,' *Modern Language Notes*, L (Jan., 1935), 32–4.

Molyneux, William. *The Case of Ireland's Being Bound by Acts of Parliament in England*. Dublin, 1698.

Moore, John B. 'The Rôle of Gulliver,' *Modern Philology*, XXV (1928), 469–80.

Moore, John Robert. 'A New Source for *Gulliver's Travels*,' *Studies in Philology*, XXXVIII (Jan., 1941), 66–80.

Nichol Smith, David, ed. *The Letters of Jonathan Swift to Charles Ford*. Oxford: Clarendon Press, 1935.

Nicolson, Marjorie, and Nora M. Mohler. ' The Scientific Background of Swift's Voyage to Laputa,' *Annals of Science*, II (1937), 229–334.

Nock, Albert Jay, and Catherine Rose Wilson, edd. *The Works of Francis Rabelais*. New York : Harcourt, Brace, 1931, 2 vols.

Oldfather, C. H., tr. *Diodorus of Sicily*. London : W. Heinemann, and New York : Putnam, 1933–47, 10 vols.

Perrot d'Ablancourt, Nicholas. *Lucien de la Traduction de N. Perrot d'Ablancourt*. Paris : Augustin Courbé, 1654, 2 vols.

Petronius. *The Satiricon*. Ed. Evan T. Sage. New York and London, 1929.

Petty, Sir William. *Sir William Petty's Political Survey of Ireland*, 1672. London, 1719.

Pons, Émile. ' Rabelais et Swift à propos du Lilliputien,' *Mélanges Offerts a M. Abel Lefranc*. Paris : E. Droz, 1936, pp. 219–28.

—— *Swift* : *les Années de Jeunesse et le Conte de Tonneau*. Strasbourg and Paris : Société d'Édition Les Belles Lettres ; London and New York : Oxford University Press, 1925.

Potter, George R. ' Swift and Natural Science,' *Philological Quarterly*, XX (April, 1941), 97–118.

Quintana, Ricardo. *The Mind and Art of Jonathan Swift*. London and New York : Oxford University Press, 1936.

—— ' Situational Satire : a Commentary on the Method of Swift,' *University of Toronto Quarterly*, XVII (1947–8), 130–6.

Redinger, Ruby V. ' Jonathan Swift, the Disenchanter,' *The American Scholar*, XV (1946), 221–6.

Rockwell, F. S. 'A Probable Source for *Gulliver's Travels*,' *Notes and Queries*, CLXIX (Aug. 24, 1935), 131–3.

Rogers, B. B., ed. *Aristophanes*. Cambridge : Harvard University Press, and London : W. Heinemann, 1938–46, 3 vols.

Ross, John F. ' The Final Comedy of Lemuel Gulliver,' *Studies in the Comic* (Univ. of California Pub. in English, vol. VIII, no. 2, 1941), pp. 175–96.

—— *Swift and Defoe : a Study in Relationship*. Berkeley and Los Angeles : Univ. of California Press, 1941.

Rossi, M. M., and Hone, J. M. *Swift, or the Egotist*. London : V. Gollancz, 1934.

Rouse, W. H. D., tr. *Lucretius, De Rerum Natura*. London : W. Heinemann, and New York : Putnam, 1924.

Schumann, Robert. *Gesammelte Schriften über Musik und Musiker.* Leipzig, 1854, 2 vols.

Scott, Temple, ed. *The Prose Works of Jonathan Swift, D.D.* London: George Bell, 1897–1908, 12 vols.

Scott, Walter, ed. *The Works of Jonathan Swift*, 2nd edition. London: Bickers and Son, 1883, 19 vols.

Sherburn, George. *The Early Career of Alexander Pope.* Oxford: Clarendon Press, 1934.

—— 'Methods in Books about Swift,' *Studies in Philology*, XXXV (1938), 635–56.

Starkman, Miriam K. *Swift's Satire on Learning in A Tale of a Tub.* Princeton: University Press, 1950.

Thompson, Elbert N. S. 'Tom Brown and the Satirists,' *Modern Language Notes*, XXXII (1917), 90–4.

Toynbee, Arnold. *A Study of History*, abridgement by D. C. Somervell. New York and London: Oxford, 1947.

Vairasse d'Alais, Denis. *The History of the Sevarambians*, anon. trans. from the French. London: Printed for J. Noon, 1738.

Warren, Austin. 'The Mask of Pope,' *Sewanee Review*, LIV (1946), 19–33.

Watkins, W. B. C. *Perilous Balance.* Princeton: University Press, and London: Oxford University Press, 1939.

Watson, John S., tr. *Justin, Cornelius Nepos, and Eutropius.* London, 1853.

Wedel, T. O. 'On the Philosophical Background of *Gulliver's Travels,* *Studies in Philology*, XXIII (1926), 434–50.

White, H. O. 'The Art of Swift,' *Hermathena*, LXIX (1947), 1–8.

Wickham, E. C., ed. *The Works of Horace.* Oxford: Clarendon Press, 1891–6, 2 vols.

Willey, Basil. *The Eighteenth Century Background.* New York: Columbia University Press, and London: Chatto and Windus, 1941.

Williams, A. Glynn, tr. Cicero, *The Letters to his Friends.* London: W. Heinemann, and New York: Putnam, 1927–9, 3 vols.

Williams, Harold. *Dean Swift's Library.* Cambridge: University Press, 1932.

—— ed. Jonathan Swift, *Journal to Stella.* Oxford: Clarendon Press, 1948, 2 vols.

Williams, Harold. ed. *The Poems of Jonathan Swift*. Oxford : Clarendon Press, 1937, 3 vols.

Williams, Kathleen M. ' Gulliver's Voyage to the Houyhnhnms,' *English Literary History*, XVIII (1951), 275–86.

Wittkowsky, George. ' Swift's *Modest Proposal* : the Biography of an Early Georgian Pamphlet, ' *Journal of the History of Ideas*, IV (1943), 75–104.

Yeats, William Butler. *Autobiography*. New York : Macmillan, 1938.

INDEX